Beethoven

Letters, Journals and Conversations

Beethoven

Letters, Journals and Conversations

Edited, translated and introduced by
MICHAEL HAMBURGER

THAMES AND HUDSON

Copyright © 1951 by Michael Hamburger

*First published in Great Britain in 1951
by Thames and Hudson Limited, London
Published in the United States of America in 1984 by
Thames and Hudson Inc., 500 Fifth Avenue, New York, New York 10110
This new paperback edition 1984
Reprinted in 1992*

Library of Congress Catalog Card Number 83-72975

Printed and bound in the United States of America

INTRODUCTION

BIOGRAPHIES, whether strictly factual or semi-fictitious, can never be wholly objective; for already by arranging and presenting his facts, the biographer is bound to emphasize those aspects of his subject which he considers more important than others, to evaluate and to interpret. The purpose of the present collection of documents is to provide the reader with a basis upon which he may construct his own biography of Beethoven.

Most of this material will be familiar to English readers of Beethoven's collected letters and of the more comprehensive biographies; but while the letters of Mozart, Mendelssohn, Schumann and Wagner (to mention only a few celebrated composers) have sufficient literary merit to appeal to the general reader, only specialists and rare enthusiasts are likely to undertake the labour of reading all of Beethoven's carelessly written letters. The reader of the present collection will be spared this labour, just as he is spared the theories, conjectures and polemics of biographers. Even accounts by contemporaries are not always reliable, especially as many of them are reminiscences of meetings already distant; but (except in the case of Bettina Brenᵗano, whose inventions were elaborately and ingeniously disguised) it is quite easy to distinguish those passages in which memory has been supplanted by imagination. There are several such passages in the account by Stumpff. Significantly, it was one of the most truly imaginative of Beethoven's visitors, the dramatist and poet Grillparzer, who had the honesty to admit that his memory had failed him here and there; for even faithful reportage is an art that requires practice and discipline.

It is usual to preface a selection from Beethoven's letters with a regret that these letters tell us so little about their author; yet, brief as it is, even the present selection should prove the absurdity of such a regret. Unlike those artists whose letters are intended for posterity, Beethoven wrote with a candour and a spontaneous impulse which are far more revealing than the studied confessions and elaborate reticences of more accomplished stylists. No one can deny that Beethoven's letters tell us a great deal about his daily life, his practical difficulties, his illnesses, friendships and aspirations; what is more, they reproduce his mental processes so faithfully that the reader may experience a sensation of almost embarrassing intimacy. Ellipsis and faulty syntax often make it difficult to follow the logic of Beethoven's communications; but these very imperfections contribute to our awareness of a "naked thinking heart that makes no show".

If we learn very little about that level of the composer's personality to which we owe his music, we should remember that music is a language incomparably more precise than the words we use to describe its effect or its inspiration. Even if Beethoven had attempted to explain the "meaning" of his more esoteric works—of the last quartets, for instance—his explanation could only distract us from the music; and Beethoven had neither the patience nor the vocabulary needed for such fatuous commentaries. From Beethoven's own statements we learn that his inspiration was often literary; but we are none the wiser for knowing that Shakespeare or Goethe stimulated Beethoven's mind. Very few of his compositions are programme music: the literary source provided no more than a vague, and entirely personal, incitement—the work itself is best appreciated if we regard it as pure music. When asked to explain the meaning of the Piano Sonatas Op. 32, No. 2 and Op. 57, Beethoven said: "Read Shakespeare's *Tempest*!"; but, interesting as it may be to know that Beethoven read and admired *The Tempest*, our appreciation of the sonatas in question is not enhanced by this knowledge. All we can say is that Beethoven's sensibility was impressed in a special way by his reading of *The Tempest* and that he was able to translate this impression into pure music; if we could understand the intermediary processes, we should be considerably wiser than Beethoven ever was. Besides, it is quite possible that Beethoven's reply was intended to be misleading; he did not suffer fools gladly and was fond of mischief at their expense.

Beethoven's insistence that he was a *Tondichter* (tone-poet) and his indignation when a correspondent had the impertinence to address him as *Tonsetzer* (tone-setter) must not be ascribed to literary pretensions on his part, but to the desire that his music should be taken seriously and he taken seriously as a musician; for while a certain dignity attached to the name of poet, musicians were commonly regarded as mere artisans—indeed, they were liable to be treated much as Beethoven treated the copyist Wolanek.

Beethoven was the first composer to claim the prerogatives of genius; by doing so, with a stubborn pride which often bordered on insolence, he helped to change the status of composers generally. It is difficult now to determine to what extent Beethoven's revolutionary sympathies and eccentric behaviour were the result of conscious reflection; but it seems probable that they were largely emotional, the result of an instinctive radicalism common to all artists. Already in his lifetime, Beethoven became the hero of a legend, the object of a new cult: the cult of genius which dominated the nineteenth century, just as the ideals of elegance, moderation and politeness had dominated preceding generations. The concept of genius had already been popularized in literature; but music, which is not subject to the same restrictions as literature, was a far more suitable medium for the expression of absolute genius.

The famous incident at Teplitz (as related by Bettina Brentano) seems almost too typical to be true; but, for that very reason, it reflects the different attitudes of Beethoven and Goethe in a magnifying (if not a distorting) mirror. Goethe, too, had begun by glorifying unfettered genius, the *daemonic*, as he preferred to call it; but as he approached maturity it became his business to acquire a wider perspective, to consider the social, moral and political implications of his youthful cult. Beethoven, as a composer, could afford to ignore these implications, to retain the uncouthness and rebelliousness of a young man— and these same qualities have come to be regarded as the attributes of genius. I do not wish to imply that Beethoven never attained maturity; but only that a great composer's maturity differs in kind from that of a great writer. Beethoven could become a great composer without obeying any laws but those of his art; Goethe was restricted by his medium, the written word, which can never exist independently, but is modified by countless associations extraneous to art.

If I have chosen to comment on an incident which may be partly or wholly fictitious, it is because this incident has given rise to endless discussion and moralizing, often at Beethoven's expense; and because, whether true or false, it has contributed more than any other to the popular conception of Beethoven's personality. His letters show that he was quite capable of prudence and self-restraint; but he did not think much of these virtues. Also, Beethoven was seriously handicapped by his deafness, which, in itself, made him unfit for social life and confirmed his eccentricities; for all we know, his music may have profited even by his vices and afflictions.

Many details of Beethoven's life are still obscure; yet, with the exception of his love affairs, about which next to nothing is known, the present collection should throw some light on all the more significant aspects of Beethoven's life and character. Needless to say, the picture will not be complete; but it will be comparatively accurate and free from those distortions of which even contemporary painters of Beethoven were too often guilty. (It is interesting, nevertheless, to see how powerful an influence the legendary Beethoven exercised on those who painted portraits of the real one; once again it was the wildness and impetuosity of genius that were emphasized and exaggerated.)

Special attention has been given to Beethoven's remarks on his own works and on music in general. The letters to Wegeler, Amenda and the Breunings (all of whom he had known since his early years in Bonn) reveal his great capacity for friendship; but it is also apparent that none of his later friendships of the Vienna period (such as those with Zmeskall, Gleichenstein and the Lichnowskys) meant as much to him as the early ones. His low opinion of the Austrians in general (whom, like many

Germans, he thought frivolous and treacherous) may have something to do with this; the letters suggest that his Bonn friends were especially dear to him because of their associations with his youth and with his native city. Most of the documents relevant to Beethoven's contact with eminent contemporaries, writers and composers, have been included; an exception has been made in the case of Haydn, because the accounts of his meeting with Beethoven are both dubious and unsatisfactory. The relationship between the two composers does not seem to have been a cordial one, though Beethoven respected Haydn's music.

Among the most revealing of Beethoven's letters are those to his various publishers; for these contain references to his own works, to financial matters and even to his personal convictions. A letter to Schott, for example, contains a cryptic allusion to the Metternich régime, followed by Beethoven's hopes for a more liberal future which, rather loosely, he connects with mechanical progress. Though usually mistrustful and suspicious, Beethoven was always eager to confide in those whom he had accepted as his friends; but the slightest offence against his ideal of friendship was enough to reawaken his suspicions and provoke him to fury. Considering that even his closest friends and his two amanuenses, Schindler and Holz, were not exempt from these sudden eclipses, it is not surprising that few of his publishers stood the test indefinitely; for Beethoven was unwilling to make a distinction between human beings and business men. What is surprising is that he remained on friendly terms with some of those publishers (such as Steiner and the Schlesingers) whom he had once accused of dishonesty. Sometimes, as in the case of the Missa Solemnis, his own dealings with publishers were not distinguished by probity; but like many impulsive and capricious persons, Beethoven was not always aware of his own inconsistencies or capable of judging his own behaviour.

Metternich's police looked upon Beethoven as a potentially dangerous revolutionary, spied on him and kept a record of his movements. Their zeal was probably excessive; there is no reason to suppose that Beethoven's opinions differed essentially from those common to his circle of noble patrons, admirers and friends. It is true that one of these, Countess Maria Erdödy, was accused of subversive activities; she was banned from Vienna and died in exile. Beethoven's outspokenness, untidy appearance and unconventional behaviour made him conspicuous; but his ideas on most subjects were those current among the educated class of his time. When Beethoven was arrested by the police in 1821, it was not as a revolutionary, but as a tramp; he was released as soon as his identity was established.

Metternich is only one of those who have taken Beethoven's ideas too seriously; but while it may have been his business to do so, moralizing critics have no such excuse. Even Beethoven's inconsistencies and heresies accorded with the fashions of the day; it was not his fault that he lived at the beginning of the age of slogans. Such general concepts as "the Good", "the Beautiful" and "the Divine" had replaced a coherent system of values; and enlightened men gaily murdered one another in the cause of Liberty, Equality and Fraternity. The rediscovery of nature had led to a revival of paganism and pantheism; the rational deism of Voltaire had been strangely concocted with the emotional primitivism of Rousseau.

As far as Beethoven had a philosophy at all, it was a jumble of odds and ends, Christian and pagan, reactionary and progressive; but he did his utmost to formulate some kind of positive creed, to the extent of reading the works of Kant (no mean achievement for a composer whose general education ceased at the age of ten). Bettina Brentano is not alone in suggesting that Beethoven treated God as an equal; and one of his letters contains the astonishing statement: "Strength is the morality of those who distinguish themselves from the rest, and it is mine too . . ."—a sentiment worthy of Nietzsche, whose superman is the direct descendant of the genius, as worshipped in Beethoven's time. Both rely on their own strength, proclaim their own morality and create their own gods. When Beethoven wrote: "The true artist has no pride; unhappily, he sees that

6

Art has no bounds", he was not advocating Christian humility, but expressing the belief (widespread in his time) that artistic inspiration is divine. It is a short step from the divinity of Art to the divinity of the artist.

In other contexts, Beethoven's frequent references to "virtue", "goodness" and "honour" may strike a modern reader as cant —but wrongly so. Beethoven sincerely and ardently desired to be good, as we can see from his private note-books. His letters to Varena prove his quite unusual eagerness to practise what he preached; he was always ready to do good works and responded generously to every appeal on behalf of "suffering humanity". Only it is difficult to define what he meant by virtue; at one moment it consisted in being strong (and ruthless) for the sake of his art or for the sake of his nephew; at the next, in not only forgiving, but helping, a defeated enemy—his sister-in-law. Such contradictions are not peculiar to Beethoven; it would be foolish to expect Beethoven to be strictly consistent in his views or in his conduct, as the effort required for this would have left him with little creative energy. When all is said and done, he was a composer, not a philosopher or a saint; all three are full-time occupations. Grillparzer, who, though reserved in his dealings with Beethoven, was one of the first to treat him with real understanding, hit the nail on the head when he wrote: "In the case of an artist, I am not interested in what he says, but in what he does." In the end, it is Beethoven's music that matters.

We can only be grateful that his music was spared the kind of criticism practised in our own time; it would have been easy enough to detect revolutionary tendencies in the choral movement of the Ninth Symphony, or irreverence in the scherzos, just as Soviet critics have discovered traces of "bourgeois decadence" in the music of Rachmaninov. Metternich's censorship, after all, seems liberal in comparison; or perhaps it is only that criticism was not so advanced in his time. Whatever the reason, not only his works, but his person were respected, as this collection of documents will show.

These must now be allowed to speak for themselves. A

7

chronological summary of Beethoven's life and work is provided; also, a number of explanatory footnotes. The index of names contains brief notes on the principal persons mentioned in the text.

Except for accounts by English visitors and the extracts from Thayer's biography, all the material in this book has been newly translated. The present version is as literal as possible; but a few passages in Beethoven's letters have been paraphrased to avoid misunderstanding: for though it seemed desirable to preserve the irregularities of Beethoven's style, this could not always be done without the risk of ambiguity. A rough equivalent has been given for untranslatable puns and idioms. No attempt has been made to improve on the style of the originals; but Beethoven's peculiar spelling, syntax and punctuation (which included dashes several inches long) have been modified.

M. H.

1770 Ludwig, second son of Johann van Beethoven, Court Musician, and his wife, Maria Magdalena, is christened in Bonn on December 17th.

1773 Beethoven's grandfather, *Kapellmeister* Louis van Beethoven, dies on December 24th.

1774 Kaspar Anton Karl, Beethoven's brother, is christened on April 8th.

1775 Maria Josepha van Beethoven, Beethoven's grandmother, dies on September 30th.

1776 Nikolaus Johann, Beethoven's brother, is christened on October 2nd.

1778 First public appearance as a pianist, of Ludwig v. B., described as "six years old", in Cologne on March 26th. Takes lessons with van den Eeden.

1779 Takes lessons with Tobias Friedrich Pfeiffer.
In October, Christian Gottlob Neefe settles in Bonn.

1780–81 Takes lessons with Franz George Rovantini (violin and viola).
Takes lessons with Willibald Koch, a Franciscan (organ?).

1781 Beethoven leaves school (the *Tirocinium* in Bonn). Travels to Rotterdam by ship with his mother to appear as a child prodigy, in October or November.

1782 Takes lessons with Neefe, who appoints him organist in his absence.
Becomes acquainted with Franz Gerhard Wegeler and, through him, with the von Breuning family.
At the end of the year, publication of "Variations on a March of Dressler" for pianoforte, "par un jeune amateur Louis van Beethoven, âgé de dix ans".

1783   On March 2nd, Neefe publishes a short article on Beethoven in a musical review.
In Neefe's absence, Beethoven becomes "cembalist in the orchestra".
Publication of three sonatas for pianoforte.

1784   On June 25th, Beethoven is appointed Court Organist with a fixed salary.

1784   Piano Concerto in E flat (piano part).

1787   Beethoven travels to Vienna in the spring, returns to Bonn early in July, because of his mother's mortal illness.
May have taken lessons with Mozart in Vienna.
Death of his mother on July 17th.

1789   Nominated member of Court Orchestra in Bonn. On November 20th, as a result of his petition to the Elector, Beethoven receives half of his father's salary for the education of his brothers, while his father is ordered to leave Bonn.

1790   Haydn visits Bonn on December 25th.
Composes a cantata on the death of Emperor Joseph II of Austria: another for the coronation of Leopold II.

1791   On October 20th, Beethoven travels with the orchestra; meets the famous pianist Abbé Sterkel.
Mozart dies in Vienna on December 5th.

1792   Haydn visits Bonn in July, on his way back from England; is shown Beethoven's two cantatas.
Early in November Beethoven leaves Bonn, settles in Vienna.
Beethoven's father dies on December 18th.

1793-94   Lessons with Haydn, also with Johann Schenk (unknown to Haydn).
From January 1793 to April 1794, takes lessons in counterpoint with Johann Georg Albrechtsberger; lessons in dramatic composition with Salieri, until 1802.

1793   Three Piano Trios, Op. 1 (published in 1795).

1795 Piano Concerto in B flat, Op. 19, which Beethoven plays at his first concert in the *Burgtheater* on March 29th. The song "Adelaide".

1796 Journey to Prague, Nuremberg and Berlin, where Beethoven plays to King Frederick II. Two Sonatas for Violincello, Op. 5.

1797 First performance of Quintet, Op. 16, in April.

1798 New version of Second Piano Concerto in B flat, Op. 19. Composes First Piano Concerto in C, Op. 15; Rondo in B flat for piano and orchestra.

1799 First Symphony (published in 1801); Sonata in C minor (Pathétique), Op. 13; two Piano Sonatas, Op. 14; three Sonatas for Violin and Piano, Op. 12.

1800 On April 2nd, Beethoven's first concert in the *Hoftheater*, where his First Symphony, a piano concerto and the Septet in E flat, Op. 20 were performed.
In the summer, Prince Lichnowsky grants Beethoven an annual retaining fee of 600 guilders.

1801 Completion of Six String Quartets, Op. 18; Piano Sonatas Op. 22, 26, 27 (Moonlight); Third Piano Concerto in C minor.
The Ballet "Prometheus" performed on March 26th, repeated ten times. The oratorio "Christ on the Mount of Olives"; Quintet in C, Op. 29.
Beethoven teaches Ferdinand Ries and Carl Czerny.

1802 Romance in G for violin and orchestra, Op. 40; in F, Op. 50; Second Symphony in D; Three Sonatas for violin and piano, Op. 30; Three Piano Sonatas, Op. 31.

1803 On April 5th, concert at *Theater an der Wien*. First performance of oratorio, Second Symphony, Third Piano Concerto.
On May 24th, first performance of Violin Sonata, Op. 47 (Kreutzer) by G. A. P. Bridgetower.
Beginning of correspondence with the publisher George Thomson in Edinburgh about Scottish songs.

Six Spiritual Songs (words by Gellert); Third Symphony (Eroica).

1804 Napoleon proclaimed Emperor on May 18th, crowned December 2nd; occupies Vienna on November 13th. "Fidelio".
Piano Sonatas, Op. 53, 54, 57 (Appassionata); Andante Favori in F; Triple Concerto, Op. 56, drafted.

1805 On April 7th, first public performance of Third Symphony.
In November, three performances of "Fidelio" with "Leonora Overture, No. 2"; these were unsuccessful.
Triple Concerto completed.

1806 In March and April, performances of "Fidelio" (Second Version) with "Leonora Overture, No. 3".
In July, meeting with Vogler and Cherubini.
Second French occupation of Vienna in November.
Beethoven's nephew Karl (son of his brother Karl Kaspar) born on September 4th.
In October, quarrel with Prince Lichnowsky, whom Beethoven visits in Silesia.
On December 23rd, first performance of Violin Concerto by Franz Clement.
Thirty-two Variations in C minor; Fourth Piano Concerto; Violin Concerto; Fourth Symphony; Three String Quartets, Op. 59.

1807 First performance of Mass in C at Eisenstadt on September 13th.
Violin Concerto arranged as piano concerto; Fifth Symphony; Coriolan Overture; Mass in C, Op. 86.

1808 Haydn's "Creation" performed on March 27th.
In the spring, Beethoven has a septic finger, undergoes operation.
At the end of October, King Jérôme offers Beethoven appointment in Kassel.
Grand concert on December 22nd; performance of Fifth

and Sixth Symphonies and Choral Fantasia, Op. 80; "Gloria" and "Sanctus" from Mass in C; Fourth Piano Concerto, etc.

Fantasy in C for piano, chorus and orchestra, Op. 80; Sixth Symphony (Pastoral) completed; four settings of Goethe's "Nur wer die Sehnsucht kennt" (Mignon's Song); 'Cello Sonata in A, Op. 69; Two Trios, Op. 70.

1809   In February, annual grant permits him to refuse appointment at Kassel.

On May 12th, third French occupation of Vienna.

Haydn dies on May 31st.

On September 8th, Beethoven conducts the Third Symphony at a charity concert.

Illness in December.

Fantasia, Op. 77; Piano Sonata in F sharp, Op. 78; Piano Sonata in G, Op. 79; Piano Sonata in E flat, Op. 81a (Les Adieux); Fifth Piano Concerto (Emperor); String Quartet in E flat, Op. 74; Four Goethe Songs, Op. 75.

1810   Proposes marriage to Therese Malfatti (?).

On May 24th, first performance of music to "Egmont". At the end of the year, first performance of Fifth Piano Concerto in Leipzig.

Piano piece "Für Elise".

1811   Devaluation of currency; heavy financial loss to Beethoven.

In August, goes to Teplitz, then on to Silesia, to stay with Prince Lichnowsky, at whose residence the Mass in C is performed.

In September, Prince Lobkowitz (one of the contributors to Beethoven's annual grant) is declared bankrupt; another loss.

Seventh Symphony begun (completed May, 1812); Eighth Symphony begun (completed October, 1812); Trio in B flat, Op. 97; "The Ruins of Athens"; "King Stephen".

1812 February 12th, first performance in Vienna of Fifth Piano Concerto, with Carl Czerny as soloist.

In July, meeting with Goethe at Teplitz.

In November, Prince Kinsky dies in Prague, after a riding accident.

Beethoven's grant is suspended until March, 1815.

Against Beethoven's will, his brother Johann marries Therese Obermeyer on November 8th.

The Violin Sonata in G, Op. 96, composed in this year, is performed by Pierre Rode and Archduke Rudolph on December 29th. Piano Trio in G, Op. 97.

1813 On June 21st, Wellington's victory at Vittoria.

On December 8th, first performance of the Seventh Symphony and of the "Battle Symphony"; repeated four days later.

"Wellington's Victory at Vittoria", Op. 91 (Battle Symphony).

1814 Grand concert of works by Beethoven on January 2nd; another on February 27th, at which the Eighth Symphony is given its first performance.

On April 11th, last public appearance as a player of chamber music, during which he performs the Trio, Op. 97, for the first time.

In April, makes the acquaintance of Anton Schindler.

Prince Karl Lichnowsky dies on April 15th.

First performance of "Fidelio" (Third Version) on May 23rd; Beethoven conducts with the help of Umlauf.

During the Congress of Vienna, "Fidelio" is performed in the presence of the visiting monarchs (on September 26th). In November it is performed in Prague, conducted by C. M. von Weber.

On November 29th, another grand concert in the *Redoutensaal*, with Seventh Symphony, Battle Symphony and the cantata, "The Glorious Moment"; repeated three days later.

Polonaise in C, Op. 89; Piano Sonata in E minor, Op.

90; Overture in E, "Fidelio"; Overture in C, "Namens-feier", Op. 115; Cantata "The Glorious Moment"; Elegiac Song, Op. 118.

1815 On January 25th, audience with the Empress of Russia, to whom Beethoven presents the Polonaise in C, com-posed for her.
Financial settlement with Kinsky's heirs and with Lobkowitz.
On November 15th, Beethoven's brother Karl dies in Vienna.
Two Sonatas for 'cello and piano, Op. 102; the cantata "Meeresstille und glückliche Fahrt" (words by Goethe).

1816 On January 19th, Beethoven becomes guardian to his nephew Karl, but not officially; in February, he places Karl in the institute directed by Giannatasio del Rio.
In the summer, operation for rupture; catarrh from the winter until the following spring.
Prince Joseph Franz Lobkowitz dies on December 16th.
Piano Sonata in A, Op. 101; Song Cycle, Op. 98.

1817 The lawsuit against Mälzel (accused of pirating the Battle Symphony) is settled in Beethoven's favour (in May).
Beethoven conducts the Eighth Symphony in the *Redoutensaal* on December 25th.
Quintet in C minor, Op. 104 (arrangement of Trio, Op. 1, No. 3).

1818 Beethoven takes Karl out of the institute in January; they now live together.
On February 3rd, Beethoven thanks Thomas Broadwood for his present of a grand piano.
In September, Karl's mother brings an action against Beethoven; he wins the case.
On December 3rd, Karl runs away from Beethoven and goes to his mother's; the police bring him back, and Beethoven puts him into the institute once more.
On December 10th, Karl's mother brings a second action.

The case is passed on to the Magistracy. On December 18th, Beethoven takes Karl home again.

Sonata in B flat, Op. 106 (Hammerklavier); "Dernière Pensée Musicale" in B.

1819 On January 7th, Beethoven appears before the Magistrate's Court. Karl is sent to Joseph Kudlich's educational institute.

On January 17th, Beethoven conducts the Seventh Symphony at a charity concert.

He resigns his guardianship of Karl at the end of March. In May, del Rio refuses to admit Karl to his institute; Karl is sent to one directed by Joseph Blöchlinger. In July, von Tuscher, who had taken over the guardianship, resigns, and Beethoven takes over once more. In September, the Magistrate transfers the guardianship from Beethoven to Karl's mother and Leopold Nussböck. On October 31st, Beethoven protests against this action; he is represented by Dr. Bach. His protest is rejected; he applies to the Court of Appeal.

1820 On April 8th, the Court of Appeal decides in Beethoven's favour; the guardianship reverts to Beethoven, jointly with *Hofrat* Peters. Karl's mother appeals to the Emperor, but in vain.

Another illness in the winter.

Piano Sonata in E, Op. 109.

1821 In July and August, ill with jaundice.

In the autumn, Beethoven is arrested as a tramp and taken to a police station, where he is identified by Herzog, Musical Director in Wiener Neustadt on the following morning, and released.

Piano Sonata in A flat, Op. 110.

1822 On January 1st, elected honorary member of Steiermark Musical Society.

Rossini, in Vienna for the performance of his "Zelmira", visits Beethoven in April.

On October 3rd, opening of Josephstadt Theatre with

Beethoven's overture "The Consecration of the House", Op. 124, completed in that year.

After three years, "Fidelio" is performed once more on November 3rd. During the general rehearsal he has to cease conducting because of his deafness.

On November 9th, Prince Galitzin writes from Petersburg, asking for three string quartets.

Piano Sonata in C minor, Op. 111; Bagatelles, Op. 119; sketches for an overture on B-A-C-H. Temporary completion of Missa Solemnis in D, Op. 123, at which Beethoven has been working since 1818. It was published in 1827.

1823 On January 25th, Beethoven accepts Galitzin's offer and asks to be paid 50 duc. for each quartet.

In February, Beethoven raises ten subscriptions for the Mass in D, at 50 duc. each.

Beethoven plans a Mass in C minor.

In February sells a security, because of heavy debts.

On March 19th, hands a copy of the Mass in D to Archduke Rudolph.

On April 29th, first performance of "Fidelio" in Dresden, Weber conducting.

From April onwards, illness; eyes and abdomen.

In August, Karl passes his final examinations at Blöchlinger's. Returns to Beethoven's house before going on to the university; stays with him at Baden till October, then both return to Vienna, where Karl continues his studies and lives with Beethoven.

Thirty-Three Variations in C on a Waltz by Diabelli, Op. 120; Bagatelles, Op. 126; Six Ecossaises; Ninth Symphony (begun in 1817).

1824 Beethoven helps Karl's mother by relieving her of the legal obligation to contribute to Karl's support (January 8th).

On February 20th, Louis XVIII sends Beethoven a gold medal.

The Missa Solemnis has its first performance, in St. Petersburg on April 6th.

Concert on May 7th; first performance of Ninth Symphony. Repeated on May 23rd.

On July 19th, Schott & Sons acquire the Mass (1000 guilders), the Ninth Symphony (600 g.) and the String Quartet, Op. 127 (50 duc.).

On December 20th, Charles Neate invites Beethoven to London on behalf of the Philharmonic Society; offers him 300 guineas for this. Beethoven asks for 400; his demand is rejected.

String Quartet in E flat, Op. 127.

1825 On March 6th, first performance of the String Quartet, Op. 127, by the Schuppanzigh Quartet; a bad performance, poor reception. Two better performances later in the month (by Joseph Böhm).

Seriously ill from April to May ("inflammation of the bowels").

At Easter, Karl gives up university studies; goes to Polytechnic.

Johann v. B. invites his brother to his estate at Gneixendorf, takes charge of Beethoven's affairs; the invitation is refused.

In September, Karl disappears for a time; Beethoven very anxious.

String Quartet in A minor, Op. 132; String Quartet in B flat, Op. 130; Grosse Fuge, Op. 133.

1826 Illness in January; eyes, lumbago, arthritis, until March.

First public performance of the String Quartet, Op. 130, on March 21st, by the Schuppanzigh Quartet.

On July 30th, Karl attempts suicide, probably because of debts.

At the end of September Beethoven and Karl travel to Gneixendorf, where they stay with Johann. Beethoven unwell; first signs of dropsy. On December 2nd, Beethoven, seriously ill, arrives in Vienna; pneumonia is diagnosed.

On December 14th, Karl joins Stutterheim Regiment; Breuning takes him there and provides his equipment.
On December 20th, first operation.
"Ludwig van Beethoven's Last Musical Thought" in C, Op. Post; sketches for a Tenth Symphony; String Quartet in C sharp minor, Op. 131; String Quartet in F, Op. 135; Finale of Op. 130.

1827 On January 2nd, Karl leaves for his regiment at Iglau.
On January 3rd, Beethoven writes his will.
On January 8th, second operation.
On February 2nd, third operation.
On February 27th, fourth operation.
Pasqualati, Breuning and Streicher provide him with food and drink during his last illness.
On March 24th, Beethoven receives the Last Sacrament.
Last signature for Schott (contract for Quartet, Op. 131).
Loses consciousness in the evening.
On March 26th, dies at 5 p.m., during a thunderstorm.

NOTE

Where place of origin and/or date of letters, etc. have been supplied by the editor, these are printed in italics.

BEETHOVEN

Letters, Journals and Conversations

FROM "MOZART", BY OTTO JAHN

Beethoven, who as a very promising young man came to Vienna in the spring of 1787, but had to return home (to Bonn) after a brief stay, was taken to see Mozart, who asked him to play something. Mozart, thinking that he was listening to some studied show-piece, praised it rather coolly. Beethoven, who noticed this, asked Mozart for a theme suitable for improvised variations. As he always played excellently when excited and, at this moment, was also inspired by the presence of a master whom he respected greatly, Beethoven began to perform upon the piano in such a manner that Mozart, whose attention increased to the point of fascination, at last went quietly to his friends sitting in the next room and said emphatically: "Keep your eyes on that fellow; one day he'll give the world something to talk about."

TO COUNCILLOR VON SCHADEN

Bonn, Autumn, 1787

Noble and most esteemed friend,

I can easily imagine what you are thinking of me; and I cannot deny that you have good grounds for not thinking favourably of me; yet I shall not attempt to excuse myself till I have pointed out my reasons for hoping that my excuses will be accepted. I must confess to you that ever since the time when I left Augsburg my good spirits and, with them, my health began to decline. The nearer I came to my native city, the more letters I received from my father, asking me to travel faster than usual, as my mother was not in a good state of health; I therefore hurried on as fast I could, though far from well myself. The desire to be able to see my sick mother in time helped me to overcome every obstacle and to endure the

21

hardest privations. I found my mother still alive, but in the most wretched state: she was ill with consumption and died about seven weeks ago after much pain and suffering. She was such a kind and lovable mother to me, my best friend. Oh, who was happier than I when I could still utter the sweet name of mother! and it would be heard, and to whom can I say it now? To the dumb images that resemble her, put together by my imagination? I have spent very few pleasant hours since I came here: all the time I have been afflicted with asthma which, I have reason to fear, may even turn into consumption. In addition to this, there is melancholy, which, to me, is an evil almost as great as my illness itself. Just imagine yourself in my place and I shall hope to obtain your forgiveness for my long silence. As for the extreme kindness you showed to me in Augsburg in lending me three Carolins, I must beg you to be indulgent with me a little longer: my journey has been a great expense and there is no hope of obtaining the least compensation in this place; fate is not well disposed to me, here in Bonn.

You will pardon me for detaining you with so much chatter; all of it was relevant to my apology.

I beg you not to deprive me of your valuable friendship in future, for I desire nothing so much as to become worthy of your friendship in some way.

With the highest respect,

I am

Your obedient servant and friend,

L. v. Beethoven
Court Organist to the Elector of Cologne

LINES INSCRIBED IN A FRIEND'S ALBUM (*about 1792-3*)

I am not wicked—fiery blood
Is all my malice, and my crime is youth.
Wicked I am not, truly I am not wicked;
Though wild up-surgings often may plead against my heart,
My heart is good.—

To help wherever one can,
Love liberty above all things,
Never deny the truth
Even at the foot of the throne!

TO ELEONORE VON BREUNING

Vienna, November 2nd, 1793

Admirable Eleonore, My dearest friend,

Only now that I have spent almost a whole year in the capital do you hear from me, and yet I have preserved you in my memory both vividly and constantly. Very often I conversed with you and with your dear family, only often without the inner calm for which I would have wished. It was then that I remembered the fatal quarrel, during which my behaviour appeared so despicable. But it could not be undone. Oh, what would I not give to be able to root this whole episode out of my life, this past conduct of mine, so dishonouring to myself, so much opposed to my true character. Certainly, there were several circumstances that always kept us apart and, I imagine, it was mostly the whispered speeches of one against the other that prevented an understanding. Each one of us believed that he was speaking with true conviction, and yet it was only anger kindled by others, and we were both deceived. It is true, my dear friend, that your noble character assures me of your forgiveness; but it is said that the most sincere repentance is that in which one admits his own faults; this was my intention. Now let us draw the curtain on this whole episode and only stop to point the moral: that when friends become involved in differences, it is always better not to employ any middlemen in such matters, but to turn to one's friend in person. Herewith you will receive a dedication[1] from me to you and I only wish that the work were greater and more worthy of you. Here I was plagued with requests to publish this little work, and I am

[1] The Variations on the Theme "*Se vuol ballare*" from Mozart's "Figaro", 1793.

23

availing myself of this opportunity, my admirable Eleonore, to give you some token of my esteem and friendship for you and of my everlasting memories of your house. Accept this trifle and bear in mind that it comes to you from a very admiring friend. Oh, if it gives you a little amusement, all my wishes will have been granted. It should serve to recall the time when I spent so many delightful hours in your house; perhaps it will help to preserve your memory of me until my return, which certainly will not take place in the near future. Oh, how we shall rejoice then, my dear friend! You will see a happier man in your friend, for time and better fortune have smoothed out the furrows left by his repellent past.

If you should see B. Koch, please tell her that it isn't at all kind of her never to write me. After all, I have written to her twice; to Malchus also I have written three times and—no reply. Tell her that if she doesn't want to write she should at least induce Malchus to do so.

At the end of this letter I shall venture another request: it is that I should very much like to be happy enough once again to possess an angora wool waistcoat knit by your own hand, my dear friend. Forgive your friend for making so immodest a request: it arises from his great preference for all things made by your own hands, and perhaps I may tell you in confidence that a certain vanity is at the root of it, that is, the pleasure of being able to say that I possess something made for me by one of the best, most admirable girls in Bonn. It is true, I still have the first, which you were kind enough to present me with in Bonn, but fashion has made it so unfashionable that I can only preserve it in my wardrobe as something most dear to me and given to me by yourself.

You would give me great pleasure by doing me the favour of writing to me soon. Should my letters give you pleasure, I promise you with all certainty that, as far as it is possible for me, I shall oblige you in this, for I welcome all things whereby I can prove to you how entirely I am

Your true and admiring friend,

L. v. Beethoven

TO ELEONORE VON BREUNING

I was most surprised to receive the lovely scarf worked by your own hands; it aroused melancholy feelings in me, agreeable as the thing was to me in itself; remembrance of past times was its effect upon me, also shame on my part on account of your generosity towards me. Truly, I did not think that you still consider me worthy of your attention. Oh, if you had been able to witness the sensations evoked in me yesterday by this event, you would certainly not think it an exaggeration if perhaps I tell you now that to recall you to my mind made me weep and very sad. Little as my deserts may appear in your eyes, I beg you to believe, dear friend (let me call you so still) that I have suffered greatly and still suffer because of the loss of your friendship. I shall never forget you or your dear mother: you were so kind to me that it will take me long to find compensation for losing you. I know what I have lost and what you meant to me, but in order to fill this gap, I should have to revert to scenes as unpleasant for you to hear about as they are unpleasant for me to reconstruct.

By way of a small return for your kind attention to me, I take the liberty of sending you these Variations and this Rondo for Violin.[1] I am extremely busy, otherwise I should have copied the long promised sonata for you; in my manuscript it is little more than a sketch and it would have been difficult even for the otherwise so skilful Paraquin to copy it. You can have the rondo copied and then return the score to me. Of all my things, the two I send you are the only works that might be useful to you, and as you are about to travel to Kerpen in any case, I thought that these trifles might give you some pleasure.

Farewell, my dear friend; it is impossible for me to call you by any other name. Indifferent as you may be to me, do believe me when I say that I revere yourself and your mother as much as ever. Should I be able to make any other contribution to your well-being and pleasure, I beg you not to pass me by; for this

---

[1] For piano and violin, in G major.

remains the only means of expressing my gratitude for the privilege of enjoying your friendship. May your journey be a happy one and may your mother's health be wholly restored by it. Think occasionally of your still true and admiring friend

Beethoven

P.S. The variations will be somewhat difficult to play, expecially the trills in the coda; but do not let this discourage you. It has been devised in such a way that you need play nothing but the trill; you may omit the other notes, as they occur also in the violin part. Never would I have set down a thing of this kind; but I have often observed that from time to time there was someone[1] in Vienna who, when in the evening I had been improvising, usually spent the next day in noting down and preening himself with many of my peculiarities. Now, as I foresaw that soon he would produce similar things, I resolved to forestall him. There was yet another reason: to embarrass the Viennese piano virtuosi. Many of them are my mortal enemies and so I wished to take my revenge in this manner, for I knew in advance that these variations would be submitted to them now and again and that these gentlemen would give a poor account of themselves on these occasions.

TO NIKOLAUS SIMROCK

Vienna, August 2nd, 1794

Dear Simrock,

I deserve something of a dressing-down from you for holding back the variations[2] for so long; but, truly, I am not lying when I tell you that a heap of accumulated business prevented me from correcting them sooner. You will see for yourself what is lacking in them; by the way, I must congratulate you on the engraving, which is pleasant to look at, clear and legible; seriously, if you continue in this way, you will soon be the very

[1] Gelinek, a prolific composer of variations.
[2] Variations in C for four hands, on a theme of Count Waldstein.

26

paragon of all engravers, I mean engravers of music,[1] of course. I promised you in my last letter to send you something of mine, but you interpreted this as mere cavalier clap-trap; what reason have I ever given you for applying this epithet to me? Fie upon you, who would put up with such language in our democratic times? In order to shake off this epithet, I shall make sure of sending you something, which you will certainly engrave, as soon as I have accomplished the great ceremonial inspection of my compositions—that is, in the very near future.

I have also been looking out for an agent and have found an extremely decent, efficient man for you. His name is Traeg. All you need to do now is to write to me or to him, proposing your terms. He asks for a third discount. May the devil understand your bargaining, I wash my hands of it.

Here it is very hot; the Viennese are afraid that soon they will have no more ice cream: as the winter was so rarely cold, ice is scarce now. Here they have been arresting several persons of importance; they say that a revolution was about to break out —but I believe that as long as the Austrians have brown beer and sausages, they'll never revolt. They say that the gates to the suburbs are to be locked at ten o'clock each night. The soldiers keep their arms well loaded. One must not talk too loudly, or the Police give him lodgings for the night.

Are your daughters grown up yet? Educate one of them to be my bride; for if I should go to Bonn without being married, I certainly should not stay there very long. You also must be living in fear now. How is dear Ries?[2] I shall write to him soon. He cannot have a very good opinion of me, but this cursed writing of letters, it seems that I shall never change in this respect! Have you performed my piece[3] yet? Write to me from time to time.

Your Beethoven

If you could send me a few copies of the first set of variations![4]

[1] There is an untranslatable pun here, for the German word *"Stecher"* has several meanings besides that of "engraver".

[2] Franz Ries, violinist in Bonn, the father of Ferdinand Ries.

[3] The Octet for Wind Instruments, composed while Beethoven was still in Bonn, but published only posthumously as Op. 103.

[4] Variations for piano solo on a theme from Dittersdorf's *"Rotkäppchen"* ("Little Red Riding Hood").

TO FRANZ WEGELER

Dearest, best of friends,

In what an abominable light you have exhibited me to my-self! Oh, I admit it, I do not deserve your friendship: you are so noble, so indulgent, and now, for the first time, I am un-worthy of you. I have fallen far below you. Oh, for eight weeks I have annoyed my best friend. You think I have lost some of my goodness of heart: no, thank Heaven! It was not calculated, intentional malice on my part that caused me to act in this way towards you: it was my unpardonable thoughtlessness, which prevented me from seeing the matter in the proper light. Oh, how ashamed I am, not only on your account, but on my own. I hardly dare to ask for your friendship again. Oh, Wegeler, my only consolation is that you have known me almost since my childhood, and yet, let me say so myself, I have always been good at heart and always aspired to be upright and moderate in my actions—how could you have loved me otherwise? Could it be that in such a short time I have changed so horribly, so much for the worse? Impossible! This sense of greatness, of goodness, could it have forsaken me so suddenly? My Wegeler, dear, best of friends, oh try once more to throw yourself wholeheartedly into the arms of your Beethoven: rely on the good qualities which you found in him formerly. I swear to you that the new temple of holy friendship which you will reconstruct there shall stand firm, for ever: no accident, no tempest will ever be able to shake its foundations—firm—for ever our friendship! Forgiveness, oblivion, a rebirth of our dying, sinking friendship! Oh, Wegeler, do not reject it, this hand held out for reconciliation! Place yours in mine—Oh God!—— But enough! I shall come to you myself and throw myself into your arms, imploring you to restore my lost friend, and you will give yourself to me, to your penitent, affectionate, never forgetting

Beethoven once again

FROM A DIARY (*December, 1795*)

Courage. Even with all the frailties of my body, my spirit shall dominate. Twenty-five years have come: this year must decide the mature man. Nothing must remain.

TO NIKOLAUS ZMESKALL VON DOMANOVETZ

Vienna, about 1798

Dearest Baron Mucksplasher,

Je vous suis bien obligé pour votre faiblesse de vos yeux. By the way, I declare that henceforth none shall be permitted to damp the good spirits in which I sometimes indulge; for yesterday I grew quite sad with your Zmeskall-Domanovetzian chatter. The devil take you, I am not at all interested in your moralizing. Strength is the morality of those who distinguish themselves from the rest, and it is mine too, and if you start again to-day I shall plague and torment you till you approve of everything I do; for I shall be at the Swan, though I prefer the Ox, but this depends on your Zmeskall-Domanovetzian decision (*réponse*). Farewell, baron ba . . . . ron ron/ nor/ orn / rno / onr / (*voilà quelque chose* from the old pawnshop).

FROM KARL CZERNY'S REMINISCENCES OF BEETHOVEN

. . . Yet at that time (1798–9) he did not show the slightest sign of being hard of hearing. I had to play something at once and as I felt too shy to begin with one of his own compositions, I played Mozart's great C major Concerto, which begins with a series of chords. Beethoven soon became attentive, came closer to my chair and, in those passages in which I had only to accompany, played the orchestral theme with his left hand. His hands were densely covered with hair and the fingers, especially at the tips, were very broad. When he expressed his satisfaction I summoned up enough courage to perform the "Sonate pathétique", which had just been published, and at last his "Adelaide", which my father sang with his rather good tenor voice. When I had ended, Beethoven turned to my father and said: "The boy has talent, I'll teach him myself and accept him as my pupil. Send him to me once a week. But, above all, get him Emanuel Bach's text-book "On the true manner of performing upon the pianoforte", which he must bring with him next time already."

Now all those who were present congratulated my father on this favourable decision, especially Krumpholz, who was quite enchanted, and my father hurried away at once to find Bach's manual.

During the first lessons Beethoven occupied me exclusively with scales in all the keys, showed me the only right position of the hands, still unknown to most players at that time, the position of the fingers and particularly the use of the thumb — rules the usefulness of which I did not fully appreciate until a much later time. After this, he made me play through the exercises given in this manual and, above all, drew my attention to the *legato*, which he himself mastered in so incomparable a manner and which at that time all other pianists considered impracticable, as it was still the fashion (dating from Mozart's time) to play in a clipped, abrupt manner. . . ..

On one of these mornings[1] Beethoven, who had not seen me for two years and was angry with my father for discontinuing our lessons, came to Prince Lichnowsky's and seemed quite satisfied with my progress. "Didn't I say so at once," he said, "the boy has talent: but", he added, smiling, "his father didn't treat him strictly enough." "Oh, Herr von Beethoven," my father replied good-humouredly, "after all, he's our only child." He was satisfied, too, with my *a vista* playing, when he gave me the manuscript of the C major Sonata, Op. 53, to play at sight.

From this time onwards Beethoven remained well disposed

[1] When Czerny was playing at the house of Prince Lichnowsky.

towards me and treated me as a friend until his last days. I had to correct all the proofs of his new publications and when, in the year 1805, his opera "Leonora" was performed[1] he asked me to arrange it for the piano. . . .

He once told me that as a boy he had been careless and rarely made to work and that his musical education had been a very bad one. "However," he continued, "I had some talent for music." It was touching to hear him say these words quite seriously, as if no one had known this before him. On another occasion the conversation turned to the subject of the fame which his name had acquired in the world. "Oh, nonsense!" he said, "I have never dreamed of writing for fame and honour. What weighs on my heart must come out, and that's why I've written."

FROM WENZEL TOMASCHEK'S REMINISCENCES

. . . The unusual and the original seemed to concern him most as a composer; this is amply confirmed by his reply to a lady, who asked him whether he often attended performances of Mozart's operas. He said that he did not know them and did not like to hear other people's music, as he did not wish to sacrifice his originality.

TO JOHANN NEPOMUK HUMMEL

about 1798–99

Let him[2] not come to see me again! He is a treacherous dog, and may the knacker take all treacherous dogs.

Beethoven

[1] On November 20th.
[2] This, of course, refers to Hummel; the third person was used in formal intercourse.

My dearest Nazerl,

You are an honest fellow and I can see now that you were in the right; so come and see me this afternoon. You will find Schuppanzigh here as well and the two of us will tease, cuff and shake you to your heart's delight.

A kiss from

Your Beethoven, also known as Mehlschöberl[1]

AN ACCOUNT BY GEORG AUGUST GRIESINGER
(*from Seyfried's reminiscences*[2])

When we were still young, I an attaché, Beethoven famous only as a pianist and hardly known as a composer, we met at the house of Prince Lobkowitz. A man who considered himself a great connoisseur of art drew Beethoven into a conversation which centred around the social standing and the inclinations of poets. "I wish", said Beethoven with endearing candour, "that I were above having to wrangle and bargain with the publishers and that I could find one who would decide once and for all to pay me an annual salary, in return for which he would have the right to publish everything I compose, and I shouldn't be slothful in composing. I believe that Goethe has an arrangement of this kind with Cotta and, if I'm not mistaken, Händel's London publisher had a similar one with him." "My dear young man," said this gentleman, putting Beethoven in his place, "you must not complain, for you are neither a Goethe nor a Händel, nor is there any reason to suppose that you will ever be either; for such minds are not born a second time." Beethoven clenched his teeth, cast a contemptuous glance at the gentleman and would not speak another word to him, indeed, even much later he spoke of this man's impudence in no uncertain terms. Prince Lobkowitz endeavoured to calm

[1] A Viennese dish: a kind of pancake or soufflé added to beef broth.
[2] *Charakterzüge und Anekdoten.*

Beethoven and once, when the subject of this gentleman was raised, said to Beethoven in a friendly way: "My dear Beethoven, this gentleman never intended to insult you; almost traditionally most people refuse to believe that one of their younger contemporaries will ever achieve as much as the older ones or the dead, who have already won their reputation." "Unfortunately that's true, Your Grace," replied Beethoven, "but I will not and cannot have any truck with persons who will not believe in me simply because I haven't yet established a general reputation."

TO FRIEDRICH VON MATTHISSON

Vienna, August 4th, 1800

Most estimable Sir,

Herewith you will receive one of my compositions which has been published and engraved already for a number of years but of which, to my shame, perhaps you have no knowledge at all. I cannot excuse myself or explain why I dedicated something to you with such warm and heartfelt respect without even informing you of it, unless it were by telling you that at first I did not know your place of residence, while partly my failure was due to my shyness, as I believed that I had been too impetuous in dedicating to you a work of which I did not know whether you approved.

Even now it is with timidity and apprehension that I send you my "Adelaide". You must know well enough how great a change the lapse of a few years can work in an artist who is always progressing. The greater one's progress in art, the less he is satisfied by his older works. My most ardent wish will have been fulfilled if the musical setting of your divine "Adelaide" is not wholly displeasing to you, and if this will induce you to compose another similar poem soon and if you should not condemn as immodest my request to send such a poem to me at once, I shall do my very utmost to render the beauty of your poems. Please regard the dedication partly as a token of the pleasure which the composition of your "Adelaide" afforded me, partly as a token of my gratitude and respect for the blissful pleasure which your poetry has always given me and will continue to give me.

When hearing A. played through, sometimes recall your truly admiring

Beethoven

TO FRANZ ANTON HOFFMEISTER

Vienna, January 15th (or thereabouts), 1801

It is with the greatest pleasure, dearest brother and friend, that I have read your letter. I thank you most heartily for having formed such a good opinion of myself and of my works, and hope that I shall often deserve it; please convey to Herr Kühnel also the gratitude due to him for his polite and friendly conduct towards me. Your enterprises, too, please me greatly and I wish that, if these works can be of profit to Art, this profit should fall to genuine, true artists rather than to mere grocers. Your intention to publish the works of Sebastian Bach rejoices my heart, which is full of admiration for the great art of this progenitor of harmony, and I hope that your intention will soon be realized; I hope that I myself shall be able to do something for you here, as soon as we hear that golden peace has been declared and as soon as you are ready to collect subscriptions for these works. Now, as far as our business proper is concerned, since you have asked for details, the following may be of use to you. For the time being I propose to you the following items; Septet (which I have already mentioned to you) 20 duc., Symphony 20 duc., Concerto 10 duc., grand solo sonata[1] Allegro, Adagio, Minuetto, Rondo 20 duc. This sonata is not to be sniffed at, dearest brother!

Now for my comments: you may be astonished that here I make no distinction between sonata, septet, symphony; because

1 The works mentioned here are the following: the Septet in E flat, Op. 20; the First Piano Concerto, Op. 21; the Second Symphony, Op. 19, and the Piano Sonata in B flat, Op. 22.

I find that there is less demand for a septet or a symphony, that is why I do so, although undoubtedly a symphony should count for more. (N.B. The septet consists of a brief introductory Adagio, then Allegro, Adagio, Minuetto, Andante with variations, Minuetto, again a brief introductory Adagio and then Presto.) I ask only 10 duc. for the concerto because, as I have already informed you, I do not regard it as one of my best. I do not suppose that you will consider this sum excessive, the total amount, I mean; at least I have endeavoured to make the prices as moderate as possible for you. As for the remission, this could be made to Geymüller or to Schüller, since you left me free to choose. The total sum, then, would be 70 ducats for all the four works; I can use no currency other than Viennese ducats. As for how many of your gold talers this sum amounts to, all such matters are not my concern, as I am really a bad businessman and mathematician.

Well, that's the end of this unpleasant business; I call it so because I wish that it could be done differently in this world. There should be only a single Art Exchange in the world; the artist would simply send his works there, to be given as much as he needs; as it is, one has to be half a merchant on top of everything else, and how badly one goes about it! Yes, by Jove! I do call it unpleasant. As for those asses in Leipzig,[1] it's best simply to let them talk, for they certainly will not make anyone immortal with their chatter, any more than they will take away his immortality from one to whom it has been granted by Apollo.

Now may Heaven protect you and your partner; I have been unwell for some time and it is even a little difficult for me now to write down music, much more so to write letters. I hope that we shall often have occasion to assure one another how truly you are my friends and how truly I am

Your brother and friend,

L. v. Beethoven

Hoping to hear from you soon. Adieu.

---

[1] The reviewers of the *Allgemeine Musikalische Zeitung*.

TO BREITKOPF UND HÄRTEL, MUSIC PUBLISHERS IN LEIPZIG

Vienna, April 22nd, 1801

P.P.

You will excuse this belated reply to your letter, I have been continually unwell for some time and, at the same time, over-whelmed with business, and as, altogether, I am not the most industrious of correspondents, this, too, may serve to excuse me. As for your request regarding works of mine, I am very sorry to say that at this moment I cannot offer you satisfaction. You need only do me the favour of informing me what kind of works it is that you wish to have, namely: Symphony, Quartets, Sonata, etc., so that I may dispose accordingly and, in case I should have that which you need or desire, I may submit it to you. Mollo, if I remember rightly, is publishing some eight works; Hoffmeister at Leipzig is likewise publishing four. In this connection I should like to observe that one of my first concertos is being brought out by Hoffmeister, and it follows that it is not one of my best works, that Mollo, also, is publishing a concerto which, though written later, is likewise not yet among the best of my works in that class. This is intended only as a hint for your Musical Review in connection with the judgment of these works, although when one can hear them, that is: played well, it will be easier to judge them. Musical politics demands that the best concertos should be withheld from the public for a time. Advise your reviewer to show more discretion and more intelligence, especially with regard to the products of younger authors, for these reviews could easily discourage men who might otherwise do better work; as for myself, it is true that I am far from having attained such perfection as would exempt me from all criticism, yet at first your reviewer's outcry against me was so humiliating that, by beginning to compare myself with others, I could scarcely be affected by it at all, but remained quite calm and thought, they do not understand it; I could remain all the more unmoved by it all when I observed how elsewhere your reviewer exalted men who have little importance in this place among the better artists—indeed, who are almost lost here, decent and hard-working as they may be. But now *pax vobiscum*; peace be with you and with myself; I should never have breathed a word of all this if you had not raised the matter yourself. When recently I went to see a good friend of mine and he showed me the sum that had been collected for the daughter of the immortal god of harmony,[1] I was astonished at the insignificant amount which Germany, and especially your Germany, had granted to a person whom I honour for her father's sake; this gave me the idea, what about publishing something by subscription for this person's benefit, submitting this sum and the annual revenue from it to the public's attention, so as to guard ourselves against every possible attack? You could do more than anyone to support me in this scheme. Write to me quickly, telling me the best way of going about it, so that it may happen before this Bach dies on us, before this brook[2] dries up and we can no longer water it. It goes without saying that you must publish this work of mine.

With great respect, I am your devoted

Ludwig van Beethoven

TO KARL AMENDA

Vienna, June 1st, *1801*

My dear, good Amenda, my true friend,

With the deepest emotion, with a pleasure mingled with pain I received and read your last letter. With what can I compare your fidelity, your devotion to me? Oh, it is a fine thing indeed that you have always remained so well disposed towards me; and I am well aware that you have proved your worth more entirely than all the others, a distinction I shall always observe. You are not one of those Viennese friends, no, you are one of that kind which my native soil has always produced. How often

---

[1] Susanna, the youngest daughter of J. S. Bach.
[2] A pun on the name of Bach, which is German for "brook".

I wish that you were with me, for your Beethoven lives most unhappily, in discord with nature and with the Creator. More than once I have cursed the latter for exposing his creatures to the slightest accident, so that often the loveliest blossoms are destroyed and broken by it. You must be told that the finest part of me, my hearing, has greatly deteriorated. Already then, at the time when you were still with me, I felt signs of this and kept quiet about it: now it has grown progressively worse. Whether it can ever be cured, remains to be seen. They say that it is occasioned by the condition of my bowels: but as far as these are concerned, I have almost entirely recovered. Whether my hearing, too, will now improve—I sincerely hope so, but it is unlikely: illnesses of this kind are the most incurable.

How miserably I must now live, avoid all that is dear and precious to me, and then among such despicable, egotistic people as ——, etc. I can say that of all my friends Lichnowsky[1] has proved the worthiest: since last year he has set aside the sum of 600 guilders for me. This and the good sale of my works relieves me of all worries regarding my livelihood. Everything that I write now I can immediately sell five times over and get a good price for it as well. I have written a good deal recently. As I hear that you have ordered pianos at ——'s, I shall be sending you something from time to time inside the lid of one those instruments, where it will not cost you much.

Now, to my great comfort, once again I have met with a person[2] with whom I can share the pleasure of social intercourse and disinterested friendship: he is one of the friends of my youth. Often already I have talked to him about you and told him that, since I left my native land, you have been one of those chosen by my heart. He, too, cannot approve of ——, who is, and always will be, too feeble for friendship. I look upon him and —— as mere instruments on which I play when I feel so inclined; but never can they become true witnesses of my outer and inner activities, no more than they can have any

[1] Prince Karl Lichnowsky (1758–1814), a pupil of Mozart's; one of Beethoven's most generous patrons.
[2] Anton Reicha (1770–1836), flautist and composer, who had played in the orchestra at Bonn.

38

real part in my life: I assess their value by what they are worth to me, and that's all. Oh, how happy I should be now if only I had the full use of my ears! Then I should hasten to join you; but, as it is, I must refrain from all such escapades. The best years of my life will pass away without achieving all that my talent and my powers would have promised me.

Sad resignation, in which I must take refuge! True enough, I have resolved to overcome all these impediments, but how will it be possible? I tell you, Amenda, if in half a year's time my complaint turns out to be incurable, then I shall call upon your help, then you must leave everything behind and come to me. Then I shall travel (in my playing and composing my defect matters least, most of all in social intercourse) and you shall be my companion. I am convinced that my luck will not run out: have I not reached the stage at which no one and nothing can prevail against me? Since the time when you left I have written everything except operas and church music. Surely you will not refuse me this, you will help your friend to bear his sorrows and his afflictions. My piano-playing, too, has improved immensely and I hope that this journey may perhaps make your fortune as well; after that, you will remain with me for good.

I have received all your letters satisfactorily; little as I have replied to them, I have always borne you in mind and my heart beats for you as tenderly as ever. I beg you to treat the matter of my hearing as a great secret, which you must not betray to anyone at all. Write to me very often. Your letters, however brief they may be, console me, soothe me, and I expect to hear from you again in the very near future, my dear friend. By no means pass on your quartet,[1] as I have altered it greatly; for only now have I learned to write quartets as they should be written, as you will see for yourself when you receive them.

Now farewell, my dear, good‧friend. If you should think of any favour I might do you here, it goes without saying that you yourself will at once inform

Your faithful, truly affectionate,

Beethoven

[1] Op. 18, No. 1, published in 1801, but composed in 1798 or 1799.

Vienna, June 29th, 1801

My dear, good Wegeler,

How grateful I am to you for thinking of me. I have deserved it so little and done so little to deserve it, and yet you are so very kind and let nothing, not even my unpardonable remissness, come between us, but always remain my faithful, kind and honourable friend. That I should ever forget you, any of you, indeed, who were once so close and dear to me, no, this I do not think possible. There are moments at which I long for you and even long to be with you for a while. My native country, the beautiful scenery in which I first saw the light of day, is still as lovely and vivid in my sight as when I left you. In short, I shall consider that occasion one of the happiest events of my life when I shall see you again and greet Father Rhine. When this will be, I cannot yet be sure. All I can tell you is that you will only see me again as a truly great man. Not only shall you find me greater as an artist, but better, more nearly perfect as a man. And if the prosperity of our country improves, my art shall be exhibited only in the service of the poor. Oh, happy moment, how fortunate I think myself to be able to further, if not to create such a moment! You would like to know something about my situation: well, it could be worse. Ever since last year, Lichnowsky, who—unbelievable as it may seem to you when I tell you so—has always been, and remains, my most ardent friend (of course there have been slight differences between us, but didn't these serve to cement our friendship even more?) has set aside a fixed sum of 600 guilders, on which I can draw as long as I have found no suitable employment. My compositions bring in a good deal of money and I can say that I receive more commissions than I can possibly accept. Besides, I have six or seven publishers for every item, and more if I wish: they no longer bargain with me: I demand, they pay. You can see that it's a pleasant situation: for example, I see that one of my friends is in need and just at that moment my purse does not allow me to help him at once, so I have only to sit down and in a short time help is forth-coming. Also, I am more economical than formerly. If I should stay here for good, I shall probably succeed in giving one concert a year: I have already given several.

Only the jealous daemon, my poor health, has put a spoke in the wheel: for three years my hearing has been growing steadily worse and this, they say, is due to my abdomen, which, as you know, has always been in a bad state, but has deteriorated even more in this place, where I have been continually troubled with dysentery and an extraordinary weakness occasioned by it. Frank wanted to tone up my body with strengthening medicines and restore my hearing with the help of almond oil, but *prosit*! Nothing came of it, my hearing grew worse and worse and my abdomen remained in the same state. This lasted till the autumn of last year, when I was sometimes in despair. Then a medical ass came along and prescribed cold baths for my condition, while a more sensible one prescribed the usual lukewarm Danube bath: this worked wonders, my belly improved, my hearing remained as it was or became even worse. This winter I was in a really miserable state; then I had some really terrible colics and quite relapsed into my former condition, and so it went on until about four weeks ago, when I went to see Vering, thinking that this condition demanded a surgeon as well and, besides, I have always had confidence in him. Now he succeeded almost completely in stopping this violent dysentery. He pre-scribed the lukewarm Danube bath, into which every time I had to pour a bottle of some strengthening stuff, gave me no medicine, except some pills for the stomach about four days ago and a kind of tea for my ears, and I must say that I have been feeling better and stronger since; except for my ears, which whistle and roar incessantly, night and day. I can say that I am leading a miserable life; for two years, almost, I have been avoiding all the social functions, simply because I feel incapable of telling people: I am deaf. If I belonged to any other pro-fession, it would not be quite so bad; but in my profession this is a terrible affliction. Then, there are my enemies, by no means few in number: what would they have to say about this?

To give you some idea of this strange deafness, let me tell you that in the theatre I have to keep quite close to the orchestra, lean against the railings, in fact, to understand the actors. The high notes of instruments, singing voices, I do not hear at all if I am at some distance from them. As for conversation, it is a marvel that there are people who have never noticed my deafness; as I have always been absent-minded, it is attributed to this. Sometimes, too, I scarcely hear those who are speaking softly, I hear the tones, but not the words: and yet I cannot bear to be yelled at. Heaven only knows what will come of it. Vering says it will certainly get better, if not quite well. Often already I have cursed the Creator and my existence. Plutarch has taught me resignation. If it is only possible, I am determined to resist my fate, although there will be moments when I shall be God's unhappiest creature. I beg you not to say anything about my condition to anyone, not even to Lorchen;[1] it is only as a secret that I entrust it to you. I should be very glad if you would have some correspondence about this matter with Vering. If my condition remains unchanged, I shall come to see you in the spring: you will rent a house for me somewhere in the country, in beautiful surroundings, and then for half a year I shall turn peasant; perhaps this will work some change. Resignation! what a wretched refuge, and yet it is the only one left to me. You will forgive me for burdening you with this friendly duty in spite of your own unhappy situation.

Steffen Breuning is now staying here and we meet almost every day; it does me so much good to revive the old feelings. He has really become a good, splendid fellow, with something in his head and—as we all have more or less—his heart in the right place. I have now got a very fine apartment that looks out on the bastions and is doubly valuable in view of my health. I do think that I shall be able to make it possible for Breuning to come and stay with me.

You shall have your *Antioch*[2] and also a great many more of

[1] Wegeler's wife, *née* Eleonore von Breuning.
[2] A picture by Füger, Director of the Academy of Painting in Vienna.

my musical scores, if you don't think that these will be too expensive for you. Your love of art still gives me great pleasure. Only let me know how it can be done, and I shall send you all my works, which, however, are pretty numerous and increasing daily. In exchange for the portrait of my grandfather, which I beg you to send as soon as possible by mail coach, I am sending you that of his grandson, your devoted and affectionate Beethoven; it is being published here by Artaria, who, like many other art dealers here and abroad, have often asked me for permission to publish my portrait. As for Stoffel,[1] I intend to write to him in the near future, not without giving him a piece of my mind in connection with his stubbornness. I intend to deafen him with reminders of our old friendship: he must promise me solemnly not to inflict more injuries on you all in your present gloomy state. I shall write to dear Lorchen too. Never have I forgotten a single one of you, my dear, good friends, even though I may not have written a word to you: but writing, as you know, has never been my forte: even my best friends have not heard from me for years. I live only in my scores, and when one thing is hardly completed, another is already on the way. As I compose at present, I often write three or four works at the same time.

Write to me more often from now on. I shall do my best to find time to write to you occasionally. Give my regards to everyone, not forgetting the good *Frau Hofrätin*, and tell her "that I still occasionally get into a frenzy". As for the Kochs, I am not at all surprised by the change in them: fortune is round as a ball and does not, therefore, always fall on the noblest or the best.

Concerning Ries, to whom I send my kindest regards, in the matter of his son, I shall write to you more fully later, though I do believe that Paris would be a better place than Vienna for one who wishes to make his fortune. Vienna is overcrowded with people and it is therefore difficult even for the most deserving to maintain their success. By the autumn or the winter

[1] Christoph von Breuning.

43

I shall know what I can do for him, as at that time everyone hurries back to town.

Farewell, my dear, faithful Wegeler, rest assured of the love and friendship of your

Beethoven

TO FRANZ WEGELER

Vienna, November 16th, 1801

. . . Now my life is a little more agreeable again, because I spend more time with others. You would hardly believe how dreary, how sad my life has been in the last two years: my bad hearing haunted me everywhere like a ghost, I fled from men, had to appear a misanthropist, though I am far from being one. This change has been brought about by a charming, fascinating girl,[1] who loves me and whom I love. At last, after two years, there have been some moments of complete bliss, and this is the first time I have ever felt that marriage could make one happy. Unfortunately she is not of my social standing and, besides, I could not marry at present, I must still struggle valiantly. If it were not for my hearing, I would have travelled half-way round the world by now, and this I must do. For me there is no greater pleasure than to pursue and display my art.

Do not think I should be happier with you: what, indeed, should make me happier? Even your care for me would hurt me, I should always be conscious of the compassion on your faces and feel only more unhappy. What did those fine native surroundings of mine bestow on me? Nothing but the hope of a better state: and this would have been fulfilled now—were it not for this affliction. Oh, if I were free from this, I should embrace the world! My youth—yes, I feel it, is only beginning now. Have I not always been a sickly person? My physical strength has been increasing more than ever for some time, and so are my mental powers. Every day I draw nearer to the goal which I can sense, but not describe. Only in this can your

---

[1] Probably Countess Giulietta Guicciardi.

44

Beethoven live. Do not mention rest! I know of no other kind than sleep and it pains me enough to be obliged to give up more of my time to it than before. Grant me only partial release from my affliction, and I shall come to you as an accomplished, mature man to renew our old feelings of friendship. You shall see me as joyful as it is possible to be here on earth, not unhappy—no, I could not bear that. I shall seize Fate by the throat, it shall never wholly subdue me. Oh, it is good to live one's life a thousand times! As for a quiet life, no, I feel I am no longer made for it. . . .

TO HOFFMEISTER

Vienna, April 8th, 1802

May the devil ride the whole lot of you, gentlemen—what, suggest to me that I should write a sonata of that sort? At the time of the revolutionary fever—well, at that time it would have been worth considering, but now that everything is trying to get back into the old rut, Buonaparte has made his concordat with the Pope—a sonata of that sort? If at least it were a *Missa pro Sancta Maria a tre voci* or a Vespers, etc.—well, in that case I should immediately take hold of the brush and write down a *Credo in unum* in enormous notes weighing a pound each —but good heavens, a sonata of that sort at the beginning of this new Christian age—ho ho!—count me out of that, for nothing will come of it.

Now my reply in very quick time. The lady can have a sonata of mine, and indeed I will follow her general plan as far as the aesthetics of the thing is concerned—and without keeping to the suggested keys. The price about 5 duc.—for that she can enjoy the sonata for a year, during which neither I nor she may publish it. When that year has elapsed the sonata is mine exclusively— i.e. I can and shall publish it, while she can insist, if she thinks that this will redound to her honour, that I dedicate it to her.

Now God preserve you, gentlemen.

My sonata has been well engraved, but you've certainly taken your time. Be a little more prompt in sending my septet out into the world, because the rabble is waiting for it—and, as you know, the Empress has it and there are scoundrels in the Imperial city as well as at the Imperial court, I cannot offer you any guarantee in this matter, so make haste.

Lately Herr Mollo has once again published my quartets full of mistakes and errata on a large and a small scale, they teem in it as fish do in water, i.e. ad infinitum. *Questo è un piacere per un autore*—that's what I call engraving, for truly, my skin has been gravely cut and ripped over these fine editions of my quartets. Now farewell and think of me as I do of you. Even unto death, your faithful

L. v. Beethoven

TO BREITKOPF UND HÄRTEL

Vienna, July 13th, 1802

. . . With respect to the transcriptions and arrangements, I am now sincerely pleased that you refused them. The unnatural fury, by which we are possessed, to transplant even things written for the piano to string instruments, instruments so entirely opposed to each other, should certainly come to an end. It is my firm opinion that only Mozart could translate his own works from the piano to other instruments, and Haydn likewise, and without wishing to join company with these two great men, I believe that it also true of my piano sonatas. As not only whole passages must be omitted or changed, there is this additional difficulty, and this is the great stumbling-block which can be overcome only by the Master himself or at least by one who has no less skill and inventiveness. I have transformed only a single one of my sonatas[1] into a quartet for string instruments, because I was asked to do so most urgently, and I know for certain that this was a feat which others will imitate at their peril. . . .

[1] Sonata in E major, Op. 14, No. 1, which appeared in 1802 transcribed for string quartet.

FROM THE "BIOGRAPHICAL NOTES"[1] OF
FERDINAND RIES

In the year 1802 Beethoven was in Heiligenstadt, a village about an hour and a half's journey from Vienna, composing his Third Symphony (now known by the name of "Sinfonia eroica"). When composing, Beethoven often had some specific matter in mind, although he frequently laughed at musical painting and condemned it, especially trivial examples of this genre. In this connection he did not spare Haydn's "Creation" and "The Seasons", although Beethoven did not fail to pay tribute to Haydn's greater achievements, and accorded well-deserved praise to many choruses and other works of Haydn. In writing this symphony Beethoven had been thinking of Buonaparte, but Buonaparte while he was still First Consul. At that time Beethoven had the highest esteem for him and compared him to the greatest consuls of ancient Rome. Not only I, but many of Beethoven's closer friends, saw this symphony on his table, beautifully copied in manuscript, with the word "Buonaparte" inscribed at the very top of the title-page and "Luigi van Beethoven" at the very bottom, but not another word. Whether and how this gap was to be filled, I do not know. I was the first to tell him the news that Buonaparte had declared himself Emperor, whereupon he flew into a rage and exclaimed: "So he is no more than a common mortal! Now, too, he will tread under foot all the rights of man, indulge only his own ambition; now he will think himself superior to all men, become a tyrant!" Beethoven went to the table, seized the top of the title-page, tore it in half and threw it on the floor. The first page had to be re-copied and it was only now that the symphony received the title "Sinfonia eroica".

. . . Once, during a walk, I spoke to him of two pure fifths which produce a notable and lovely effect in one of his first string quartets, the one in C minor. Beethoven did not know of them and insisted that I was wrong in saying that they were fifths. As it was his custom always to carry music paper, I asked

[1] *Biographische Notizen über Ludwig van Beethoven* (in collaboration with Wegeler), 1838.

for some and wrote down the passage in question for him, complete with all the four parts. When he saw that I was right, he said, "Well, and who has forbidden them?" As I did not know how to take this question, he repeated it several times, till at last, full of amazement, I replied: "But it's one of the elementary rules." He repeated his question once more, whereupon I said: "Marpurg, Kirnberger, Fux, etc., etc., all of them theorists!" "In that case, I permit them!" was his reply.

THE HEILIGENSTADT TESTAMENT
(*To Karl and Johann van Beethoven*)

For my brothers Karl and (Johann) Beethoven.

O, you men who believe or declare that I am malevolent, stubborn or misanthropic, how greatly you wrong me! You do not know the secret cause behind the appearance. From childhood onwards my heart and my mind have tended towards a gentle benevolence. I have always been disposed even to accomplish great deeds. Yet only consider that for six years I have been suffering an incurable affliction, aggravated by imprudent physicians. Year after year deceived by the hope of an improvement, finally forced to contemplate the prospect of a lasting illness, whose cure may take years or may even be impossible, born with a fiery, impulsive temperament, sensible, even, to the distractions of social life, I was yet compelled early in my life to isolate myself, to spend my life in solitude. Even if at times I wished to overcome all this, oh, how harshly I was driven back by the doubly grievous experience of my bad hearing, and yet I could not prevail upon myself to say to men: speak louder, shout, for I am deaf. Oh, how could I possibly admit to being defective in the very sense which should have been more highly developed in me than in other men, a sense which once I possessed in its most perfect form, a form as perfect as few in my profession, surely, know or have known in the past. Oh, I cannot do it. Therefore you must forgive me if you should see me draw back when I would gladly mingle with you. My affliction is all the more painful to me because it leads to such misinterpretations of my conduct. Recreation in human society, refined conversation, mutual effusions of thought are denied to me. Almost quite alone, I may commit myself to social life only as far as the most urgent needs demand. I must live like an exile. When I do venture near some social gathering, I am seized with a burning terror, the fear that I may be placed in the dangerous position of having to reveal my condition. So, too, it has been with me during the past half-year, which I spent in the country. When my reasonable physician ordered me to spare my hearing as much as possible, he almost accorded with my natural disposition, although sometimes, overpowered by the urge to seek society, I disobeyed his orders. But what an humiliation when someone standing next to me heard a flute in the distance and I heard nothing, or when someone heard the shepherd sing and, again, I heard nothing. Such occurrences brought me to the verge of despair. I might easily have put an end to my life. Only one thing, Art, held me back. Oh, it seemed impossible to me to leave this world before I had produced all that I felt capable of producing, and so I prolonged this wretched existence—truly wretched, (because I am cursed with) a body so irritable that a somewhat sudden change can plunge me from the best into the worst of states. Patience—so I am told, it is patience that I must now choose to be my guide: I have patience enough. My determination to hold out until it pleases the inexorable Fates to cut the thread shall be a lasting one, I sincerely hope. Perhaps there will be an improvement, perhaps not: I am prepared. Already in my 28th year I have been compelled to become a philosopher; this is no easy matter, more difficult for an artist than for anyone else. Divine one, thou canst see into my inmost thoughts, thou knowest them; thou knowest that love of my fellow men and the desire to do good are harboured there. O, men, when one day you read these words, reflect that you did me wrong; and let the unhappy man take comfort in his meeting with one of his kind; one who, despite all his natural disabilities yet did everything in his power to be admitted into the ranks of worthy artists and men. You, my brothers Karl and (Johann) as soon as I am dead (if) Professor Schmidt[1] is still alive, ask him in my name to describe my illness, and add this document to his account, so that, as far as possible, the world may be reconciled with me after my death. At the same time I declare you both to be the heirs to my small fortune (if one can call it such). Divide it fairly, bear with and help each other. The evil you have done me, as you know yourselves, has long been forgiven you. To you, brother Karl, I give special thanks for the devotion shown to me in these recent times. It is my wish that you may lead lives better and more free from cares than my own. Recommend virtue to your children: for virtue alone, not money, can grant us happiness; I speak from experience. It was virtue that raised me up even in my misery; it is owing to virtue, and to my art, that I did not end my life by suicide. Farewell and love each other! I give thanks to all my friends, but especially to Prince Lichnowsky and to Professor Schmidt. I desire that the instruments given to me by Prince Lichnowsky[2] be preserved by one of you; yet let no quarrel arise among you on this account. However, as soon they can be of more use to you in this way, by all means sell them. How glad I am at the thought that even in the grave I may render you some service!

Now it is done. It is with joy that I hasten to meet my death. Should death come before I have had time to develop all my artistic faculties, then, in spite of my cruel fate, it will come too soon and I would wish that its coming might be delayed. Yet even then I shall be content: does not death liberate me from a state of endless suffering? Come whenever it pleases thee to come: bravely I shall come out to meet thee. Farewell and do not quite forget me when I am dead. I have deserved this of you, for often in my lifetime I thought of you, wondering how I could make you happy; be so!

Heiligenstadt, October 6th, 1802.

Ludwig van Beethoven

[1] Johann Adam Schmidt, an eye specialist and professor of medicine at Vienna University, had been treating Beethoven.

[2] Prince Lichnowsky had made Beethoven a present of a set of old string instruments, enough for a string quartet; the makers were Amati and Guarneri.

So I must bid you farewell—though sadly. Yes, the cherished hope—which I brought with me when I came here, of being healed at least to a certain degree, must now abandon me entirely. As the leaves of autumn fall and are withered, so, too—my hope has dried up. Almost as I was when I came here, I leave again—even the courage—which often inspired me on lovely summer days—is vanished. O Providence—let a single day of untroubled joy be granted to me! For so long already the resonance of true joy has been unknown to me. O when —O when, Divine one—may I feel it once more in the temple of Nature and of mankind? Never?—no—that would be too hard!

TO BREITKOPF UND HÄRTEL

October 18th, 1802

I should like to add the following comments to the letter that my brother has written to you. I have composed two sets of Variations,[1] one of which consists of eight variations, the other of thirty. Both have been worked out in an entirely new manner, each in another, different way. I should prefer to see them engraved by you, but on no other condition than an inclusive payment for both of them, about fifty ducats. Make sure that this offer has not been made in vain, for I assure you that you will not regret having accepted these two works. In them, every theme is elaborated in a manner peculiar to itself, different from that of the rest. Usually it is only others who tell me that I have had a new idea, as I never know it myself, but this time I myself must assure you that the manner in these two works is a complete innovation on my part. I cannot accept what you

[1] In spite of the inconsistencies, Beethoven was probably referring to the Six Variations in F major (Op. 34) and the Fifteen Variations and Fugue in E flat, on a theme from his ballet "Prometheus", Op. 35, both of which were published by Breitkopf and Härtel in 1803.

have told me about the attempted sale of my works. Surely there is sufficient proof of the demand for my works when nearly all the foreign publishers write incessantly to ask me for new works, and even the piratical engravers, as you rightly complain, are among this number, while Simrock has written to me several times to ask for works which would be his exclusive property and is willing to pay me quite as much as any other publisher for such works. You may regard it as a kind of favour that I have personally made this offer to you, rather than to others, for, indeed, your firm deserves to be so distinguished.

Your

L. v. Beethoven

TO? (Zmeskall or Count Moritz Lichnowsky)

Vienna, 1802

Dearest, victorious though sometimes fallible Count, I hope that you will have rested soundly, dearest, most charming of Counts! Dearly beloved, most extraordinary of Counts!

("Count Count Count . . . dearest Count, dearest Sheep,
best of Counts, best of Sheep.")

When can we meet at Walter's to-day? I am entirely
dependent on your ability or inability in this matter.

Yours,

Beethoven

TO BREITKOPF UND HÄRTEL

December, 1802

Instead of all the din about a new method of variations, such
as our neighbours, the Gallo-Franks would raise, just as, for
example, a certain French composer presented me with fugues
après une nouvelle méthode, which new method consists in that the
fugue is no longer a fugue, etc.—I did wish, nonetheless, to draw
the non-expert's attention to the fact that these Variations do
at least differ from others, and I thought that this could be done
least ostentatiously and least affectedly in the form of this little

53

prefatory note, which I ask you to affix both to the smaller and the greater set of Variations; in which language or in how many languages, this I leave to you to decide, since we poor Germans are obliged to talk in all languages and must accept the fact.

FROM KARL CZERNY'S REMINISCENCES

About the year 1803, when Beethoven had composed Op. 28, he said to his intimate friend Krumpholz: "I am far from satisfied with my past works: from to-day onwards I will turn over a new leaf." Shortly after this incident he published the three sonatas, Op. 31, in which one can detect the partial realization of his intention.

His improvisation was most brilliant and amazing: in whatever kind of society he might find himself, he was able to make such an impression on every one of his listeners that often not a single eye remained dry, while some began to sob loudly; for, apart from the beauty and originality of his ideas and his ingenious manner of expressing them, there was something magical about his playing. When he had ended an improvisation of this kind, he was capable of laughing noisily and of ridiculing the emotion which he had aroused in his listeners. "You're a crowd of fools", he would say. Sometimes he even felt offended by such signs of their interest and sympathy. "Who can live among such spoilt children?" he exclaimed, and it was only for this reason (as he told me) that he refused an invitation which the King of Prussia sent to him after one of those improvisations described above. . . .

Far more valuable still (than his written remarks on theoretical matters) were Beethoven's oral statements about musical matters of every sort, about other composers, etc., whom he always judged with great assurance, pertinent, often caustic, wit and invariably from the high standpoint which his genius allocated to him and from which he surveyed the whole of Art. For that reason, his assessment, even of classical names, was always a strict one and was uttered in the manner of one who feels himself to be their equal. On one occasion, while I was giving his nephew a lesson, he said to me: "You mustn't think that you're doing me a favour by giving him my own stuff to play. I am not childish enough to desire that. Give him whatever you think is good for him."

I mentioned Clementi. "Yes, certainly", he said. "Clementi is quite good." Laughing, he added: "For the time being you'd better give Karl the regular things, until he's ready for the irregular."

After such conceits, with which nearly all his conversation was generously spiced, he would roar with laughter. As in former times the critics had often accused him of irregularities, he would readily allude to this in a humorous and merry fashion.

FROM A SKETCH-BOOK (1804)

June 2nd—Finale more and more simple, likewise all my piano music. God knows why still my piano music always makes the worst impression upon me, especially when it's badly played.

TO GOTTLIEB WIEDEBEIN

Baden, July 6th, 1804

I am glad, Sir, that you have done me the honour of approaching me, although I regret that I cannot offer you as much help as I should like to do. It is not as easy as you imagine to make one's way here, since Vienna is full of master musicians who earn their living by giving lessons. If, however, there were any certainty of my remaining here, I should ask you to take the risk of joining me. But as I shall probably be leaving as early as next winter, I should no longer be able to do anything for you. To give up your position is a course I cannot possibly recommend to you, since I cannot promise you another.

Your claim that it is impossible to obtain even moderately good tuition in Brunswick seems to me somewhat exaggerated. Without the least intention of holding myself up as a model to you, I can assure you that I have lived in a small, unimportant place—and that, there as well as here, I have become what I am almost entirely by my own efforts. I tell you this only for your consolation in case you should feel the need to make some progress in your art. Your variations show promise, yet I assume that you have changed the theme; why did you do that? What a man loves must not be taken from him—and this means making an alteration even before beginning the variations. Should I be in a position to do anything else for you, you will find me ready to do so, as in all such cases.

Your devoted servant,

Ludwig van Beethoven

TO FERDINAND RIES

Baden, about the middle of July, 1804

Dear Ries,

As Breuning did not have the decency to refrain from exhibiting my character to you and to the tutor in such a light that I appear as a pitiable, wretched and petty creature—all this by his inexcusable behaviour—I have chosen you, firstly, to convey my answer to Breuning orally, though only to one, the first, point in his letter, which I am answering only so that it may justify my character in your eyes. Tell him, therefore, that it never occurred to me to reproach him for not giving notice in time and that, if it had really been Breuning's fault, still I value every harmonious relationship far too dearly ever to give offence to one of my friends because of a few hundred or more. You yourself know that I reproached him entirely in jest with being responsible for the delay in giving notice. I am certain that you will remember this; as for me, I had entirely forgotten the whole matter. Then, during dinner, my brother began again by saying that he thought Breuning responsible; I denied it immediately and said that you were responsible. I should think it is clear enough that I do not blame Breuning for it. Thereupon Breuning jumped to his feet like a raving maniac, saying that he would have the tutor called. This behaviour, a kind of behaviour to which I am not accustomed on the part of anyone with whom I have any dealings, upset my balance completely; I, too, jumped up, threw over my chair, left the room and did not return. This conduct on my part induced Breuning to paint me in such lovely colours to you and to the tutor, also to send me a letter which, by the way, I can answer only by silence. To Breuning I have nothing more to say. His manner of acting and thinking with regard to me proves that no friendly relationship should ever have been established between us and certainly will not be maintained in future. I wished to acquaint you with this, as your testimony has debased my whole manner of thinking and acting. I know that you would certainly not have done so if you had been acquainted with the above evidence, and I am satisfied with that.

Now, dear Ries, I beg you to go straight to my brother, the chemist, as soon as you receive this letter and to tell him that I shall be leaving Baden already within the next few days and that he should find me lodgings in Döbling without delay. I very nearly went straight there, already to-day: this place disgusts me, I am sick of it. For Heaven's sake see to it that he takes lodgings for me at once, as I wish to move in at once, as soon as I get to Döbling. As for Breuning, neither tell nor show him anything of what is written on the other side of this letter; I wish to show him in every possible way that I do not think as pettily as he does himself, and wrote my controlled letter to him only after writing this, although my decision to end our friendship is firm and shall remain so.

Your friend,

Beethoven

TO FERDINAND RIES

Baden, July 24th, 1804

. . . This business about Breuning has probably astonished you. Believe me, dear Ries, my outburst was nothing more than the accumulated effect of several unpleasant experiences that I have had with him in the past. I have the gift of being able to hide and restrain my irritability in a great many things; if, however, a single provocation is offered to me at a time when I am more easily angered, I inevitably explode with greater violence than any other man. Doubtless Breuning has some excellent qualities, but he imagines that he has no faults at all, when in fact he usually suffers most from the very faults he claims to have discovered in others. In him there is a spirit of pettiness which, ever since my childhood, I have despised. My judgment had already warned me of the course that our relationship was likely to take, for our ways of thinking, acting and feeling are too far apart. Yet I had believed that these obstacles, too, could be overcome—experience has proved me wrong. And now I am cured of friendship, too. I have found only two persons[1] in the world with whom I have never had so much as a misunderstanding; but, then, what fine people they were, too! One of them is dead, the other still alive. Although for nearly six years each has known nothing of the other, I do know that I occupy the foremost place in his heart, as he does in mine. A well-founded friendship demands the greatest affinity of heart and soul between two persons. I should like nothing more than to let you read the letter I wrote to Breuning and his letter to me. No, never again will he be able to claim the place which he had formerly occupied in my heart. Anyone who is capable of attributing such a base mentality to his friend and equally capable of such base conduct towards him is not worthy to be my friend. Don't forget the matter of my lodgings. My best wishes to you. Don't spend too much time tailoring,[2] give my regards to the loveliest of the lovely, send

[1] Lorenz von Breuning, Stephan's brother, who died in 1798; and Franz Wegeler.
[2] Ries occupied rooms in the house of a tailor who had three beautiful daughters.

me half a dozen darning needles. Never in my life should I have believed that I could be as lazy as I am here. Should this be followed by an outburst of industry, something really good may come of it.

Vale!

Beethoven

FROM THE "BIOGRAPHICAL NOTES" OF FERDINAND RIES

Beethoven needed a great deal of money, though he enjoyed little benefit from it; for he lived very simply. When he was composing "Leonora" he had been given free lodgings for a year in the *Wiedener Theater*; but as these lodgings faced the court-yard, he did not like them. At the same time, therefore, he rented another apartment in the "Red House" near the Alser Barracks, where Stephan von Breuning was also living. When the summer came, he took lodgings in the country, at Döbling, and as a result of his quarrel with Stephan von Breuning (to which Beethoven's letter to me of July 24th, 1804 refers—about Breuning's conduct with the private tutor, whom Breuning called as a witness in support of his allegation), he asked me to find him lodgings on the Bastions. I chose an apartment in Pasqualati's house on the *Mölkerbastei*, on the fourth floor, from which there was a very fine view, and so Beethoven had four apartments at the same time. He even left the last of these several times, but always returned to it, so that, as I heard later, whenever Beethoven moved out, Baron Pasqualati would remark, good-naturedly enough: "The apartment will not be let: Beethoven is sure to come back."

. . . Beethoven was always glad to see women, especially beautiful, youthful faces, and usually when we walked past a rather attractive girl he would turn round, look at her again sharply through his glasses, and laughed or grinned when he found that I had observed him. He was very frequently in love, but usually only for a very short time. When once I teased him with his conquest of a beautiful lady, he confessed that she had charmed him more powerfully and longer than any other— that is, for no less than seven whole months.

. . . Beethoven was very clumsy and awkward in his movements; his gestures were totally lacking in grace. He seldom took up anything without dropping or breaking it. Thus he repeatedly threw his inkwell into the piano that stood next to his writing-desk. No piece of furniture was safe with him, least of all a valuable one: everything was knocked over, dirtied and destroyed. It is difficult to understand how he succeeded in shaving himself, even without taking into account the frequent cuts on his cheeks. He could never learn to dance in time.

TO STEPHAN VON BREUNING
(*With a portrait of Beethoven*)

1804?

Behind this portrait, my dear, good Steffen, all that happened between us for a time shall be hidden for ever. I know, I have rent your heart. My own emotion, which you must surely have noticed, has been sufficient punishment for the offence. Whatever it was that turned me against you, I assure you it was not malice. No, I should never again be worthy of your friendship; it was passion on your part and on mine—but I did feel mistrust of you. Persons who will never be worthy of you or me came between us. I have long intended to send you my portrait; you know well that it has always been intended for someone. To whom else could I give it with whole-hearted friendship but to you, my good, faithful, noble Steffen! Forgive me, if I hurt you; I suffered no less than you. When for such a long time I did not see you about me, I felt all the more clearly how dear you are to me, and always will be.

Yours . . .

I am sure that you will be as eager to embrace me as before.

TO SIMROCK

Dear, most excellent Herr Simrock,

For a long time already I have been waiting impatiently for a copy of the sonata which I gave you, but in vain. Kindly let me know what exactly is being done about it and whether you acquired it from me only to give the moths a feast. Or are you waiting to receive a special Imperial licence for it? This, I should say, could have been obtained long ago. What is happening to the slow devil who is to see that my sonata is published? Usually you are the quick devil, are notorious for being in league with the black devil, as Faust was once, and are no less loved for it by your fellows. Once again: where is the devil, and what sort of a devil is it, who is sitting on my sonata and with whom you have no understanding? Hurry, therefore, and send me news as to when I shall see the sonata delivered. As soon as you let me know the time, I shall send you a note for Kreutzer which you will be good enough to enclose with a copy (as you are sending copies to Paris in any case or are even having them engraved there). This Kreutzer is a fine, an excellent fellow who gave me much pleasure during his stay here; his modesty and unaffected manner please me more than the exterior or interior of most virtuosi. As the sonata has been written for a capable violinist, the dedication to him is all the more fitting. In spite of the fact that we keep up a correspondence (i.e. a letter from me every year or so), I hope that he has heard nothing about it yet.

I hear continually that you are establishing your position more and more securely; I am heartily glad to hear it. Remember me to all the members of your family and to all others who, in your opinion, would be pleased to be remembered by me. I beg you to reply soon.

Your Beethoven

REPORT FOR KARL CZERNY

We, the undersigned, cannot refuse to testify that the youth
Karl Czerny has made such extraordinary progress on the
piano, progress far in advance of what is normally expected
of one aged fourteen years, that in this respect as well as
in view of his admirable memory he should be deemed
worthy of all possible support, the more so as his parents
have devoted their fortune to the musical education of this
promising son.

Vienna, December 7th, 1805.

Ludwig van Beethoven

FROM GRILLPARZER'S "RECOLLECTIONS OF BEETHOVEN"[1]

. . . The first time I saw Beethoven I was still a boy—it was
probably in 1804 or 1805—and the occasion was a musical
soirée at the house of my uncle, Joseph Sonnleithner, who at
that time was a partner in a firm of art and music dealers in
Vienna. Apart from Beethoven, Cherubini and Abbé Vogler
were among those present. Beethoven at that time was still
slim, dark and, contrary to his later habit, most elegantly
dressed; he wore spectacles, a detail which I remember so well
because in later years he ceased to make use of this aid to his
rather short sight. I cannot recall whether he himself or
Cherubini played during this *soirée*, but only that, when the
servant had already announced supper, Abbé Vogler seated
himself at the piano and began to play endless variations on an
African theme which he himself had brought back from its
country of origin. The company gradually drifted off to the
dining-room during his musical exercises. Only Beethoven and
Cherubini remained behind. At last the latter also went away
and Beethoven stood alone beside the toiling artist. Finally

[1] *Erinnerungen an Beethoven*, 1844–45.

62

Beethoven, too, lost patience, while Abbé Vogler, now left quite alone, did not cease to caress his theme in every possible shape. I myself had remained behind in dull amazement at the monstrous aspect of the thing. As is apt to be the case with youthful reminiscences, my memory quite fails me after this point. Who sat next to Beethoven at table, whether he talked to Cherubini, whether later they were joined by Abbé Vogler —it seems as if a dark curtain had descended upon all this in my mind.

A year or two later I was living with my parents in Heiligenstadt, a village near Vienna. Our apartment faced the garden, while Beethoven had rented the rooms facing the street. A communal passage, leading to the stairs, connected the two partitions. My brothers and myself cared little for this extraordinary man—he had grown stouter in the meantime and walked about in untidy, even dirty clothes—when, grunting, he shot past us; but my mother, a passionate music-lover, from time to time, when she heard him play, yielded to the impulse to step out into the communal passage, not near his door but immediately in front of ours, and to listen with religious awe. This may have occurred a few times when suddenly Beethoven's door was opened, he himself stepped out, observed my mother, hurried back and, immediately afterwards, rushed down the stairs with his hat on his head and out of the house. From this moment onwards he never touched his piano. In vain my mother, when all other means of communication had failed, asked his servant to assure him that not only would no one ever eavesdrop on him again, but that our door to the passage would be kept locked and all the members of our household, instead of using the communal stairs, would make a long detour by using only the garden exit: Beethoven remained unrelenting and left his piano untouched until at last late autumn took us back to town.

TO THE IMPERIAL THEATRE, VIENNA

Vienna, December, 1806

Most honourable Directorate of the I.R. Theatre,

The undersigned may certainly flatter himself that during his past sojourn in Vienna he has obtained some favour and recognition from the high nobility, as well as from the general public, and that his works have been granted an honourable reception both in this country and abroad. Notwithstanding all this, he has been obliged to grapple with difficulties of every kind and has never yet been fortunate enough to establish himself here in a position compatible with his desire to live entirely for his art, to develop his talents to a higher grade of perfection—the ultimate end of all true artists—and to secure the purely fortuitous advantages accorded to him in the past for an independent future.

As generally the undersigned has been concerned not so much with merely earning his daily bread as with the interests of Art, the ennoblement of taste and the impulse of his genius to rise to greater heights of the ideal and of perfection, it followed inevitably that often he sacrificed his gains and his advantages to the Muse. Nevertheless, works of this kind won him a reputation in distant countries, a reputation which assures him of the most favourable reception in several eminent places and a status commensurate with his talents and acquirements.

In spite of this, the undersigned cannot deny that the many years spent in this city, the favour and applause accorded to him by high and low, the desire to fulfil those expectations which, in the past, he has been fortunate enough to arouse and, he may add, the patriotism of a German have made this city more estimable and more desirable than any other.

Before realizing his decision to leave this place, therefore, he cannot refrain from following up the intimation which His Grace, the reigning Prince of Lobkowitz, was kind enough to give to him when he observed that an honourable Directorate of a theatre were not disinclined to engage the undersigned on suitable conditions for service in the theatres under their management and to ensure his further sojourn here by offering him the means of a permanent livelihood more favourable to the exercise of his talents. As this intimation is in perfect accord with the desires of the undersigned, he takes the liberty to submit both his readiness to accept such an engagement and the following conditions for the gracious consideration of the honourable Directorate:

1. He agrees and contracts to compose every year at least one grand opera, to be selected jointly by the honourable Directorate and the undersigned; in return he demands a fixed yearly salary of 2,400 guilders and the gross receipts of the third performance of every such opera.

2. He agrees and contracts to deliver gratis every year one small operetta or divertissement, choruses or occasional pieces according to the desire and requirements of the honourable Directorate; yet he trusts that the honourable Directorate will not hesitate to grant him one day each year for a benefit concert in one of the theatre buildings, in return for such special works.

If one considers what an expenditure of time and effort is required for the completion of an opera, to the virtual exclusion of every other mental exertion, and if, further, one considers how in other cities, where the author and his family have a share in the receipts of every performance, a single successful work has at once established an author's fortune—and, again, how few are the advantages accorded to an artist here in view of the unfavourable exchange and the high prices for all the necessities, when foreign countries are open to him—the above conditions can certainly not be considered excessive or immoderate.

In any case, whether or not the honourable Directorate confirm and accept this offer, the undersigned adds the request that one of the theatre buildings be placed at his disposal for one day in every year; for in the case of his application's being accepted, the undersigned would immediately require all his time and faculties for the composition of the opera and could not, therefore, work for profit in any other way. In the event of a rejection of the present application, on the other hand, since the permission to hold a concert granted to him last year could not be utilized because of various unforeseen obstacles, the undersigned would regard the future fulfilment of the previous year's promise as the very last token of the great favour enjoyed by him in the past, and requests that in the first case the appointed day be that of the Feast of the Annunciation, but in the second case one of the approaching Christmas holidays.

Ludwig van Beethoven, m.p.

NOTE. *It appears that Beethoven never received a reply to his appeal.*

TO IGNAZ TROXLER

April, 1807

To Herr von Troxler in Vienna.

Dear Doctor,

A thousand thanks for your exertions on my behalf; if your news had come a little sooner, I should have been spared some wretched days. The Baden mail service is the worst imaginable, it resembles the whole State; I did not receive your letter until to-day. If possible, expect me at your house to-morrow morning, between 9 and 10 o'clock. I shall be coming to Vienna. I very much want you to go to Clementi's with me on Tuesday, as I am better able to communicate with foreigners by my music than by my conversation; once again, my sincere thanks for all your kindness and helpfulness towards me. My very best wishes to Malfatti.

Remain well disposed towards your friend

Beethoven

TO CAMILLE PLEYEL

Vienna, April 26th, 1807

My dear, esteemed Pleyel,

What are you doing, how is your family? I have often wished that I were with you: until now it hasn't been possible, partly because of the war. If one is further prevented from going there, or longer, most probably one will never see Paris.

My dear Camillus (that, if I am not mistaken, was the name of the Roman who chased the wicked Gauls out of Rome: at that price I, too, should like to have that name, if I could chase them away from all those places to which they don't belong!) What are you doing with your talent, dear Camill? I hope you are not simply leaving it to look after itself; I suppose that you are doing something to help it. I embrace you both, father and son, with all my heart and wish that besides the business matters of which you have to write to me you will let me know much of that which concerns yourself and your family. Farewell and do not forget your true friend

Beethoven

TO BARON IGNAZ VON GLEICHENSTEIN

Vienna, 1807 or 1808

You live on a calm, untroubled sea or already in the safety of the harbour. The need of your friend, who is out in the gale, you do not feel—or must not feel. What will they think of me on the star of Venus Urania, how will they judge me, without seeing me? My pride is so badly damaged that even uninvited I would gladly travel there with you. Let me see you here early to-morrow morning, I expect you at about 9 o'clock for breakfast. Dorner[1] could accompany you at some other time. If only you would be more truthful! You are certainly hiding something from me, you wish to spare my feelings and are yet causing me more pain in this uncertainty than you would in the most fatal of certainties. Farewell! If you can't come, let me know in good time. Think and act for me! On paper I can reveal nothing more of what is going on inside me.

[1] A Viennese doctor.

67

TO GLEICHENSTEIN

Vienna, 1807 or 1808

Your news plunged me from the regions of highest rapture, back to the depths. Why did you need to add that you would let me know about it as soon as there is another musical reunion? Am I, then, nothing more than your musical adviser, or that of the others? That, at least, is the most likely construction. Once again, therefore, I must look for support nowhere but in my own breast, for outside there is none whatever. No, friendship and kindred feelings can give me nothing but wounds. So be it, then! For you, poor Beethoven, there is no happiness to be found outside; you must create everything for yourself, within yourself, you will find no friends anywhere but in the world of ideals. I beg you to reassure me as to whether yesterday's happenings were my fault, or, if you cannot do that, tell me the truth: I hear it as gladly as I speak it. Now there is still time, truths can still be of use to me. Farewell! Don't tell your only friend Dorner anything about all this.

FROM THE SKETCH-BOOKS: NOTES ON THE PASTORAL SYMPHONY   *1807*

It is left to the listener to discover the situation. *Sinfonia caracteristica* or a reminiscence of country life. Every kind of painting loses by being carried too far in instrumental music. *Sinfonia pastorella.* Anyone who has the faintest idea of country life will not need many descriptive titles to be able to imagine for himself what the author intends. Even without a description one will be able to recognize it all, for it is (a record of) sentiments rather than a painting in sounds.

1808

Pastoral Symphony not a painting, but an expression of those sentiments evoked in men by their enjoyment of the country, a work in which some emotions of country life are described.

TO MARIE BIGOT

Vienna, 1808

My dear, admirable Marie,

The weather is so divinely beautiful, and who knows whether it will be so to-morrow. I therefore suggest that I call for you at about noon and that we go for a drive. As Bigot has presumably gone out already, we can certainly not take him with us; but Bigot himself would not demand that we drop the whole matter only for this reason. Only, the mornings are now at their best: why not seize the moment, since it passes so soon? It would be quite contrary to the nature of this enlightened, educated Marie to refuse me this pleasure only for the sake of mere scruples. Oh, whatever reasons you may give us, if you do not accept my suggestion, I shall ascribe this refusal to no other cause but a lack of confidence in my character and shall never believe that you harbour true feelings of friendship for me. As for Karoline, you can swathe her in napkins from top to toe, so that nothing may happen to her.

Let me know, my dear Marie, whether you can come. I do not ask whether you wish to come, as such a question could only be detrimental to me. So simply write yes or no in so many words. Farewell and grant me the selfish pleasure of sharing the enjoyment of serene and lovely Nature with two persons so dear to me.

Your friend and admirer,
L. v. Beethoven

TO MARIE BIGOT

A few days later

Dear Marie, dear Bigot,

With the deepest regret I observe that the purest, most innocent of feelings can often be misinterpreted. Affectionately as you have received me in the past, it never occurred to me to assume anything other than that you were honouring me with your friendship. You must think me very vain and very petty

69

if you suppose that the favourable disposition of even so excellent a person as you are would cause me to conclude at once that I have won her love. Besides, it is one of my first principles never to maintain a relationship other than one of friendship with another man's wife. Never would I permit such a relationship to fill my heart with mistrust of those who might, perhaps, play an important rôle in my life one day, and so deprive myself of the best and purest of joys. It may be possible that at times my jesting with Bigot was lacking in refinement; but then, I told him myself that sometimes I am extremely ill-mannered. I am always most natural with all my friends and detest every kind of inhibition. Now, I counted Bigot among my friends: if something I do offends him, his friendship and yours demand that you should tell me so, and I shall certainly be careful never to hurt him again. But how can this good Marie interpret my actions in such a bad light! As for my asking you and Karoline to go out for a drive, it was natural—when on the previous day Bigot had objected to your going out with me alone—for me to assume that both of you might consider it unseemly or even scandalous, and when I wrote to you I had no other intention than to make it clear to you that I did not see it in this light. If now I declared also that I attached great value to your not refusing my request, I did so only to induce you to enjoy the splendid, beautiful day. I was always more concerned with your and Karoline's pleasure than with my own and, by describing mistrust on your part or a refusal to accept my invitation as nothing less than an insult to me, I hoped almost to force you into acceptance. You would do well to reflect how you may make up for the harm that you have done me by spoiling this day for me, by depriving me both of my peace of mind and the fine weather.

If I said that you misjudge me, your present opinion of me proves all too clearly that I was right, even without considering your own thoughts on this occasion. If I said that my coming to see you would have evil consequences, this was little more than a jest intended to show you how greatly I am attracted by everything about you. Even my saying that I desired nothing more than to live in your house for ever, this, too, is the truth. Let us even suppose that this statement implied a hidden meaning: even the most sacred of friendships can often contain much that is hidden, but, nevertheless, you should not misinterpret your friend's secret only because you cannot immediately unravel it.

Dear Bigot, dear Marie, never, never will you find me guilty of ignoble sentiments. From my childhood onwards I learned to love virtue and all that is fine and good. You have sorely wounded my heart. May this serve only to make our friendship more and more secure. I am really not well to-day, and I shall hardly be able to see you. My sensibility and my imagination, ever since yesterday, after the quartets, have been persuading me that I made you suffer. To-night I went to the Redoute to distract myself, but in vain: everywhere the image of you all pursued me. Always it said to me: they are so good and may be suffering on your account. Discontented, I hurried away. Write me a few lines. Your true

Friend Beethoven

Embraces you all.

FROM GRILLPARZER'S "RECOLLECTIONS OF BEETHOVEN"

During one of the following summers I often visited my grandmother, who occupied a country residence in Döbling, not far from Heiligenstadt. Beethoven, too, was living in Döbling at the time. Facing the windows of my grandmother's house was the dilapidated house of a peasant notorious for his slovenliness, Flehberger by name. Besides his wretched house, this Flehberger possessed a daughter who, though very pretty, did not enjoy a reputation much better than his own: her name was Liese. Beethoven seemed to take a great interest in this girl. I can still see him walking up the *Hirschgasse*, a white handkerchief, which trailed on the ground, in his right hand, then stop at Flehberger's gate, while beyond it the flighty *belle*, standing on a cart laden with hay or manure, sturdily wielded her pitchfork amidst incessant laughter. I never saw Beethoven speak to her, but he would stand there in silence, looking in, until at last the girl, whose taste was rather for young farm labourers, roused him to fury either by her mockery or by stubbornly ignoring his presence; then he would suddenly turn away, quick as lightning, yet never failed to stop at the gate on the next occasion. Indeed, his interest went so far that when the girl's father was put in the village prison (known as the *Kotter*) because of some drunken brawl, Beethoven himself endeavoured to persuade the Village Council to release the prisoner, on which occasion, however, he treated these dignitaries in his usual tempestuous manner, so that he only just avoided having to join his imprisoned protégé.

DRAFT OF A CONTRACT

February, 1809

It must be the aspiration and the aim of every true artist to place himself in a position in which he can occupy himself exclusively with the composition of larger works and will not be prevented from doing so by other duties or by economical considerations. A tone-poet, therefore, can have no more urgent desire than to be able to devote himself undisturbed to the invention of larger works and to be able to present these to the public upon their completion. Meanwhile he must also bear in mind his old age and endeavour to make adequate provision for that period of his life.

The King of Westphalia has offered to Beethoven a salary of 600 ducats in gold for life and 150 ducats for travelling expenses, on the sole condition that he agree to play for him occasionally and that he conduct his chamber concerts, both of which functions will be infrequent and require little time. This offer is certainly wholly to the advantage of the artist and of his art.

Nevertheless, Beethoven has so strong a predilection for his life in this capital, feels so much gratitude for the many tokens of goodwill given to him there and so much patriotism for his second fatherland that he will never cease to count himself among the Austrian artists and that he will never choose another domicile as long as he can be reasonably sure of enjoying the said advantages here. As persons of high and of the highest rank have invited him to declare the conditions under which he would be prepared to remain here, he responds to this request with the following:

1. Beethoven should receive from an exalted nobleman the assurance of a salary for life, even if several persons of high rank were to contribute to the sum fixed for this salary. This salary, in view of the present high cost of living, could not amount to less than 4000 fl. per annum. Beethoven desires that the donors of this salary might then look upon themselves as having a share in the authorship of his new larger works, because they make it possible for him to devote himself to such works and relieve him of the need to attend to other duties.

2. Beethoven should always retain the liberty to travel in the interests of his art, because only on such travels can he become very well known and acquire some wealth for himself.

3. It would be his greatest desire and his most fervent wish one day to enter into the actual service of the Emperor and by means of the salary to be expected in such a position to be enabled to renounce the benefits set forth above either wholly or in part. Meanwhile even the title of Master of the Emperor's Music would make him very happy: should it be possible to obtain this title for him, his sojourn here would be even dearer to him.

Should this wish be fulfilled one day and should His Majesty grant him a salary, Beethoven will give up so much of the 4000 fl. mentioned above as accrues to him from the Imperial salary; and should this salary even amount to 4000 fl., he would then entirely renounce his claim upon the 4000 fl. mentioned above.

73

4. As Beethoven also wishes to perform his new, larger works in the presence of a wider public, he requests an assurance from the Directorate of the Court Theatre and from their successors that on Palm Sunday every year the *Theater an der Wien* shall be placed at his disposal for a concert to be performed for his own benefit. In return, Beethoven would bind himself to devise and conduct a charity concert every year or, if unable to do so, to contribute a new work of his own to such a concert.

NOTE. *This contract was accepted. The sum of 4000 fl. per annum was assured to Beethoven by three of his patrons; it was made up as follows:*

His Imperial Highness, Archduke Rudolph	*Fl. 1500*
His Highness, Prince Lobkowitz	*Fl. 700*
His Highness, Prince Ferdinand Kinsky	*Fl. 1800*

TO GLEICHENSTEIN

Vienna, March 18th, 1809

You can see from the enclosed, my dear, good Gleichenstein, how honourable my staying here has become for me. The title of Imperial *Kapellmeister*,[1] etc., will also follow. Write to me now as soon as possible whether you think that I should travel in the present war-like circumstances and whether you are still firmly resolved to travel with me. Several people have advised me against it, yet I shall rely entirely on your opinion as to whether each of us should travel part of the distance that divides us. Write to me quickly!

Now you can help me to look for a wife. If you should find a good-looking one there in Freiburg—one who might occasionally spare a sigh for my harmonies (but she must not be another Elise Bürger[2])—then prepare the connection in advance. But she must be good-looking: I cannot love anything

[1] Roughly: Conductor of the Imperial Orchestra, but other duties were entailed.
[2] Elise Hahn, third wife of the poet Gottfried August Bürger; they were divorced in 1792 on the grounds of her misconduct.

that is not beautiful, or I should love myself. Be happy and write soon. My regards to your parents, your brother.

I embrace you with all my heart and am your faithful friend

Beethoven

TO BREITKOPF UND HÄRTEL

Vienna, July 26th, 1809

My dear Sir,

You were surely mistaken in believing that I was so well—in this recent period we have suffered the most concentrated misery—when I tell you that since May 4th[1] I have produced little that is coherent, scarcely more than a fragment here and there. The whole course of events has affected me physically and spiritually; even now I cannot partake of rustic life, a delight quite indispensable to me. My mode of existence, only lately established, rests upon a loose foundation—even during this short period I have not seen any confirmation of the promises made to me. I have not received a farthing from Prince Kinsky, one of those who takes an interest in me—and that at a time when one needs it more than ever. Heaven knows how it will work out. I may also be faced with the removal to some other place. The contribution begins as from to-day. What a destructive and savage life is raging all around me! Nothing but drums, cannons, human misery of every kind! . . . Herewith a fine collection of misprints to which, as I no longer trouble myself with works I have already written, a good friend of mine has drawn my attention (I refer to the 'cello sonata). . . . Only now do I thank you for the really excellently translated tragedies of Euripides. Among the poetry intended for me I have made a note of certain things in "Callirroe"[2] which I intend to set to music, sung or otherwise—only I wish to know the name of the author or translator of this tragedy. At Traeg's I took the Messiah as a privilege which you had already granted to me here in your presence; it is true that by

[1] On May 4th the Imperial Family left Vienna; on the 10th the French laid siege to the city, which they occupied on the 12th.
[2] A tragedy by August Apel, 1806.

taking the work away I may have stretched it. I had begun several times to hold weekly soirées devoted to vocal music at my house; but this unhappy war has put a stop to everything. For this purpose and generally I should be grateful if from time to time you would send me most of the scores that you have, as, for example, Mozart's Requiem, etc., Haydn's Masses, in fact all such scores as those of Haydn, Mozart, Bach, Johann Sebastian Bach, Emanuel, etc. . . . I have only a few of Emanuel Bach's piano works, and yet some of them must yield to every true artist not only noble enjoyment, but instruction, too, and it is my greatest pleasure to play works which I have never or only seldom studied, at the house of a true patron of Art. I shall surely devise some means of compensating you in such a manner that you will be satisfied. . . . Perhaps it is the will of Heaven that I need not wholly cease to regard Vienna as my lasting place of residence. Farewell, I wish you all that is good and beautiful, as far as our wild century permits; remember

Your most devoted servant and friend,

Beethoven

FROM THE MEMOIRS OF BARON DE TREMONT

I consulted Reicha: "I'm afraid", he said to me, "that my letter will be of no use to you. Ever since France became an Empire, Beethoven has had such a hatred for Napoleon and for the French that Rode, the best violinist in Europe, who passed through Vienna on his way back from Russia, spent a whole week in Vienna without being received by him. He is retiring, sullen and misanthropic and, to give you some idea how little respect he has for the conventions, let me tell you that the Empress[1] asked him one morning to call on her; he replied that he was busy all that day but would try to look her up on the following one."

This information made me feel quite sure that all my endeavours to make Beethoven's acquaintance would be in

[1] Princess of Bavaria, the second wife of Francis II.

vain. I could make use neither of my reputation, nor of my title, and it was all the more likely that I should be rejected when I was coming to a Vienna bombarded by the French army for the second time and as, besides, I belonged to Napoleon's Council. And yet I wished to try it. I went to the house of the inaccessible composer and it occurred to me at the door that I had chosen the day badly: for, since later I had to make an official call, I was wearing the uniform of a Councillor of State. Unfortunately he lived on the Ramparts and, as Napoleon had ordered their destruction, a mine had been laid just below his window.

The neighbours showed me his quarters. "He's at home", they said, "but at this moment he has no maid-servant, as he's always changing them, and it's doubtful whether he'll open the door." I rang the bell three times and was just about to leave when a very ugly and evidently ill-humoured man opened the door and asked me what I wanted. "Have I the honour to address Herr Beethoven?" "Yes, sir, but I should like to let you know at once," he replied in German, "that I don't understand French at all well." "Nor do I understand German any better, sir, but my message consists only in hand-ing you a letter from Herr Reicha, which he gave me in Paris." He looks at me, takes the letter and motions to me to enter. His apartment, I think, consisted only of two rooms. The first contained an enclosed alcove, in which his bed stood, so small and dark that he had to perform his toilet in the next room or in the drawing-room. Imagine all that is most filthy and untidy: puddles on the floor, a rather old grand piano covered in dust and laden with piles of music, in manuscript or en-graved. Beneath it (I do not exaggerate) an unemptied chamber-pot. The little walnut table next to it was evidently accustomed to having the contents of the inkwell spilled over it. A mass of pens incrusted with ink—and more musical scores. The chairs, most of them straw chairs, were covered with plates full of the remains of the previous evening's meal and with clothes, etc. Balzac or Dickens would spin out this description over two whole pages and would need as much space again to describe the famous composer's appearance and costume to you. But as I am neither Balzac nor Dickens, I limit myself to saying this: I was at Beethoven's.

I spoke only broken German, but understood it a little better, nor was his French much more fluent. I expected him to dismiss me as soon as he had read the letter and so put an end to our acquaintanceship. I had seen the bear in his cage, and that was more than I had dared to hope. I was therefore most astonished when he continued to look at me, put down the letter unopened on the table and offered me a chair. I was even more astonished when he began to talk. He inquired about my uniform, my profession, my age, the purpose of my journey; whether I was a musician and whether it was my intention to spend some time in Vienna. I replied that Reicha's letter would explain all this much better than I could explain it myself. "No, no, speak," he said, "but speak slowly, for I'm very hard of hearing, but I shall understand you." Unbelievable linguistic exertions on my part, a great deal of goodwill on his—my bad German and his bad French produced the strangest of mixtures. But we understood each other, the visit lasted three-quarters of an hour and he invited me to visit him again.

I left, prouder than Napoleon when he entered Vienna: I had conquered Beethoven.

Do not ask me how! What should I answer? The reason lies only in his extraordinary character. I was young, gentle, polite, was unknown to him, was different from him; somehow, by some whim, I don't know how, he took a liking to me. And as with crotchety people such sudden likings are rarely luke-warm, he gave me many opportunities of meeting him during my stay in Vienna, and for my own benefit he improvised for no less than one whole hour, no, two whole hours. When he had a maid-servant, he ordered her not to open the door when the bell rang, and, if one could hear the sound of a piano being played, to say that he was composing and must not be disturbed.

A number of musicians with whom I became acquainted would hardly believe it. "Will you believe me", I said to them, "if I show you a note which he's written to me in French?"

"In French? Impossible! He hardly knows it and writes even German illegibly! He's incapable of such an exertion."

I produced my evidence. "In that case, he must have a veritable passion for you," they said. "What an unfathomable man!" . . .

Beethoven's improvisations were certainly the deepest of all my musical experiences. I am quite sure that no one who has not heard him improvise freely and spontaneously can wholly grasp the vast extent of his talent. Sometimes, quite on the spur of the moment, he would say to me, after striking a few chords: "I can't think of anything, let's leave it for another time." Then he talked about philosophy, religion, politics and especially about Shakespeare, his idol, and always in a language which would have made any listener, had there been one, burst out laughing. Beethoven was not an *homme d'esprit*, in the sense of making polished and witty remarks. He was too taciturn by nature to permit a conversation with him to be spirited. He uttered his thoughts in jerks, they were exalted and generous, though often erroneous. There is this similarity between him and Jean-Jacques Rousseau in the matter of their mistaken views: owing to their misanthropic disposition, they created imaginative worlds for themselves, without adapting these very closely to human nature or to social conditions. But Beethoven was cultured. The solitude of his unmarried state, of his poor hearing and his retirements to the country had induced him to devote himself to the study of the Greek and Latin writers and to become an enthusiastic reader of Shakespeare. Because of the peculiar, but real tension created by erroneous opinions expounded or stated in good faith, conversations with him, if not very attractive, were at least original and memorable. And as he was well disposed towards me, in his splenetic humour he sometimes desired that I should contradict him, rather than defer to his own views. . . . I asked him whether he did not feel inclined to get to know France. "I have always ardently desired to see France," he replied, "but that was before France acquired an Emperor. Now I've lost my inclination. However, I should very much like to hear Mozart's symphonies in Paris," (he did not mention either his own or those of Haydn in this connection) "for the Conservatoire there, I'm told, performs them very much better than they are performed anywhere else. Besides, I'm too poor to be able to make such a journey merely out of curiosity, and also such a journey would have to be very short." "Travel with me, then, I'll take you with me." "Why not, indeed! I could never accept such a sacrifice from you." "Believe me, it would be a matter of no consequence. My travelling expenses have been paid and I'm alone in my carriage; if you would be satisfied with a small room, I can put one at your disposal. Do say 'yes' without any further ado! I assure you that it's worth while to spend a fortnight in Paris. You would have no other expense than that of your return journey, and this would hardly amount to more than fifty guilders." "You are leading me into temptation; but I'll think about it."

I tried to persuade him to decide very quickly. His irresoluteness was due to his morose disposition. "I shall be besieged by visitors." "You will simply refuse to receive them." "Overwhelmed with invitations." "You will not accept them." "They will pester me with requests to play for them, to compose." "You will say that you have no time." "You Parisians will think me a bear." . . .

. . . And yet the greatness of Napoleon preoccupied him and he often spoke to me about it. In spite of his ill humour, I observed, he admired Napoleon's ascent from such a low beginning. It suited his democratic ideas. One day he said to me: "If I should go to Paris, should I be obliged to pay a call on your Emperor?" I assured him of the contrary, unless he were expressly invited to do so. "And do you think that he would order me to attend on him?" "If Napoleon could judge who you are, then he would undoubtedly do so—but you've learned from Cherubini that he knows next to nothing about music." This question led me to infer that, in spite of his convictions, Beethoven would have been flattered by distinctions bestowed upon him by Napoleon. Thus human pride bows down to that which flatters it.

TO BREITKOPF UND HÄRTEL

. . . Perhaps you could let me have copies of the collected works of Goethe and Schiller; surely many such things come in with your other literary treasures, and I shall then send you various items in return, i.e. something which will go out into the whole world. These two poets are my favourite poets, besides Ossian, Homer, the last of whom, unfortunately, I can read only in translation; as you need only pour these authors—Goethe and Schiller—out of your literary treasury, you will give me the greatest pleasure. N.B.—if you send them to me soon—by making me a present of them, all the more so as I hope to be able to spend the rest of the summer in some happy corner of the countryside. The sextet[1] is among my earlier things and, besides, was written in one night; really one cannot say more for it than that it was written by an author who did, at least, produce some better works—yet some persons regard such works as my best.

TO BREITKOPF UND HÄRTEL

Vienna, on the 19th of the vintage month, 1809

. . . Kindly let me know the cost of these editions of Schiller, Goethe in convention coin, also the whole edition of Wieland (in smaller format). If I must buy them, then I prefer to get them there, for here all editions are botched and expensive. Later, more about the quartets I am writing. I do not like taking on sonatas for piano solo, but I promise you some. Have you heard that I have become a member of the Society of the Arts and Sciences? So I've received a title after all! Ha, ha, that makes me laugh. . . .

[1] The Sextet for Wind Instruments, Op. 71.

TO BREITKOPF UND HÄRTEL

Wednesday, on the 2nd of the winter month, 1809

At last I am writing to you; after this wild destruction, a little peace, after all this unthinkable discomfort which we have endured—I have been working for some weeks at a stretch, rather, it seemed, for death than for immortality, and so I received your parcel without a letter and gave very little attention to it. Only some days ago I picked it up, and I now reproach you most severely, why this very beautiful edition not without errors???? Why not first a proof copy, as I have often demanded? Errors creep into every transcription, errors which any skilful proof-corrector can easily rectify, although I am almost sure that there are few or none at all in the copy I sent you. As yet I have not been able to let you know anything about Dr. Apel;[1] meanwhile assure him of my respect. Another thing! You will not easily find a treatise that is too learned for me; without laying claim to any genuine learning, I yet accustomed myself from childhood onwards to grasp the spirit of the best and wisest in every age. Shame on the artist who does not consider it his duty to achieve at least so much.

What do you say to this dead peace?[2] I no longer expect anything stable in this age; one can be certain of nothing but blind chance. . . .

TO THERESE MALFATTI

Vienna, Spring, 1810

Herewith, admirable Therese, you will receive what I promised you, and, had it not been for the most serious impediments, you would receive more, so that I might prove to you that I always do more for my friends than I have promised to

[1] Johann August Apel (1771–1816), author of the tragedy mentioned on p. 75, wished to write an opera or an oratorium for Beethoven.

[2] The peace between Napoleon and Austria, concluded on October 14th, 1809, in Vienna.

do. I hope and do not doubt that you are as usefully employed as you are pleasantly diverted—yet not too much of the last, so that you will think of us, too. I suppose that I should be asking too much of you or overestimating my own value if I credited you with this thought: "Persons are not only together when they are in each other's company; even those who are distant, departed, live within us." Who would ascribe such a thought to my hasty Therese, who skims so lightly over all the things of this life?

Whatever you do, never let your other occupations make you neglect the piano or, indeed, the whole of music generally. You have such a fine talent for it: why not cultivate it thoroughly? You, that have so fine a sense for all that is good and beautiful, why should not you apply this sense in order to attain the higher perfections of so beautiful an art, perfections which never cease to cast their reflection back at us?

I live a very calm and solitary life. Although now and then a light would wish to rouse me, yet the departure of you all has left a gap in my life, a gap that can never be filled and over which even my art, usually so faithful and reliable, has not been able to triumph. I have ordered your piano and you will have it soon. What a difference you will have found between the treatment of the theme as invented one evening and the present version recently written down for you! Find your own explanation for this, but without resorting to punch for help.

How fortunate you are to have been able to go to the country so early in the year! Not before the 8th shall I be able to enjoy this delight: I look forward to it with childish anticipation. How glad I shall be to wander about amidst shrubs, forests, trees, herbs and rocks! No man can love the country as I do. For it is forests, trees and rocks that provide men with the resonance they desire.

Please be kind enough to give this song, transcribed for guitar, to your dear sister Nanette. Time was too short, else the voice, too, would have been entered.

Soon you will receive some other compositions of mine which should give you less cause to complain of difficulties. Have you read Goethe's *Wilhelm Meister?* or Schlegel's translation of Shakespeare? In the country one has so much leisure; I imagine it would be agreeable to you if I sent you these works. It so happens that I have an acquaintance in your vicinity. Perhaps one morning you will see me at your house for an hour or so, but no longer. You can see that I wish to bore you as little as possible. Commend me to the kindly disposition of your father and your mother, although I have not yet won the right to lay any claim to it, also to your sister Nanette.

Now farewell, admirable Therese. I wish you all that is good and beautiful in this life. Think of me, and gladly, forget my follies, rest assured: no one can wish your life to be more carefree, more cheerful than I do, even if you should feel no concern at all for your most devoted servant and friend

Beethoven

N.B. It would be very kind of you to let me know in a few lines in what way I could be of service to you here.

AN ACCOUNT BY DR. JULIUS BECHER
(*from Seyfried's reminiscences*)

One day, at the Viennese inn *zum Goldenen Lamm*, Beethoven observed that several musicians and literary men were engaged in a very lively discussion. He asked one of them what was going on. "These gentlemen maintain that the English can neither produce good music, nor appreciate it," Mayseder[1] replied, "but I don't agree with them." Beethoven said sarcastically: "The English have commissioned several of my works for their concerts and offered me decent payment for them, the Germans, with the exception of the Viennese, are only just beginning to perform my works, and the French consider my music impracticable: consequently it is clear that the English know nothing about music. Isn't that so? Ha, ha!" He laughed heartily and the discussion came to an end at once.

[1] Joseph Mayseder, a distinguished violinist and a member of the Schuppanzigh Quartet.

TO ARCHDUKE RUDOLPH

Vienna, 1810

I can see that Yr. Imperial Highness wish to try out the effect of my music even on the horses. So be it! I will do my best to make sure that the riders, too, turn some skilful somersaults. Well, well, it really makes me laugh to think how Your Imperial Highness consider me even on this occasion; for this, assuredly, my whole life long I shall remain
                        Your most obliging servant,
                                Ludwig van Beethoven

N.B.—The desired horse music will reach Yr. Imperial Highness at full gallop.

TO FRANZ WEGELER

Vienna, May 2nd, 1810

My dear old friend,

Almost, I can imagine, these lines will surprise you, and yet, although you have no written proof of it, you are always vividly present in my mind.

A year or two ago my more quiet, restful life came to an end, and I was dragged by force into worldly affairs, the result, up to now, has been negative rather than positive. But who could be immune from the effect of the external storms? Yet I should be happy, perhaps one of the happiest of men, had not the daemon pitched his camp in my ears. Had I not read somewhere that men must not part voluntarily from this life as long as they are capable of doing a single good deed, I should have ceased to exist long ago, and this by my own hand. Oh, life is so lovely, but with me it is poisoned for ever. . . .

BETTINA BRENTANO TO GOETHE

When I saw this man of whom I now wish to speak to you, I forgot the whole world. . . . It is Beethoven of whom I now wish to speak to you and in whose presence I forgot you and the world; true, I have not reached my majority,[1] yet I am not mistaken when I declare (though now, perhaps, no one will understand or believe me) that he is far in advance of all educated humanity —shall we ever catch up with him? I doubt it; may he survive until the mighty and exalted secret latent in his spirit has ripened to its highest perfection, may he attain his highest end: then, undoubtedly, he will leave us the key to a heavenly revelation, which will bring us one stage nearer to true bliss.

To you I may surely confess that I believe in a divine spell which is the element of spiritual nature: this spell Beethoven exercises in his art; all that you can learn from him about it is pure magic, every phase is the organization of a higher existence, and so Beethoven feels himself to be the founder of a new sensuous basis for the spiritual life; you will surely divine what it is I wish to say and discern the truth in it. Who could take the place of such a man? of whom could we expect the like?

Like clockwork, the whole of human activity moves within him, he alone creates the undivined, the unformed freely from his own depths: what could worldly intercourse mean to him, who already before sunrise works at his holy craft and after sunset scarcely looks about him, who forgets to nourish his body and is borne over the banks of our flat quotidian lives on the wings of ecstasy? He himself said: "When I open my eyes, I

[1] This is untrue; Bettina Brentano was well over twenty-one and about to get married. But the above is taken from Goethe's "Correspondence with a Child", for the purpose of which Bettina concealed her true age.

It is impossible here to discuss all the controversial aspects of Bettina's dealings with both Goethe and Beethoven. The authenticity of the above has been disputed; and there is no doubt that Beethoven's other conversations are in a very different vein. Yet, whatever may be said against Bettina, there is no denying that she had a flair for discovering geniuses and, up to a point, for understanding them; and as level-headed a writer as Thayer was convinced that Bettina did not unduly distort Beethoven's utterances. On the other hand, two of the three letters which Bettina claimed to have received from Beethoven are undoubtedly forged; only the genuine one appears in this book.

must sigh, for what I look upon is contrary to my religion, and I must despise the world which never divines that music is a greater revelation than the whole of wisdom and philosophy; music is the wine that incites us to new creation and I am the Bacchus who presses this glorious wine for mankind and grants them drunkenness of the spirit; when they are sober again they will have fished up much which they may take with them on to dry land. I have no friend, must live alone with myself; yet I know well that God is nearer to me in my art than to others, I consort with Him without fear, have always recognized and understood Him, nor am I at all anxious about the fate of my music; its fate cannot be other than happy; whoever succeeds in grasping it shall be absolved from all the misery that bows down other men."

All this Beethoven said to me when we met for the first time; I was filled with a feeling of reverence for the friendly candour with which he expressed himself to me, when I must have been utterly insignificant to him; also, I was astonished, for I had been told that he was very retiring and refused to be drawn into conversation with anyone. People were afraid to take me to his house, I had to look him up alone; he has three different apartments, in which he hides alternately, one in the country, one in town and one on the Bastions: it was there I found him, on the third floor; I entered unannounced, he was seated at the piano; I told him my name; he was very kind and asked me whether I should like to hear a song which he had just composed; then he sang *"Kennst du das Land?"*, sharply and incisively, so that the sadness of this song affected the listener. "It's beautiful, isn't it?" he said, enthusiastic, "very beautiful! I'll sing it again." He was pleased with my cheerful applause. "Most people are moved by something that's good, but not if they're artists by nature: artists are fiery, they don't weep," he said. Then he sang another song with words by you, also composed within the last few days: *"Trocknet nicht, Tränen der ewigen Liebe."* He escorted me home and it was on the way that he said all these fine things about art. But he raised his voice so much and so often stopped walking suddenly that I needed courage to listen to him: he spoke with great passion and far too surprisingly for me to remember where I was. . . .

Yesterday he accompanied me to a garden in full flower, all the hothouses were open, the scent was intoxicating. Beethoven stood still in the sweltering heat of the sun and said: "Goethe's poems exercise great power over me not only by their content, but by their rhythm. His language is such that it stimulates me and puts me in a mood to compose, for, as if with the aid of spirits, it attains a higher order and contains the secret of harmony within it. So, from the focal point of enthusiasm, I must discharge melody in all directions. I pursue it, passionately catch up with it again, see it flee from me and vanish in the crowd of diverse excitements; now I seize it with renewed passion, cannot bear to part with it, must multiply it in all its modulations in a quick ecstasy, and at the last moment I triumph over the first musical idea. You see, that's a symphony; yes, indeed, music is truly the link between the life of the spirit and the life of the senses. I should like to speak about this to Goethe: would he understand me, do you think? Melody is the sensual life of poetry. Is it not its melody that transforms the intellectual content of a poem into pure sensation? In Mignon's song, does not the melody reveal the whole state of her emotions? and does not this sensation in turn incite us to new creativeness? Here the spirit desires to expand to boundless generality, where all within all becomes the bed of the emotions which spring from a simple musical idea and which would otherwise die away, never even imagined. This is harmony, this is expressed in my symphonies in which the confluence of many-sided forms surges along in one bed to its destination. In them, one can feel that something eternal, infinite, never wholly comprehensible is contained in every product of the spirit, and although my works always give me a sense of having succeeded, I feel an insatiable hunger to recommence like a child—even though the last work seemed to have been exhausted with the last beat of the kettle-drum which inculcated my joy and my musical convictions upon the audience. Speak to Goethe about me, tell him to listen to my symphonies, for then he will admit that music is the only entrance to the higher world of knowledge which, though it embraces me, a man cannot grasp. A rhythm of the spirit is needed in order to grasp the essence of music; for music grants us presentiments, inspiration of celestial sciences, and that part of it which the mind grasps through the senses is the embodiment of mental cognition. Although minds live on it, as we live on air, it is still a different thing to be able to grasp it intellectually. Yet the more the soul takes its sensuous nourishment from music, the more prepared does the mind grow for a happy understanding with it. Yet few ever attain this stage; for just as thousands marry for love and love is never manifested in these thousands, although they all practise the craft of love, so thousands have intercourse with music and never see it manifested. Like all the arts, music is founded upon the exalted symbols of the moral sense: all true invention is a moral progress. To submit to its inscrutable laws, and by means of these laws to tame and guide one's own mind, so that the manifestations of art may pour out: this is the isolating principle of art. To be dissolved in its manifestations, this is our dedication to the divine which calmly exercises its power over the raging of the untamed elements and so lends to the imagination its highest effectiveness. So always art represents the divine, and the relationship of men towards art is religion: what we obtain through art comes from God, is divine inspiration which appoints an aim for human faculties, which aim we can attain. We do not know what it is that grants us knowledge. The grain of seed, tightly sealed as it is, needs the damp, electric warm soil in order to sprout, to think, to express itself. Music is the electric soil in which the spirit lives, thinks and invents. Philosophy is a striking of music's electric spirit; its indigence, which desires to found everything upon a single principle, is relieved by music. Although the spirit has no power over that which it creates through music, it is yet joyful in the act of creation. Thus every genuine product of art is independent, more powerful than the artist himself, and returns to the divine when achieved, connected with men only inasmuch as it bears witness to the divine of which they are the medium. Music relates the spirit to harmony. An isolated thought yet feels related to all things that are of the mind: likewise every thought in music is intimately, indivisibly related to the whole of harmony, which is oneness. All that is electrical stimulates the mind to musical, flowing, surging creation. I am electrical by nature. I must interrupt my indemonstrable wisdom, or I shall miss the rehearsal. Write to Goethe about me, if you understand me, but I cannot accept responsibility for anything and will gladly yield to his better judgment." I promised him that, as far as I can grasp it, I shall write all this to you.

. . . I wrote all this down last night without delay; this morning I read it to him. He said: "Did I say that?—well, in that case, I must have been in a frenzy." He read it again attentively and crossed out what you see above and wrote between the lines; for he thinks it important that you should understand him. . . .

Bettine

GOETHE TO BETTINA BRENTANO

Your letter, dearly beloved child, reached me at a happy hour. You have made a praiseworthy effort to describe to me a great and admirable nature in its achievements and in its aspirations, its needs and its superfluity of talent; it gave me great pleasure to take in this picture of a true genius; without wishing to classify him, I do think that a veritable feat of psychological calculation would be needed to extract the true sum of agreement from your account; yet I do not feel in the least compelled to contradict what I can grasp of your quick explosion; on the contrary, I should like to admit for the present that there is an inner connection between my own nature and that which can be deduced from these manifold utterances; the ordinary human mind would probably discover incongruities in it, but a layman must feel reverence for the utterances of one possessed by such a daemon, and it should be a matter of indifference whether he speaks from feeling or from knowledge, for here the gods are at work, scattering seed for future revelations, and our only wish should be that they may thrive and develop undisturbed; yet before they can become common property, the fog that surrounds the human mind must disperse. Give my most sincere regards to Beethoven and tell him that I would gladly make sacrifices in order to meet him personally, when an exchange of ideas and sentiments would surely be to our greatest advantage; perhaps you have sufficient influence over him to persuade him to make a journey to Karlsbad where, after all, I go nearly every year and should have most leisure to listen to him and to learn from him; as for instructing him, this would surely be insolent even on the part of persons endowed with insight greater than mine, as his genius lights his way and often illuminates him as with lightning, while we sit in the dark and scarcely guess from which direction the day will break upon us.

It would give me the greatest joy if Beethoven were to send me the two songs composed to words by myself, but very clearly written; I am very eager to hear them—it is one of my greatest pleasures, and one for which I am most grateful, to have such a poem, with its moods that belong to the past, newly embodied in a melody (as Beethoven quite rightly says).

Lastly, I thank you once again most sincerely for your communications and for the manner in which you have done me this favour; for you succeed so well in everything and seem to derive instruction, as well as pleasure and enjoyment, from all things. What wishes could I add to this but that you may continue in this way for ever, also in relation to me, for I do not fail to appreciate the privilege of being counted among your friends. Therefore remain what you have been in the past with such fidelity, often as you moved from one place to another, often as the objects around you changed and became more beautiful. . . .

G.

June 6th, 1810

BETTINA BRENTANO TO GOETHE

June, 1810

Dearest friend,

I have communicated your fine letter to Beethoven, as far as it concerned him. He was full of joy and exclaimed: "If there's anyone who can make him appreciate music, I'm the man!" He seized upon the idea of looking you up in Karlsbad with enthusiasm, struck his forehead and said: "Couldn't I have done that sooner? but, to be honest, I did think of it before, but refrained from doing it out of timidity, which sometimes afflicts me as if I weren't quite human, but now I'm no longer afraid of this Goethe." You may therefore count upon seeing him next year. . . .

I have enclosed both of the songs by Beethoven, the two others are by myself, Beethoven has seen them and said many pleasant things about them, to the effect that if I devoted myself to this art I could hope for great things; yet I only grazed its surface in passing, for my art is to laugh and sigh at the same time—and that's all the art I am fit for. . . .

Bettine

TO NIKOLAUS ZMESKALL VON DOMANOVETZ

Vienna, July 9th, 1810

Dearest Zmeskall,

You are travelling, I also am to travel and this because of my health. Meanwhile everything else, too, is going topsy-turvy with me; his Highness wants my company, and so does Art. I am half at Schoenbrunn, half here. Every day there are new enquiries from foreigners, new acquaintances, new relationships, even with regard to art. Sometimes my undeserved fame is enough to drive me mad: fortune is seeking me out, and this almost makes me fear some new misfortune. As for your Iphigenia, the facts are these: I haven't seen it for at least three and a half years, have lent it to somebody, but to whom? That's the great question. I've sent for it here, there and everywhere, and haven't discovered it yet, though I still hope to retrieve it; if it is lost, you shall suffer no damage. My best wishes to you, dear Zmeskall. I hope that we shall meet again in circumstances that give you reason to think that my art has made further progress in the mean time.

Remain my friend, as I remain yours,

Beethoven

TO BREITKOPF UND HÄRTEL

Baden, on the 21st, summer month (*August*), 1810

... It is not my final purpose, as you believe, to become a musical usurer in Art, who writes only to enrich himself. God forbid! Yet I am fond of an independent life; this I cannot lead without a little wealth and, besides, even his fee must yield an artist some honour, even as honour must surround everything that he undertakes. I would not dare to tell anyone that Breitkopf and Härtel have given me 200 ducats for these works. You, being a more humane and a far more educated person than any other publisher, should also make it your purpose not only to pay the artist as meagrely as you can, but rather to make it possible for him to achieve undisturbed all that he has in him to achieve and all that is expected from him externally. It is no mere inflation if I tell you that I give you precedence over all other publishers. Even those in Leipzig have often approached me and others here have done so, the former through representatives and lately in person, on which occasions they were willing to give me as much as I demanded. Yet I rejected all offers in order to prove to you that I deal with you gladly and prefer you to all others, and this because of your head (of your heart I know nothing), and that I am even prepared to suffer some loss in order to maintain this connection.

If, in the matter of the Song of the Flea from Faust, it was not clear to you what I meant by my remarks, you have only to look up the passage in Goethe or send me a copy of the tune, so that I may look through it. ... The concerto is to be dedicated to the Archduke Rudolph. . . . Likewise the Egmont; as soon as you have received the score of the latter, you yourself will know best to what use you should put it and how you should draw the public's attention to it. I wrote it purely out of love for the poet and, to prove that this was so, accepted nothing for it from the management of the theatre, who accepted it, too, and, as a reward, treated my music as carelessly as ever. Nothing in the world is smaller than our great men, yet I make an exception of Archdukes. . . .

TO BREITKOPF UND HÄRTEL

Vienna, on the 15th, autumn month (*October*), 1810

. . . Should the last piece in the Egmont not bear the heading Triumphal Symphony, have this entered above it. Make haste to get this done and kindly inform me as soon as you no longer need the original score, as I shall then ask you to despatch it straight from Leipzig to Goethe, to whom I announced it long ago. I hope that you will raise no objection to this, for I suppose that you are as great an admirer of this poet as I am. I should have despatched a copy from here, but as I have not yet found a copyist so practised as to be wholly reliable and nothing is certain but the torment of revising his copy, I consider this the better course and the one likely to waste less of my time. . . .

. . . In addition, I want all the works of Karl Philipp Emanuel Bach, all of which, I know, you are publishing; also, a Mass by J. Sebastian Bach in which, I am told, there occurs the following Crucifixus with a Basso ostinato, said to resemble yourself, that is:

Also, you are said to have the best copy of Bach's tempered clavier -[*sic*]; this, too, I beg you to let me have.

94

TO COUNTESS THERESE BRUNSWICK

Vienna, January, 1811

Even without being sought out, the better among us bear one another in mind: this, too, is the case with you and me, worthy and admirable Therese. Still I owe you sincere thanks for your beautiful picture, and even while I accuse myself of being your debtor I must at once appear as a beggar by entreating you, whenever you may feel the genius of painting within you, to renew that little drawing for me, the one I was unfortunate enough to lose. An eagle looked up at the sun, that was it, I cannot forget it. But do not imagine that such a thing makes me think of myself, though, indeed, things of that kind have been ascribed to me: for many, after all, contemplate an heroic subject with pleasure, without bearing the slightest resemblance to it. Farewell, worthy Therese, and think at times of your truly admiring friend.

Beethoven

TO BETTINA BRENTANO

Vienna, February 10th, 1811

Dear, dear Bettine,

I have already received two letters from you and see from your letters to Toni[1] that you are still thinking of me, and far too favourably at that. I carried your first letter about with me all the summer, and it often made me feel quite blissful. Even if I do not write to you very often and even though you never see me at all, I yet write you a thousand letters a thousand times in my thoughts.

I could have imagined how you are faring in Berlin, confronted with the dregs of humanity, even if I had not read your own account of it. A great deal of talk and chatter about art, and no actions!!!! The best description of this is to be found in Schiller's poem 'The Rivers', in which the Spree speaks. You

---

[1] Antonie Brentano, the wife of Bettina's stepbrother Franz.

are about to marry,[1] dear Bettine, or have already done so, and I did not even have the opportunity of speaking to you previously. May all the joy with which marriage blesses the married be heaped upon you and upon your husband! What shall I tell you about me? "Pity my fate," I exclaim with Joan.[2] Should a few more years be granted to me, I shall give thanks to the All-Embracing, to the Highest, as for all the past blessings and afflictions.

If you should write to Goethe about me, choose all those words which will convey my most sincere respect and admiration. I am just about to write to him myself about "Egmont", to which I have composed some music, and this purely out of love for his writings, which give me such happiness. But who can thank a great poet enough, the most precious treasure of a nation?

No more now, dear, good Bettine! Not until four o'clock this morning did I come home after a Bacchanal at which I did a good deal of laughing, only to weep as much to-day. A great upsurge of joy often drives me back into myself all the more violently. About Clemens, many thanks for his readiness to oblige me! As far as the cantata[3] is concerned, the subject is not weighty enough for us here; it is different in Berlin. As for my affection, the sister has taken so great a part of it that very little remains for the brother; will he be satisfied with this?

Now farewell, dear, dear Bettine. I kiss your forehead and, in so doing, imprint all my thoughts of you upon it, as with a seal. Write soon, soon and often to your

Friend,

Beethoven

---

[1] Bettina was married to Achim von Arnim, the poet, on March 11th, 1811.
[2] Joan of Arc in Schiller's drama *The Maid of Orleans*.
[3] Clemens Brentano, Bettina's brother, had sent Beethoven the text for a cantata on the death of Queen Louise of Prussia, in the hope that Beethoven would set it.

TO GOETHE

Vienna, April 12th, 1811

Your Excellency,

This pressing occasion offers me only a moment in which to write to you—for a friend of mine, and a great admirer of yours (like myself), is leaving here in great haste—and to thank you for the long time that I have known you (for I have known you since my childhood): that is so little for so much. Bettine Brentano has assured me that you would receive me graciously, or even as a friend. Yet how could I think of such a reception when I can only approach you with the greatest reverence, with an unspeakable, profound feeling for your splendid creations. You will soon be receiving the music to "Egmont" from Leipzig through Breitkopf and Härtel, this glorious "Egmont" which, just as warmly as I read it, I have thought over once more, felt and set to music in sympathy with yourself. I should be very glad to have your judgment on it; even your adverse criticism would be profitable to me and to my art and accepted as readily as your highest praise.

Your Excellency's

great admirer,

Ludwig van Beethoven

GOETHE TO BEETHOVEN

Karlsbad, June 25th, 1811

Your kind communication, my most honoured Sir, has been delivered to me by Herr Oliva, to my great satisfaction. I am sincerely grateful for the sentiments expressed therein and can assure you that I reciprocate them in all truth, for I have never heard any of your works performed by accomplished artists or amateurs without wishing that one day I might have occasion to admire you in person at the pianoforte and to delight in your extraordinary talent. Our good Bettina Brentano surely deserves the interest which you have shown in her. She speaks of you with enthusiasm and with the keenest regard for you

97

and counts the hours which she has spent with you among the happiest of her life.

I shall probably find the music to Egmont, which in your thoughts you have dedicated to me, when I return home, and I am grateful for it in advance—for I have already heard it favourably mentioned by many and hope to be able to perform it this winter in our theatre, as an accompaniment to the said play, whereby I hope to afford the greatest pleasure to myself, as well as to your numerous admirers in these parts. Most of all, however, I desire that I have properly understood Herr Oliva, who gave us reason to hope that on a projected journey you might be able to visit Weimar. May such a visit occur at a time when both the Court and the entire music-loving public are assembled. You would certainly be accorded a reception worthy of your achievements and of your sentiments. No one, however, can feel more concern in this than I, who, with the wish that you may fare well, commend myself to your kind thoughts and thus offer you my most sincere thanks for so many favours already bestowed upon me.

TO COUNT FRANZ BRUNSWICK

Vienna, June 18th, *1811*

A thousand thanks, my dear little friend, for your nectar— and how can I thank you enough for your willingness to travel with me! I am sure that somehow my resounding heart will find a way of expressing my gratitude. As I want to avoid anything that might not be in accordance with your wishes, I must tell you that my doctor has ordered me to spend no less than two whole months at Teplitz. I could not, therefore, go with you before the middle of August; you would then have to make the journey alone or, as you could easily do if you wish, with someone else. I await your friendly decision in this matter. If you think that it would not suit you to travel back alone, do whatever is most convenient to you. Dear as you are to me, much as I value and enjoy your company, I do not want it to be a source of unpleasantness to you. Since in any case, even if you come with me, you will have to return by the middle of August, I shall take my manservant, who is a really decent, reliable fellow. I beg you to see to it that you will be here on the first or second of July at the latest, as otherwise it will be too late for me and even now the doctor is angry with me for delaying so long, although he himself agrees that the company of such a dear, good friend would have a good effect on me. Have you a carriage? Now let me have your reply at lightning speed, as I shall be writing for lodgings for us two as soon as I know whether you want to come with me and I hear that the place is becoming very crowded. My best wishes, my dear, good friend, let me have your reply at once and love

Your true friend

Beethoven

TO BREITKOPF UND HÄRTEL

Teplitz, August 23rd, 1811

While, for the past 3 three weeks, I have been attempting to restore my health in this place, I received your letter of August 2nd; most probably it has been lying about in Vienna for a while. I had just begun the revision of the oratorio[1] and the songs and you will receive both within a few days. Here and there the text must remain as it was originally. I know that the text is extremely bad; but when one has finally succeeded in thinking of a bad text as a whole, it is difficult to avoid upsetting this wholeness by making individual alterations; and even where a word is misplaced but great weight has been attached to this word, it must remain and it is a (poor) author who does not seek and contrive to make as good a thing as possible even out of a bad text. And if this is the case, alterations will surely not improve the whole. Some of the corrections I have preserved, because they are real improvements. Farewell and let me hear from you soon. Oliva is here and intends

[1] *Christ on the Mount of Olives*, which appeared in 1811.

to write to you. The good reception of Mozart's "Don Juan" pleases me as much as if it were my own work. Although I know enough unprejudiced Italians who do justice to the German composers, if the nation itself has lagged behind, this is probably due to the backwardness and laxity of the Italian musicians; but I have made the acquaintance of many Italian lovers of music who prefer our music to their Paisiello—indeed, I was fairer to him than his own countrymen.

Your

most devoted servant,

Ludwig van Beethoven

TO BREITKOPF UND HÄRTEL

Vienna, October 8th or 9th, 1811

. . . Another experience for me was the Hungarians. As I was getting into my carriage, about to leave for Teplitz, I received a parcel from Ofen with the request to write something[1] for the opening of the new theatre in Pest. After spending three weeks at Teplitz, feeling passably well, I sat down in spite of my doctor's orders to the contrary so as to help the moustaches,[2] who are heartily fond of me, sent off my parcel to Pest on September 13th, thinking that the thing was to take place on October 1st. Meanwhile, however, the whole business drags on for another month. Owing to misunderstandings, I do not receive the letter in which this was to be intimated to me until I reach this place, and yet even this theatrical experience has confirmed my intention to return to Vienna. On the other hand, a delay is not necessarily a cancellation. I have sampled the taste of travelling and it has done me good, indeed, I am already impatient to be off again. I have just received the Farewell,[3] etc. I see that you (have engraved) other copies as well with the title in French. Why did you do that? Farewell is something quite different from *les adieux*: the first is something

[1] *King Stephen* and *The Ruins of Athens*.
[2] The Hungarians.
[3] Piano Sonata in E flat, Op. 81 a, known as "*Les Adieux*".

which one says only from one's heart, when one is alone, the other something which one says to a whole assembly, to whole cities. As you are having me reviewed in so shameful a manner, you, too, shall be taken to task. Also, you could have used far fewer plates and this would have facilitated the now so difficult process of reversing, but let this suffice! But how, in heaven's name, does my Fantasia with Orchestra[1] come to be dedicated to the King of Bavaria? Kindly answer this question at once. If it was your intention to make me an honourable present in this way, I will thank you for it; otherwise I do not like such things at all. Is it perhaps you yourselves who have affixed this dedication? How does all this hang together? Even to kings one cannot dedicate things with impunity. Nor was the Farewell dedicated to the Archduke. Why did you not print the date, year, month and day, as I wrote them on my score? You will give me a written assurance that in future you will preserve all headings just as I wrote them. You will have the Oratorio reviewed by whomever you wish, as, indeed, is the case with all my works. I am sorry to have written even a single word about the miserable review. Who can take any notice of such reviews when he sees how the most pitiable of scribblers are raised to the skies by reviewers no less pitiable, and how altogether they accord the worst treatment—and are forced to do so by their incompetence—to those works of art to which they cannot immediately apply the common standards, as a cobbler applies his last. If the Oratorio calls for any comment, it is that this work was my first and earliest of the kind, written in a fortnight amidst every conceivable kind of tumult and other disagreeable, disquieting events in my life (my brother had just contracted his fatal disease). Rochlitz,[2] if I remember rightly, spoke unfavourably of the chorus of the Apostles, "We have seen him (in C major)", even before the score was handed over for engraving; he called it comical, a sentiment which certainly was not manifested by any member of the public here, even though there are critics even among my

[1] Choral Fantasia, Op. 80.

[2] The Editor of the *Allgemeine Musikalische Zeitung*, published by Breitkopf und Härtel.

friends. It goes without saying that if I wrote an oratorio now, it would be quite different. And now review to your hearts' content; I wish you joy. Even if at times it feels somewhat like a mosquito bite, it never fails to amuse. Re-re-re-re-re-view-view-view-view-view-view—not to all eternity, that you cannot do. Now God have mercy upon you! . . .

When will the Mass appear?—and Egmont? By all means send a copy of the whole score, copied at my expense if you wish, to Goethe. How can a German publisher be so impolite, so gross in his dealings with the greatest of German poets? Quickly, therefore, off to Weimar with the score! As for the Mass—the dedication[1] could be changed. The woman is married now and so the name should be changed: the dedication could, therefore, be omitted. Do let me know when you are publishing it, and then we shall soon find a patron saint for this work.

XAVER SCHNYDER VON WARTENSEE TO HANS GEORG NÄGELI

Vienna, December 17th, 1811

. . . Beethoven gave me an extremely good reception and I have already paid him several visits. He is a most extraordinary man. Great thoughts drift through his soul, but he cannot express them in any form but music; he has no command over words. His whole education has been neglected, and, apart from his art, he is coarse, but honest and unaffected; he says quite bluntly whatever he may be thinking. In his youth and even now he had to struggle with a great many difficulties and unpleasantnesses; this made him moody and gloomy. He curses Vienna and would like to leave. "From the Emperor to the boot-black," he said, "all the Viennese are worthless." I asked him whether he did not accept any pupils. No, he replied, this was a miserable sort of drudgery; he had only one, who gave him a great deal of trouble and whom he would like to get rid of, if he could. "Who is that?" "Archduke Rudolph."

[1] The Mass in C major, Op. 86, had been dedicated to Bettina Brentano; after her marriage, Beethoven substituted a dedication to Prince Kinsky.

Schnyder found Beethoven in a very good humour. He handed him the letter of recommendation from Troxler; Beethoven read it at once, shook hands with his visitor in a friendly manner and said: "You are most welcome, especially welcome because you are Swiss, for I'm very fond of the Swiss!"

"I have to deliver another message to you and should like to do so at once," said Schnyder, while he took the sonata by Liste out of his pocket. "Herr Anton Liste in Zürich has dedicated a grand solo sonata for piano to you and asked me to deliver the dedication copy to you." Beethoven did not reply, took the score and put it on the table without looking at it. Schnyder now broached the subject which concerned him personally and said: "Herr van Beethoven, I long to take lessons in composition with you." Beethoven: "I accept no pupils." Schnyder: "But, Herr van Beethoven, I have come to Vienna on your account, and your friend Troxler, too, was of the opinion that I might be fortunate enough to be accepted as your pupil." Beethoven: "I should certainly accept you, but I no longer give any lessons at all." Schnyder: "But, Herr van Beethoven! Do remember that it's only because of you that I've come to Vienna, and do make me the exception to this hard rule." Beethoven (raising his voice, very decided, but not unfriendly): "No! no! I've only one pupil left, and I can't get rid of him, much as I should like to." "Who is your pupil, then?" Thereupon Maestro Beethoven, his face grim with fury and violently stamping his feet, roared at me: "Oh! He's Archduke Rudolph!" After a little pause Beethoven said in the most endearing tone of voice: "On the other hand, I'll gladly let you have my opinion and judgment on any composition you care to submit to me." After the business part of his visit had been settled, Schnyder felt impelled to express what was on his mind and to describe the intense pleasure which Beethoven's majestic compositions had given him. He spoke to him of some of his favourites, for example of the three Piano Trios, Op. 1, of the three solo sonatas, Op. 2, of the Piano Quintet with Wind Instruments, of the Septet. Beethoven frowned and said: "Don't mention these works to me, if you're out to praise me."' Schnyder: "But they're beautiful and have given the greatest joy to thousands of people!" Beethoven (indignant): "I wish I'd never written them." Schnyder: "Why?" Beethoven: "Because I can produce better things now." I could not decently prolong my visit. Beethoven clasped Schnyder's hand, while he bade him a friendly farewell, shook it heartily, as the Swiss and the English are wont to do, and said with feeling: "Come again soon and don't hesitate to visit me frequently."

A few days later he paid another visit to Beethoven. Once again he found him in the best of spirits and, after exchanging the usual greetings, asked him: "Have you looked through the sonata which Liste dedicated to you?" "Of course," said Beethoven, rather coldly. Schnyder: "How do you like it?" Beethoven (even more coldly): "It's a good school exercise." Schnyder did not have the courage to defend the sonata and, in order to change the subject, said: "I've brought some of my own work, Herr v. Beethoven. May I show it to you?" Beethoven: "With the greatest pleasure! I've already told you that I'll gladly give you my opinion of anything you care to show to me." Schnyder showed him the very clearly written score of the song for soprano and orchestra already mentioned: "The Confederation. She to him." Beethoven took the score, perused it calmly, expressing his satisfaction at times, while Schnyder, too, glanced at the page. Towards the end, in a certain place, Beethoven, sliding his finger up and down the page, said to him: "This should be here, not there." (Saying this he moved his finger upwards.) Schnyder: "How do you mean that, Herr v. Beethoven?" Beethoven (briskly and loud): "This should be here, not there." Meanwhile he went through the same motion, but faster and more forcefully. Schnyder understood well enough what the Master meant. At this place, together with a *crescendo*, the violins soared up from a deep note to a very high one and Beethoven meant that there should rather be a downward sweep with a *decrescendo*. This was intimated by the movement of his fingers. Schnyder had the audacity to wonder whether Beethoven was incapable of expressing his opinion clearly in words, and to satisfy his curiosity he said: "I still don't know what you mean, Herr v. Beethoven." Then, in a veritable blaze of fury, the Master Musician roared at Schnyder: "I've already told you repeatedly that this should be here, not there—surely you're capable of understanding that?" At the same time he continued to run his fingers up and down the page, so that one could hear the scratching of his nails. Beethoven was soon pacified and invited Schnyder to continue his visits without fail.

Schnyder soon paid Beethoven another visit and brought his *Grave* and a string quartet. The *Grave* won Beethoven's special approval and he said: "Continue to compose in this way; this work has been thought and felt." The string quartet, of which, however, only the first movement was complete, did not please him at all. He thought it too contrapuntal and too dry.

Before Schnyder had become acquainted with the immortal Master, he had read the well-known anecdote according to which, when Beethoven was practising the violin in his garret, a spider lowered itself on a thread and alighted on him. This interested Schnyder, who was a lover and observer of spiders, and he questioned Beethoven about this anecdote. Beethoven, who knew this anecdote well, laughed and replied: "But I never play the violin."

One afternoon Schnyder and Beethoven were sitting comfortably on the latter's sofa; Schnyder said: "Dear Herr v. Beethoven, I've now visited you so many times and have never heard you play; do play me something, please!" Beethoven replied: "Oh, but I'm not a good pianist"—making the kind of face which a peasant girl might make when someone says to her: You're a very pretty child—and who then thinks she must deny the compliment and answers archly: Oh, but I'm not pretty at all! Schnyder: "I know, and everyone knows, that you play extraordinarily well." Beethoven :"Oh, no; last year I was improvising at a small social gathering in (we believe that he mentioned Karlsbad) when suddenly I saw that the fools were weeping. I ran away and never played to them again." This anecdote was evidence for, rather than against, his masterly playing. Schnyder could not prevail upon Beethoven, who diverted the conversation to a different subject. At this moment two Austrian peasants entered the room and showed Beethoven a document. It was a kind of begging letter. The peasants had lost their house in a fire and had received permission from the authorities to collect alms. Beethoven cursed and ranted, growled that something of the sort turned up every minute of the day, went to his writing-desk and took out a great deal of money which, still grumbling, he gave to the peasants, who left the room amidst the most fervent expressions of gratitude and countless bows.

Schnyder often dined in the *Mehlgrube*, because he knew that Beethoven often went there at the same time in the evening. One lovely spring night Schnyder, on entering the restaurant, saw his friend Beethoven seated at one of the tables. He sat down beside him and was greeted with quite unusual friendliness and enthusiasm. "You have certainly taken a pleasant walk this afternoon, Herr van Beethoven?" Schnyder began. Beethoven: "Yes, indeed! A splendid one, a splendid one!" Schnyder: "I've no doubt at all, you've been hunting after ideas!" "Yes," Beethoven grinned. Schnyder: "If I could have the great privilege of seeing some of it . . ." "Here you are, you can have the whole lot!" exclaimed Beethoven and drew a little wad of crumpled paper out of his side pocket. Schnyder pounced on it greedily and began to study it. "Well, how do you like the themes?" Beethoven asked, with a cunning and somewhat mocking glance. Schnyder: "I can't make head or tail of it—it's nothing but one great scrawl!" Beethoven (laughing): "Ha, ha, ha! I knew that all along, else I'd never have shown it to you."

TO AUGUST VON KOTZEBUE

Vienna, January 28th, 1812

Highly esteemed, highly respected Sir,

As I was composing music for your prologue and epilogue[1] for the Hungarians, I could not refrain from ardently desiring that I might possess an opera created by your unique dramatic genius. May it be romantic, wholly serious, mock-heroic, sentimental, in short, as you wish, yet I shall accept it with pleasure. True, I should prefer a great subject taken from history and especially from the darker ages, for instance that of Attila, etc. Yet I shall accept anything gratefully, whatever the subject, as long it comes from you, from your poetic spirit, which I can translate into my musical spirit. . . .

TO KAMMERPROKURATOR VARENA

End of January, 1812

P.P.

Did not your letter so clearly reveal the intention to aid the poor, you would have given me no little offence by immediately following your invitation with offers to repay me. Never, since my earliest childhood has my zeal to place my art in the service of suffering humanity wherever possible been content with any other course, or rather it requires nothing but the inner satisfaction which always accompanies such deeds. Herewith you will receive an *oratorio* which takes up half an evening, an Overture, a Fantasia with chorus. If in your charitable institutions there is a depot for such works, deposit these three works in my name as a contribution to the poor of your city[2] and as the property of its charitable institutions. Apart from this, you will receive an Introduction to the Ruins of Athens, the score of which I shall at once have copied for you with all possible speed; also, a grand Overture to Hungary's first benefactor[3]. . . .

[1] The music to "King Stephen" and "The Ruins of Athens", performed at the opening of the new theatre in Pest. Kotzebue was the author of these historical dramas.
[2] Graz.   [3] King Stephen.

Most worthy Sir!

Always sickly and very busy, I could not reply to your letter; but why on earth must you therefore draw inferences which do not apply to me at all (?) I should be angry with you for this. It would have been better if you had sent the musical scores immediately after the performance, for this was the moment when I could have had them performed here; as it is, unfortunately, they came too late, and I say unfortunately only because under these circumstances I could not save the reverend women the cost of copying. . . .

The score of the Overture is a present, likewise the Overture of the Egmont. You may keep the parts of the Oratorio until you have performed the same. Take anything you like for the concert which, I believe, you are now planning, and if you need the Chorus and the Overture which you have returned to me, these items will be sent to you at once. For the projected concert in aid of the reverend Ursuline nuns I at once promise you an *entirely new* symphony, this at the very least, but perhaps also an important vocal item—and as I now have the opportunity, the copying shall not cost them a penny. My pleasure at a successful concert would be boundless, if I had not been forced to occasion you any expenses; so you must content yourself with my goodwill. . . .

FROM IGNAZ VON SEYFRIED'S REMINISCENCES

Often he himself made fun of his truly illegible handwriting and added by way of an excuse: "Life is too short for me to paint letters or notes; and notes more carefully penned would hardly relieve my penury."

Beethoven rarely permitted himself to pronounce judgment on his fellow artists, even if only to his intimate friends. However, his own words will best express what he thought about the following four Masters:

"Of all the living composers of operas Cherubini is the one whom I most respect. I am also wholly in agreement with his conception of the Requiem and, if I should ever come to write one of my own, I shall borrow several passages *ad notam*."

"Karl Maria von Weber began his education too late; his art could never develop quite naturally and it was evidently his one aspiration to be considered a genius."

"'The Magic Flute' remains Mozart's greatest work; for only in this did he show himself to be a German Master. 'Don Juan' is still cut to the Italian pattern, entirely so, and, besides, Art, which is sacred, should never be debased in the service of so scandalous a subject."

"Händel is the unequalled Master of all Masters! Go and learn to produce such great effects by such modest means!"

"What is Rossini?" he was once asked. He wrote down in reply: "A good theatrical painter."

TO BREITKOPF UND HÄRTEL

Vienna, January 28th, 1812

P.P.

As a punishment for your unbroken silence, I now command you to deal with these two letters at once. Some windbag of a Livonian promised me to deliver a letter to Kotzebue, but probably—as the Russians and Livonians generally are windbags and capital braggarts—he has not done so, although he claimed to be a great friend of Kotzebue's. I therefore beg of you, although it has been imposed upon you as a punishment, and rightly so, for countless faulty editions, wrong titles, negligences, etc., and other instances of humanity, to see to this matter, so I beg of you once again in all humility to deal with these letters—and then to send off the Egmont (score) to Goethe at the same time, yet not in the usual manner, so that perhaps a piece will be missing here and there, etc., not in this manner, but quite tidily. I have given him my word and am all the more determined to keep it when I can get someone else, such as yourself, to do the work for me. Ha, ha, ha, you know quite well what sort of language you deserve that I should use against you, against such a sinner who, if I wished, would now be wearing a hair-shirt in penance for all the ruthless offences committed against my works. In spite of my note in favour of the old text, you have retained the unfortunate correction of the chorus "We have seen him" in the Oratorio. Good heavens, do they, then, believe in Saxony that the word makes the music? If an unsuitable word can spoil the music, and it certainly can, one should be glad to find that music and words are one and the same thing and, although in themselves the expressions used are vulgar, refrain from trying to improve anything. . . .

If the three songs by Goethe have not yet been engraved, make haste with them. I should like to present them soon to the Princess Kinsky, one of the prettiest, fattest women in Vienna. And the songs from Egmont, why not yet out? why not, indeed, the whole of Egmont, out with it, out, out? Should you wish to have a conclusion appended here and there to the Entreactes [*sic*], (I) could oblige, or leave this to one of the Leipzig proof-readers of the Music Review; this kind of work fits them like a glove. Kindly debit the postage for the letters to my account. It seems to me, a little bird tells me, that once again you are out for a new wife. I ascribe all the confusions of which you have been guilty in the past to this one cause. I wish you a Xanthippe, like the one that fell to the lot of holy Socrates the Greek, so that for once I may see a German publisher publicly embarrassed, deeply embarrassed both in private and in public. I hope that soon I shall have the honour of receiving a few lines from you.

Your friend,

Beethoven

FROM THE AUTOBIOGRAPHY OF LOUIS SPOHR

As, at the time when I made his acquaintance, Beethoven had ceased to perform either in public or at private gatherings, I was only given a single opportunity of hearing him, when by chance I went to see him during the rehearsal of a new trio (D major, triple time). It was hardly an enjoyable experience; for, to begin with, the piano was badly out of tune, a circumstance which troubled Beethoven little as, in any case, he could not hear the music, and secondly scarcely anything remained of the artist's once so greatly admired virtuosity, also because of his deafness. In the *forte* passages the poor deaf man struck the instrument with such violence that the strings rattled, while in the *piano* passages he played so softly that whole bars were inaudible and the music became unintelligible if one was unable to follow the pianoforte part in manuscript. I was overpowered by a feeling of deep sorrow when I considered this hard fate. If it is a great misfortune for anyone to be deaf, how can a musician endure it without despairing? Beethoven's chronic melancholia no longer puzzled me.

TO COUNT FRANZ BRUNSWICK

Vienna, Spring, 1812

Dear friend and brother,

I should have written to you sooner, in my heart I did so a thousand times.... If the waves of war should come even nearer, I shall go to Hungary; perhaps even in any case. For, after all, I have nothing to care for but my wretched person. So I shall probably struggle through; away, more noble and exalted plans! Our striving alone is infinite, vulgarity makes all things finite!

Farewell, dear brother! Be a brother to me! I have no one whom I could call by this name. Spread as many good things about you as these evil times permit.

TO ?

Teplitz, 1812

On the morning of July 6th

My angel, my all, my very self! Only a few words to-day, and those in pencil (with yours). Not until to-morrow will the matter of my lodgings be finally settled: what a shameful waste of time are all such things! Why this deep sorrow, where necessity speaks? Can our love subsist otherwise than by sacrifices, by our not desiring everything? Can you do anything to alter the fact that you are not wholly mine, that I am not wholly yours? Oh, God! gaze at the beauties of Nature and reconcile yourself to that which must be! Love demands everything and quite rightly so; that is how I feel towards you and you towards me. Only you so readily forget that I must live for me and for you. If we were wholly united you would feel the pain of it as little as I do.

My journey was terrible: I did not arrive here until four o'clock yesterday morning. As there was a shortage of horses, the mail coach chose a different route, but what terrible roads! At the stage before the last I was warned not to travel at night, told to fear a certain forest, but this only made me eager, and I was in the wrong. The coach was bound to break down on this dreadful road, a bottomless, sheer mud-track! Without four such excellent postillions as I had with me, I should still be lying somewhere on the way. Esterhazy suffered the same fate on the other, usual route with his eight horses, while I had only four. Nevertheless, I got a certain amount of enjoyment even from this, as I do whenever some great difficulty or danger has been overcome.

But to plunge from external to internal matters: we shall probably be meeting soon. But to-day I cannot tell you of the observations I have made during the past days with regard to my life. If our hearts were always close together I should scarcely have occasion to make any such observations. My heart is full of many things to say to you. Oh, there are moments when I feel that words are nothing at all. Take courage! remain my true, my only treasure, as I remain yours! The gods must send us the rest, whatever has been ordained for us and must be.

Your faithful Ludwig

Monday night, July 6th

You are suffering, you, my dearest creature. (At this very moment I learn that letters must be posted very early in the morning, on Mondays, Thursdays, the only days on which the mail-coach goes from here to K.[1]) You are suffering. Oh, wherever I am, you are with me; I speak to you and to myself. Make it possible that I may live with you! and what a life we shall live!!!! thus!!!! without you—pursued by the kindness of persons here and there, a kindness which I wish to deserve as little as I deserve it. The humility of men towards men, it hurts me. And when I contemplate myself in connection with the universe, what I am and what is he whom they call the greatest! And yet it is herein that the divinity of men resides. I weep when I reflect that you will probably receive no news of me before Saturday. Much as you love me, I love you still more. But never hide your thoughts from me!

Good night! As I am here for the baths, I must go to bed. Oh, God, so near and so far! Is it not truly a heavenly edifice, our love? but as firm, too, as the firmament of heaven.

Good morning! July 7th

Though I am still in bed, my thoughts surge towards you, my immortal beloved, now joyfully, then again sorrowfully, waiting to know whether fate will hear us. I must live with you entirely, or not at all. Yes, indeed, I am resolved to stray in distant places until that moment when I can throw myself into your arms and say that I am really at home with you, when I can send my soul, wrapped in your presence, into the realm of the spirits. Yes, unfortunately there is no other way. You will not give in, for you know my fidelity to you. Never shall another be able to possess my heart, never—never! Oh, God, why is one forced to part from her whom one loves so well! And yet my life in Vienna, as it is at present, is a wretched

[1] Karlsbad?

113

affair. Your loves makes me both the happiest and unhappiest of men. At my age I need a certain regularity, a certain balance in my life: can these be reconciled with our relationship? My angel, at this moment I learn that the mail-coach leaves every day and so I must end, to make sure that you will receive this letter at once. Be calm! Only by calmly contemplating our existence shall we be able to achieve our purpose of living to-gether. Be calm! Love me! To-day, yesterday, what a tearful desire to be with you, you, you! My life, my all! Farewell! Oh, never cease to love me, never misjudge the most faithful heart of your beloved.

Eternally yours, eternally mine, eternally ours!

L.

NOTE. *The three preceding letters, popularly known as the "Letters to the Immortal Beloved" have been the subject of endless controversies. Neither their date nor the identity of the addressee can be established with any certainty; Thayer was of the opinion that the letters were written in 1806; Leitzmann dates them 1807. Originally it was believed that these letters were addressed to Countess Guicciardi; Thayer and Leitzmann argued that they must have been addressed to Countess Therese Brunswick; Thomas-San-Galli made out a good case for a third lady, Amalie Sebald, and believed that the letters were written in 1812. A fourth possible recipient is Magdalene Willmann, a singer to whom Beethoven is said to have proposed marriage as early as 1795. The identity of the place referred to as K. is equally questionable and does not, therefore, offer any clue to the enigma. These letters were never posted; they were found in a drawer of Beethoven's desk after his death. (A more recent assertion is discussed on page 270.)*

TO EMILIE M.

Teplitz, July 17th, 1812

My dear good Emilie, my dear friend,

The answer to your letter has been long delayed: a heap of business and perpetual illness should excuse me. My presence here as a patient proves the truth of my excuse. Do not rob Händel, Haydn, Mozart of their laurel wreaths: they deserve them, I have not yet earned mine.

Your wallet will be preserved among other tokens of an esteem which I am still far from meriting, given to me by several others. Continue your progress, do not practise your art alone, but penetrate into its inner meaning. It is worth it: for only Art and science exalt men to the point of divinity. Should you ever want anything, my dear Emilie, do not hesitate to write to me confidently. The true artist has no pride; unhappily he sees that Art has no bounds. Obscurely he feels how far away he is from his aim, and even while others may be admiring him, he mourns his failure to attain that end which his better genius illumines like a distant sun. Perhaps I should prefer to stay with you, with your family, than with many of the rich who betray their inner poverty. Should I go to Hamburg one day, I shall stay with you, with your family. I know of no other advantages of human beings than those which place them in the ranks of the good and the superior; wherever I find these, there is my home.

Should you wish to write to me, dear Emilie, simply address your letter to this place, where I shall spend another four weeks, or to Vienna; it makes no difference. Regard me as your friend and as the friend of your family.

Ludwig van Beethoven

GOETHE'S COMMENTS ON HIS MEETING WITH BEETHOVEN AT TEPLITZ

From Goethe's Diary.

Teplitz, July 20th, (1812). In the evening drove to Bilin with Beethoven.

Teplitz, July 21st. In the evening, at Beethoven's. He played deliciously.

From a letter to Christiane von Goethe, July 19th, 1812

. . . Tell his Highness, Prince Frederick, that I cannot be in Beethoven's company without wishing that it might be at the

"Goldene Strauss". I have never seen an artist more concentrated, energetic and intense. I can understand quite well that his relationship to the world must be a strange one.

From a letter to Zelter, September 2nd, 1812

. . . I got to know Beethoven at Teplitz. His talent amazed me; but unfortunately his is a personality utterly lacking in self-control; he may not be wrong at all in thinking that the world is odious, but neither does such an attitude make it any more delectable to himself or to others. On the other hand, he much deserves to be both excused and pitied, for his hearing has almost failed him, which probably does more harm to the social part of his character than to the musical part. He, who in any case is laconic by nature, is now becoming doubly so because of this defect.

BEETHOVEN'S COMMENTS ON HIS MEETING WITH GOETHE AT TEPLITZ

(*From a letter by Bettina Brentano (now v. Arnim) to Prince Hermann von Pückler-Muskau.*)

He entrusted me with messages to Goethe, to the effect that he esteemed him more than anyone. In the following year they made each other's acquaintance. Goethe went to see him; Beethoven played to him. When he observed that Goethe seemed to be deeply moved, he said: "Oh, Sir, I didn't expect this of you. In Berlin, too, I was giving a concert some years ago, I made a great effort and thought I was giving a really good performance and hoped for some decent applause; but, lo and behold! when I had expressed my utmost enthusiasm, not the faintest sound of applause was to be heard. That really was too much for me: I couldn't understand it. However, the enigma soon resolved itself in this way: the whole Berlin public was so educated and refined that now they all staggered towards me with their handkerchiefs wet with emotion to assure me of their gratitude. This was quite irrelevant to a crude enthusiast like myself: I could see that I had only had a romantic audience, not an artistic one. But from you, Goethe, I won't stand for this. When your poems passed through my brain, they produced music and I was proud enough to desire that I might rise to the same height as yourself. But never in my life did I know whether I had done so, and least of all would I ever have shown it in your presence: for here enthusiasm should have a very different effect. You yourself must know how pleasant it is to be applauded by hands which one respects: if you don't recognize me and consider me as your equal, who will? To what sort of a pack of ragamuffins shall I turn for understanding?" In this way he drove Goethe into a corner; at first Goethe could not think how he might undo the damage he had done; for he was well aware that Beethoven was right. The Empress and the Austrian dukes were at Teplitz and Goethe received many tokens of distinction from them; in particular, it was no trivial matter to him to pay his respects to the Empress. He intimated this to Beethoven in solemn but modest terms. "What nonsense!" said he, "that's not the way to go about it, that will do no one any good. You must make it very obvious how valuable you are to them, else they'll never know it: there isn't a princess in the world who appreciates Tasso any longer than she's pinched by the shoes of her vanity. I behaved very differently towards them: when I had to give lessons to Duke Rainer (Archduke Rudolph), he made me wait in the ante-room. For that, I put an extra strain on the joints of his fingers: when he asked me why I was so impatient, I said I had wasted my time in the ante-room and could not, therefore, afford to lose any more by being patient. After this, he never made me wait again; furthermore, I had proved to him that this was a piece of silliness which revealed nothing but their brutishness. I told him that they might be able to hang a decoration on a man's neck but that this didn't make them any better than the next man. They could make a Privy Councillor or a Minister, but they couldn't make a Goethe or a Beethoven. Therefore they must be taught to respect that which they cannot make and which they're far from being themselves; it does them good." At this moment, while they were walking together, the Empress and the dukes approached with all their attendants. Now Beethoven said: "Keep your arm linked in mine, they must make room for us, not we for them." Goethe was not of this opinion and began to feel embarrassed; he withdrew his arm and, with his hat in his hand, stood aside, while Beethoven, his arms crossed, walked straight through the crowd of dukes, only moving his hat a little, while the dukes parted to make room for him and all of them greeted him kindly. At the other end he halted and waited for Goethe, who had let them pass by while he bowed deeply. Now Beethoven said: "I've waited for you, because I honour and revere you as you deserve; but you have done too much honour to those others." Afterwards Beethoven came running to us and told us everything with childish delight at having teased Goethe in this way. The speeches above are all literally true; nothing essential has been added to them. Beethoven told this story several times in the same manner, and in more respects than one it seemed quite important to me.

TO BREITKOPF UND HÄRTEL

Franzensbrunn, near Eger, August 9th, 1812*

Only essentials: you lack the title for the Mass, while I have too much of many things; such as taking baths, doing nothing, etc., and I am tired of these and other inevitable incidentals and accidentals. You can now visualize and think of me here. My doctor drives me from one place to the other in the hope of finally catching my health on the run, from Teplitz to Karlsbad, from Karlsbad to this place. In Karlsbad I played something to the Saxons and Prussians in aid of the burnt-out township of Baden; it was, so to speak, a poor concert for the poor. Our *Signore Polledrone* assisted me in this,[1] and once he

---

[1] A large part of the town of Baden, near Vienna, was destroyed in a fire on July 26th, 1812. Beethoven immediately gave a charity concert together with the Turin violinist Giovanni Battista Polledro.

had sweated out his fear as usual, he played well enough. "To his Grace, the high-born Prince Kinsky", something of the sort should be contained in the title. And now I must refrain from writing more; instead I must splash about once more in the water. When I have scarcely washed out my interior with a large quantity of same, I must at once submit to having my exterior thoroughly rinsed once more. I shall reply to the rest of your letter very soon. Goethe is very fond of Court air, more so than is seemly for a poet. It is scarcely worth while to discuss the absurdities of the virtuosi here, when poets, who should be regarded as the foremost teachers of the nation, can become oblivious to all else because they are dazzled by this poor glitter. . . .

Your Beethoven

* The climate here is such that one could easily write: November 9th.

TO AMALIE SEBALD

Teplitz, September 16th, 1812

I a   ir tyrant? Only a misapprehension can lead
you t   thing, even though this very judgment shows
the   tween our ways of thinking. Not that I blame
yo   ather it is fortunate for you. Already since
ye   ave not been feeling quite well; but since this
r   illness has become more pronounced; something
        I have eaten is the cause of it, and the sensitive part
        s to get hold of the bad as well as the good. Don't,
        apply this to my moral nature. What people say
amoun   to nothing, they are only people; in most cases they see only themselves in others, and this precisely is what amounts to nothing; away with it! Whatever is good and beautiful needs no people. It simply exists without anyone's help and this, too, seems to be the basis of our association.

Farewell, dear Amalie. If to-night the moon seems brighter to me than did the sun throughout the day, you will be visited by the very least of all men.

Your friend Beethoven

September 17th

This is only to report to you that the tyrant is quite slavishly fettered to his bed—that's how it is. I shall be happy to get away with the loss of no more than this one day. Yesterday's walk at daybreak in the woods, where it was very misty, has aggravated my illness and perhaps hindered my recovery. Meanwhile, frolic about with Russians, Lapps, Samoyeds, etc., and don't overdo your singing of the song "Long may he live".[1]

Your friend Beethoven

September

I cannot yet tell you anything definite about myself. Now it seems that I am better, then again the illness seems to be taking its old course or about to prolong itself indefinitely. If I could express my thoughts about this illness by signs as reliable as those by which I express myself in music, I would soon help myself. To-day, too, I am still confined to bed. Farewell, and rejoice at your good health, dear Amalie.

Your friend
Beethoven

Some days later

Dear, good Amalie, Ever since I left you yesterday my condition has been deteriorating and I have not left my bed since last night. I wished to send you news of me to-day, but then again I thought that by doing so I should be trying to make myself too important to you; so I refrained.

[1] The German song "*Er lebe hoch*".

What makes you think that you cannot be anything to me? Let us rather speak of this when we meet. Above all, I have always wished that my presence calmed and soothed you and inspired you with confidence in me. I hope to be better to-morrow, so that a few hours at least may be left to us during your stay here in which we may edify and cheer each other amidst the beauties of Nature. Good-night, dear Amalie! Very many thanks for proving your kind disposition towards

Your friend Beethoven

I shall glance at the Tiedge.[1]

FROM NOTEBOOKS AND CALENDARS
(As transcribed by Fischhoff)

1812

Resignation, the most sincere resignation to your fate! Only this can make you capable of the sacrifices which your duty and vocation demand. O hard struggle! Do everything in your power to make all the necessary arrangements for your distant journey. You must find all those things that guarantee the realization of your most treasured wish; thus, in spite of it all, you must win through by defiance, be absolutely true to your constant conviction.

You must not be human, not for yourself, only for others: for you there can be no more happiness, except within yourself, in your art. Oh, God! give me strength to conquer myself! For nothing must bind me to this life. (By behaving) in this manner, as with A. all is ruined.

1813

May 13th. To refrain from a great action, which could be accomplished, and remain content to do so! Oh, how different

---

[1] Probably the long poem *Urania*, popular at the time.

this is from the aimless and idle life which so often manifested itself in me! Oh, terrible circumstances that do not suppress my feeling for domesticity, but prevent its realization! O, God, God, look down upon this unhappy B., do not let it go on much longer in this way!

A note on the "Battle Symphony", Op. 91

I must give the English some idea of their great good fortune in possessing "God save the king".

Show me the race-course at whose distant end the palm-tree stands! Lend sublimity to my highest thoughts, enrich them with truths that remain truths for ever!

TO NIKOLAUS ZMESKALL VON DOMANOVETZ

Vienna, September 21st, 1813

August nobleman, wearer of the Grand Cross of Violincellity, should your manservant be a good fellow and know of another for me, you would do me a great favour by letting your good fellow obtain another good fellow for me. I want a married one in any case; even if no more honesty is to be expected of a married man, he is yet likely to be more orderly. At the end of this month my present brute of a manservant is leaving; the manservant could therefore begin on the first day of next month. Since yesterday I have not been allowed out because of my catarrh and shall probably be confined to my room for several more days. If you should wish to visit me, please let me know the hour. As I do not give my servants any livery other than an overcoat, my servant gets twenty-five florins a month. Dear Zmeskall, please forgive

Your friend Beethoven

NOTE OF THANKS[1]

December, 1813

I consider it my duty to thank all those honourable gentlemen who took part in the concert given on the 8th and 12th of December in aid of members of the Imperial Austrian and Royal Bavarian armies who were wounded at the battle of Hanau—for the zeal shown in such a high cause. It was a rare assembly of excellent musical artists, every one of them inspired only by the thought that his art could be of some use to the fatherland, without any distinctions of rank even in subordinate places, who contributed to the admirable execution of the whole. If Herr Schuppanzigh occupied a prominent place as leader of the first violins and impelled the orchestra to follow him by his fiery and expressive performance, Herr Kapellmeister Salieri did not disdain to conduct the drums and cannonades; Herr Spohr and Herr Mayseder, whose art has made him worthy of the highest executive functions, took part in the second and third places, and Messrs. Siboni and Giuliani were likewise content with subordinate places. The direction of the whole performance was entrusted to me only because the work was of my composition; had it been by another, I should have been just as willing as Herr Hummel to take my place beside the big drum, as every one of us was filled only with pure feelings of patriotism and of joyful self-sacrifice to those who have sacrificed so much to us. No one, however, deserves our gratitude so much as Herr Maelzl, inasmuch as he conceived the idea of this concert in his capacity of manager and as it was he who took upon himself the heaviest burden of all, the preparation, administration and planning needed for this concert. Again, I must thank him especially because by arranging this concert he has given me the opportunity, by means of works composed exclusively for this occasion and handed over to him, to fulfil my constant and ardent wish to be able to lay one of my larger works upon the altar of the fatherland in the

[1] This document refers to a concert (given on December 8th) at which the Seventh Symphony and the "Battle Symphony" received their first performance.

present troubled circumstances. Indeed, since a printed notice of all the persons concerned in this concert and of the various parts taken by them on this occasion is about to appear, the public will be able to see for themselves with how noble a self-denial many of the greatest musical artists have worked to a single and worthy end.

Ludwig van Beethoven

TO HUMMEL

Vienna, February, 1814

Dearest Hummel, I beg of you: on this occasion, too, conduct the percussion instruments and the cannonades with your excellent conductor's and field-marshal's baton! Do it, I beg of you. If ever you wish me to cannonade you, I shall be entirely at your disposal, body and soul.

Your friend

Beethoven

TO COUNT FRANZ BRUNSWICK

Vienna, February 13th, 1814

Dear friend and brother,

You wrote to me recently, I am writing to you now. I suppose that you are celebrating all these victories—and mine, too. On the twenty-seventh of this month I am giving a second concert[1] in the great *Redoutensaal*—come up. Now you know of it. So save me from my misery by degrees, for I haven't yet received a penny of my salary. Schuppanzigh has written to Michalcovics, asking whether it would be worth while to go to Ofen—what do you think about it? Certainly, such a thing should take place in a theatre. My opera, too, is being performed on the stage, but there is much to be revised. I hope you are content, for that, surely, is a great deal. As for me, good heavens, my realm is in the air; as often as the wind whirls, so do the sounds whirl and so, too, does it whirl in my soul—I embrace you.

[1] At which the Seventh Symphony received its second performance, the Eighth its first.

There is much to be done on earth; do it soon!

My present daily life must not continue! Art demands even this sacrifice. Rest in your recreations, so as to work all the more vigorously in your art!

For Fate to mankind granted long-suffering courage. (Homer)

No time passes more swiftly, rolls on faster, than the time when our spirits are wholly occupied or when I am wholly occupied with my Muse.

Never overtly show all men the contempt which they deserve, for one can never know when one may need them.

The Scottish songs prove with how little constraint a disordered melody can be treated by means of harmony.

TO JOHANN KANKA, Advocate in Prague, who had represented Beethoven in his claims against the heirs of Prince Kinsky

Vienna, 1814

A thousand thanks, my honoured friend. At last I see another advocate of justice and a man who can write and think without using those wretched formulas. You can scarcely imagine how I sigh for the conclusion of this business, for, because of it, I must live in a state of uncertainty in all matters concerning my economy, not to mention the harm it has done me in other respects. You know as well as I do that the mind, the creative mind, must not be dependent on trivial needs, and this business has deprived me of many things that lend happiness to my life. I have had to restrict, and must still restrict, even my inclination and my self-appointed duty to use my art as a means of relieving needy humanity.

About our monarchs, etc., the monarchies, etc., I shall say nothing to you; the newspapers tell you everything. My favourite realm is that of the mind and spirit and I regard it as the highest of all worldly and spiritual monarchies. Do let me know what you want of me, of my poor musical faculties, so that I may create something for your own musical sense or feelings, as far as I am able to comply. Do you not need all the papers relevant to the Kinsky affair? In that case I should send them to you, as they include the most important testimonials which, I believe, you were able to read when you came to see me. Remember me and remember that you are representing a disinterested artist against a stingy family. How ready men are to take away from an artist the very things which, in other ways, they have offered him as a tribute, and there is no longer a Zeus of whose ambrosia one may partake by inviting himself. Lend wings, dear friend, to the sluggish feet of justice. If I find myself never so exalted, if in happy moments I find myself in the sphere of my art, still the spirits of earth pull me down again; among these I must now include the two lawsuits. You, too, are troubled with disagreeable things; although with your accustomed insight and capacities and, especially, in your profession, I should never have believed this, I must yet direct your attention back to myself. I have drained a cup of bitter sufferings and have already attained martyrdom in Art with the help of my dear disciples and colleagues. I entreat you to think of me every day, and think of me as a whole world, as naturally it would be too much to expect you to think of so small an individual as myself.

Yours, with the most sincere respect and friendship,

Ludwig van Beethoven

AN ACCOUNT BY BLASIUS HÖFEL (according to Thayer)

Another consequence of Beethoven's sudden popularity was the publication of a new engraving of him by Artaria, the crayon drawing for which was executed by Latronne, a French artist then in Vienna. Blasius Höfel, a young man of 22 years, was employed to engrave it. He told the writer how very desirous he was of producing a good likeness—a matter of great importance to the young artist—but that Latronne's drawing was not a good one, probably for want of a sufficient number of sittings. Höfel often saw Beethoven at Artaria's, and when his work was well advanced, asked him for a sitting or two. The request was readily granted. At the time set, the engraver appeared with his plate. Beethoven seated himself in position and for perhaps five minutes remained reasonably quiet; then suddenly springing up went to the pianoforte and began to extemporize, to Höfel's great annoyance. The servant relieved his embarrassment by assuring him that he could now seat himself near the instrument and work at his leisure, for his master had quite forgotten him and no longer knew that any-one was in the room. This Höfel did; wrought so long as he wished, and then departed with not the slightest notice from Beethoven. The result was so satisfactory that only two sittings of less than an hour each were needed. It is well known that Höfel's is the best of all the engravings made of Beethoven.

TO ARCHDUKE RUDOLPH

Vienna, July 14th, 1814

Your Imperial Highness,

Whenever I enquire about your well-being, I hear only favourable reports. As far as my insignificant self is concerned, until now I have been continually cursed with the inability to leave Vienna, so that unfortunately I could not approach Your Imperial Highness and was likewise deprived of the en-joyment, so necessary for me, of natural beauty. The theatre management are so honest that once again, contrary to their promises to me, they have performed my opera Fidelio without giving any thought to my share of the proceeds. They would have shown the same loving honesty on a second occasion recently, had I not lain in wait for them like a former French customs official. At last, after some rather strenuous exertions on my part, I succeeded in making sure of a performance for my benefit of the same opera on July 18th. At this time of the year a good reception is the exception rather than the rule and my own profit is likely to prove a deception; yet a performance for the author's benefit, when the work has been moderately successful, can be an occasion for modest festivity. To this festivity the master obediently invites his exalted pupil and hopes—yes, I hope that Your Imperial Highness will graciously accept and add splendour to the occasion by your presence. It would be gratifying if Your Imperial Highness could persuade the other Imperial Highnesses to attend this performance of my opera. I myself shall observe such decorum as respect demands. Because of Vogl's illness I could satisfy my wish to assign the part of Pizarro to Forti, as his voice is more suitable for the part. However, there are now rehearsals daily and while these promise to be most advantageous to the performance, they will prevent me from attending on Your Imperial Highness at Baden before this occasion. Accept my communication graciously and may Your Imperial Highness think of me most graciously and with favour.

Your Imperial Highness'

True and most faithful servant,

Ludwig van Beethoven

FROM WENZEL TOMASCHEK'S REMINISCENCES

On the morning of the 10th[1] I visited Beethoven in the company of my brother. The poor man was extremely hard of hearing on this particular day, so that we had to shout rather than speak to make ourselves intelligible. The reception room, in which he welcomed me kindly, was anything but luxuriously furnished; in addition, it was quite as untidy as his hair. . . .

Myself. You will forgive me for disturbing you, Herr van Beethoven. I am Tomaschek from Prague, composer in the

---

[1] October.

service of Count Bouquoy, and have taken the liberty of visiting you in the company of my brother.

B. I am very glad to know you in person. You do not disturb me at all.

Myself. Dr. R. sends you his regards.

B. What is he doing? I haven't heard from him for a long time.

Myself. He would like to know how much progress you have made in your lawsuit.

B. With all those complications and formalities, one makes no progress at all.

Myself. I hear that you have composed a Requiem.

B. I intended to write a Requiem as soon as that business was over. Why should I write before I've won my case?

Now he began to tell me the whole story. Even now he spoke without much coherence, rhapsodically rather than methodically; at last the conversation reverted to other topics.

Myself. You seem to be very busy, Herr van Beethoven.

B. Can I help it? What would become of my reputation?

Myself. I presume that you go out very rarely?

B. Hardly anywhere.

Myself. To-night they're performing a new opera by Seyfried; I don't feel in the least inclined to listen to music of that sort.

B. Good Heavens! Someone must compose music of that sort; what would the common crowd do without it?

Myself. I was also told that a young foreign artist[1] is here at present, he is said to be a most distinguished pianist.

B. Yes, I've been told about him, too, but haven't heard him myself. My God! Let him stay with us only for a quarter of a year, then we'll hear what the Viennese think of his playing. I know how everything new is liked in Vienna.

Myself. I take it that you have met this young man.

B. I got to know him at the performance of my *Battle*, on which occasion several of the composers here each took charge of an instrument. The big drum had been allocated to this

---

[1] Giacomo Meyerbeer.

young man. Ha, ha, ha! I wasn't at all satisfied with him; he never beat it in time and was always late, so that I had to tell him off in no uncertain terms. Ha, ha, ha! That must have annoyed him. He's no good; he hasn't the courage to strike at the right time.

This idea made my brother and myself laugh heartily. Refusing his invitation to lunch with him, we left him after assuring him that we should call again before my departure.

On the 24th[1] I visited Beethoven, for I felt a great longing to see him once more before leaving Vienna. I was announced by his manservant and admitted at once. If his apartment had looked untidy during my first visit, it looked far more so now; in the middle room I met two copyists, who were hurriedly transcribing his cantata, the one he had just completed. In the second room all the tables and chairs were covered with fragments of scores, which were probably being corrected by Umlauf, whom Beethoven introduced to me. This gentleman seemed to have a happy temperament, for during our first meeting he was neither cold nor warm: the impression was reciprocated, but he excused himself, while I stayed. Beethoven received me very courteously, but seemed to be very deaf that day, for I had to exert all my strength to make myself understood.

Myself. I have come so as to see you once more before leaving.

B. I thought that you had already left Vienna; have you been here all the time?

Myself. Always, except for excursions to the Aspern and Wagram districts. Have you been well since my last visit?

B. Full of troubles, as usual; life here is becoming impossible.

Myself. I notice that you are very busy preparing for your concert: I do not wish to detain you.

B. Not at all, I'm very glad to see you. There are so many unpleasantnesses connected with a concert, and corrections without end!

Myself. I have just read the announcement saying that you have postponed your concert.

[1] November.

B. Everything had been wrongly copied. I was to have a rehearsal on the day of the performance; that's why I postponed the concert.

Myself. I am sure there is nothing more annoying or more vulgar than the preparations for a concert.

B. You're certainly right there, there is so much stupidity that one can make no headway at all. And what an expense! It is quite irresponsible, the way in which artistic matters are dealt with nowadays. I have to give a third of the proceeds to the theatre management and a fifth to the Gaol. It makes me sick! When all this business is over I shall enquire whether the art of music is a free art or not. Believe me, there's no hope for art at the present time. How much longer are you staying in Vienna?

Myself. I intend to leave on Monday.

B. In that case, I must give you a ticket for my concert.

I thanked him and asked him not to put himself to any trouble on this account; but he went into the ante-room and returned at once, saying that his servant, who was looking after the tickets, was not at home: I should simply write down my address for him, so that he could send me the ticket. As he insisted, I wrote down my address and we then continued our conversation as follows:

Myself. Have you been to Meyerbeer's opera?[1]

B. No, I'm told that it was a bad failure. I thought of you; you hit the nail on the head when you said that you didn't expect much of his compositions. I spoke to the opera singers on the evening after the performance, at the wine house where they usually go. I said to them straight out: "You've certainly distinguished yourselves again! What a braying of asses you've set up! You should be ashamed of yourselves for not understanding anything yet, for being incapable of any judgment, for making so much ado about this opera! Is it possible that a man should meet with such opinions in mature singers? I should like to take you to task over this, but you don't understand me."

[1] *The Two Caliphs.*

131

Myself. I was at the opera; it began with Halleluiah and ended in a Requiem.

B. Ha, ha, ha, ha, ha! That's exactly how it is with his playing. I've often been asked whether I've heard him—I said no; yet from the judgments of those of my acquaintances who can judge such things I could deduce that, while he is competent, he is otherwise a superficial person.

Myself. I hear that before he left for Paris he played at Herr ——'s house and was liked much less.

B. Ha, ha, ha, ha! What did I tell you? I know the whole process. Let him settle here for only half a year and then we'll hear what they say about his playing. It doesn't mean anything. It has long been known that the greatest pianists were also the greatest composers, but how did they play? Not like our pianists to-day who only run up and down the keyboard in passages learned by heart, thump—thump—thump—what's the use of that? None whatsoever! When the true virtuosi played, it was something coherent, something whole; written down on the spot, one would have regarded it as a well-executed work. That can be called playing the piano, the rest should be called nothing.

Myself. I think it's quite ludicrous that Fuss, who himself seems to have a very restricted idea of the piano, should have called him the very greatest of pianists.

B. He has no idea at all of instrumental music. He is a pitiable creature, and I shall tell him so to his face. He once praised an instrumental composition in so extravagant a manner, that one could see all the sheeps' and asses' ears sticking out; I could not help laughing at his ignorance. He does understand vocal music, and should stick to it, but apart from that he knows damned little about music.

Myself. I, too, will leave Vienna with a very low opinion of Fuss' knowledge.

B. As I said, apart from vocal music he knows nothing.

Myself. Moscheles, I am told, is attracting a great deal of notice.

B. Good Heavens! He plays prettily, prettily—apart from

that he's a . . . He will never come to anything. All these people have their circles of acquaintances, with whom they spend a good deal of time; there they are praised, praised again and again, and that's the end of their art! I tell you, nothing will come of him. I used to be too free with my judgments and made enemies in this way; now I judge no one, and for no other reason than that I want to harm no one, and in the end I say to myself: if there's something decent in anyone, it will be upheld in spite of every kind of malice and envy; if there's nothing solid in him, nothing that's durable, then he'll collapse in any case, though others support him in every possible way.

Myself. That's my philosophy, too.

Meanwhile Beethoven had got dressed and was ready to go out. I bade him farewell, whereupon he wished me a happy journey and invited me to look him up again if I should decide to remain in Vienna a little longer.

TO LOUIS SPOHR

133

pain, all pain, all pain, end - less, e - -

- ndless is re - joi - cing, is re - joi - cing, e - - - - - -

- - - - - - - ndless is re - joicing, e - - - - ndless,

e - - - ndless is re - joicing. Brief, brief,

brief, brief is all pain, all pain, all pain,

end-less, e - - - - ndless is re - joic - ing,

e - - - - - - - - - - ndless is re - joi - - - - -

- - - - - - - - - - - - - - cing.

May you be glad to think of me, dear Spohr, wherever you encounter true art and true artists,

Of your friend,

Beethoven

Vienna, March 3rd, 1815

134

TO KANKA

Vienna, April 8th, 1815

It is probably not permitted—to be as friendly with you as I believed us to be, and to live in such hostile proximity without our seeing each other!!!!!! *Tout à vous*, you wrote. Ah, you old windbag, I thought. No, no, it's too terrible! I am always wanting to thank you 9000 times for your exertions on my behalf and to curse you soundly 20,000 times for arriving in this way, leaving in this way. So it's all vanity! Friendship, Monarchy, Empire, all mere fog which any gust of wind can transform or blow away!! Perhaps I shall be going to Teplitz, but it's by no means certain; I could take this opportunity of giving the citizens of Prague a piece of my mind. What do you think about this, if you have any opinion in matters concerning me? Now that the business with Lobkowitz has also come to an end, we have reached the FINIS, though it seems to be written with a small fi, a small fie. Baron Pasqualati, I imagine, will soon be looking you up again; he too has put himself to great trouble for my sake. Yes, indeed, it is easy to talk about justice, but difficult to obtain it from others. How can I place my art at your service? Tell me, would you like to have the monologue of a fugitive king or the perjury of a usurper set and sung?—or the living next to each other of two friends who never see each other? In the hope of hearing from you soon, now that you are so far away from me and, it would seem, so much the more accessible,

I am

Your ever devoted

And respectful friend,

Ludwig van Beethoven

FROM NOTEBOOKS, CALENDARS, SKETCHBOOKS, ETC.

1815

All that is called life shall be sacrificed to sublime Art, a sacrament of Art! Let me live, even by means of artificial aids! if only such are to be found!

If possible, develop the ear instruments, then travel! This you owe to yourself, to men and to Him, the Almighty: only in this way may you be able to develop once more all that has remained latent within you. And a small Court, a small Chapel, the song of praise to be written in it by me, performed, to the glory of the Almighty, the Eternal, the Infinite! Thus may my last days pass—and for future humanity! Händel, Bach, Gluck, Mozart, Haydn's portraits in my room, they can help me to deserve indulgence.

Iliad. The Twenty-Second Book.

But Fate now conquers; I am hers; and yet not she shall share
In my renown; that life is left to every noble spirit
And that some great deed shall beget that all lives shall inherit.

Brühl at the *Lamm*. How lovely to see my native countryside, to travel to England, then to spend four weeks there!

My only decree to remain in the country. How easily this can be fulfilled in any place whatsoever. Here my wretched hearing does not plague me. Does it not seem as if every tree in the countryside said to me: Holy, holy! In the forest, enchantment! Who can express it all? Should all else fail, even in winter the country remains, like Gaden, Lower Brühl, etc. Easy to find lodgings at a peasant's, certainly cheap at that time. Sweet stillness of the forest! The wind which comes already on the second fine day cannot keep me in Vienna, though it is my enemy.

Almighty in the forest! I am happy, blissful in the forest: every tree speaks through you. Oh, God! what splendour! In such a wooded scene, on the heights there is calm, calm in which to serve Him.

TO AMENDA

My dear, good Amenda,

Your friend Count Keyserling, who is conveying this letter to you, paid me a visit and so recalled you to my mind. You were happy, he said, and had some children: neither, I fear, will ever be the case with me. It would take too long to discuss this matter in any detail; another time you shall hear more of it, when you write again. A thousand times I have thought of you and your patriarchal simplicity, and how often have I wished to have such people as yourself about me! But fate denies me the fulfilment of such wishes, whether for my own good or the good of others, I cannot tell. I can say with some truth that I live almost alone in this, the largest city in Germany, as I have to live far away from nearly all those whom I love or could love. In what sort of a state is the art of music in your part of the country? Have you heard at all of my great works? Great, I say—compared with the works of the Supreme Creator, all things are small. Farewell, my dear, good Amenda! Think occasionally of your friend

Ludwig van Beethoven

TO COUNTESS ERDÖDY

Vienna, on the 15th of the vintage month
(*October*), 1815

My dear and honoured Countess,

As I can see, I should be justified in being anxious on account of your making this journey in your partly ailing condition, but it seems that you can, in fact, realize your intention, and I therefore console myself and, at the same time, assure you of my sympathy. We finite creatures with infinite spirits are born only to suffer and to rejoice and one could almost say that the most excellent among us derive joy from suffering.

Now I am hoping to hear from you again. Your children must be a great comfort to you, for their sincere affection and striving after all that is good can amply reward their dear mother for all her sufferings. Then there is the honourable Magister, the most faithful of your shield-bearers, and a host of other rabble, amongst them the Master of the Guild, the violincellist, and dispassionate Justice in the Bailiff's Court—truly a retinue which many a king would envy you. About me, nothing—that is, nothing about nothing! May God continue to give you the strength to attain your temple of Isis, and may the pure fire there devour all your afflictions so that you may awake like a new phoenix.

In haste,
Your faithful friend,
Beethoven

TO JOHANN PETER SALOMON

Vienna, June 1st, 1815

My honoured compatriot,

I have always hoped that one day I should be able to realize my desire to see you personally in London; but always many obstacles have prevented me from doing so—and for this very reason, because, in fact, I am not in this position, I hope that you will not refuse my request, that is, to do me the favour of speaking with a London publisher and of offering him the following works of mine: grand Trio for piano, violin and violincello[1] (80 ducats), Sonata for piano and violin[2] (60 ducats), grand Symphony in A (one of my most excellent), little Symphony in F,[3] Quartet for two violins, viola and violoncello in F minor,[4] grand Opera in score (30 ducats), Cantata with chorus and solo voices[5] (30 ducats), score of The Battle of Vittoria on Wellington's Victory[6] (80 ducats), as well as the piano score if, in spite of what I am told here, it has not already been published. In passing I have appended to some of these works the sum which, I believe, would be right for England, but leave it to you, in the case of these as of the others, to determine what is the right amount. I am told that

[1] In B flat, Op. 97.   [2] In G major, Op. 96.
[3] The Seventh and Eighth Symphonies.   [4] Op. 95.
[5] "The Glorious Moment."   [6] The "Battle Symphony", Op. 91.

Cramer is a publisher also; yet my pupil Ries informed me recently that he had publicly declared his antagonism to my compositions, I hope for no other purpose than that of furthering Art, and, if so, I have no objection to make. If, however, Cramer should want to own any of these pernicious works of art, I should prefer him to any other publisher. I only reserve the right to submit these same works to an Austrian publisher, so that these works would really appear only in London and Vienna, and this at the same time.

Perhaps it is also possible for you to let me know in what manner I could obtain from the Prince Regent at least the cost of copying the Battle Symphony on Wellington's Victory in the Battle of Vittoria, dedicated to him. For I have long given up hope of anything more substantial. He did not even do me the honour of a reply as to whether I was permitted to dedicate this work to the Prince Regent in publishing it. I am even told that the work has already been published in London as a piano score. What a fate for an author!!! While the English and German newspapers are full of the success of this work, performed in the Drury Lane Theatre, and the theatre, too, has made considerable profit from it, the author cannot show as much as a few friendly lines for it, not even compensation for the copyist's bill, indeed, even the loss of all his rightful proceeds. For if it is true that the piano score has been engraved, no German publisher will take it now. It is probable that soon some London publisher will pirate it and I shall lose both honour and honorarium. Your well-known distinction of character permits me to hope that you will show some concern in this matter and actively further my cause. The bad paper currency of our State has already been debased to a fifth of its value: I was treated accordingly; after great efforts, however, I obtained the full value, though still with considerable losses. Only the moment has come when these papers have been devalued once more, to far less than one fifth of their true value, and I am confronted with the prospect of seeing my salary reduced to nothing yet again, without hope of any compensation. My compositions are my sole source of income. If I could count on their being sold in England, I should almost certainly profit by it. Rely upon my boundless gratitude. I hope that you will honour me with a speedy, a very speedy, reply.

> Your admirer and friend,
>> Ludwig van Beethoven

TO COUNTESS MARIE ERDÖDY

> *Vienna, 1815*

Dear, dear, dear, dear, dear Countess, I am taking the baths and must continue with this treatment until to-morrow; that is why I could not see you and all your dear ones to-day. I hope you are enjoying better health. It is no consolation to the better among us to be told that others, too, are suffering; yet, I suppose, comparisons must always be made, and there one may well discover that we all suffer and err, only each in his own way. Take the better edition of the quartet and give the bad one to the 'cellist together with a gentle cuff. As soon as I am able to visit you again I shall make a point of driving the latter into a corner.

My best wishes to you. Hug and kiss your dear children on my behalf! although—it occurs to me now, I may no longer kiss your daughters; for they're too old for that. In such matters I'm out of my depth, so act in accordance with your wisdom, dear Countess!

> Truly your friend and admirer,
>> Beethoven

TO ANNA MILDER-HAUPTMANN

> Vienna, January 6th, 1816

My most esteemed, unique Milder, my dear friend,

This letter to you has been long delayed. How gladly I would contribute in person to the enthusiasm of the Berlin public evoked by your performance in "Fidelio". A thousand thanks on my part for your fidelity to my "Fidelio"!

If you would ask Baron de la Motte-Fouqué on my behalf

to devise a great subject for an opera, and one which, at the same time, would be suitable for you, you would be rendering a great service to me and to the German stage. Also, I should wish to write such an opera exclusively for the Berlin theatre, as I shall never succeed in putting on a new opera here, because of the stingy management. Reply to me soon, with all speed, as soon as possible, with all possible speed, as speedily as possible, whether this is practicable. The conductor Weber has praised you to the skies, and he is right. Happy is the man whose lot it is to profit by your Muse, your genius, your splendid qualities and distinctions! Not excluding myself! Be that as it may, all those who surround you may call themselves only next men; I alone have the right to bear the venerable name of head man,[1] and only quite silently at that.

Your true friend and admirer

Beethoven

(My poor unhappy brother has died—that is the reason for my long failure to write.)

As soon as you have replied to me, I shall also write to Baron de la Motte-Fouqué. I am sure that your influence in Berlin will easily make it possible for me to write a whole opera for the Berlin theatre, with special attention to your part and acceptable terms. Only, reply soon, so that I can fit this in with my other writings.

(*Follows music to the words:*

I kiss and hug, press you close to my heart!
I the head man, the head man)

(Away with all the other usurping head men!)

AN ACCOUNT BY KARL FRIEDRICH HIRSCH
(*from Frimmel's biography*)

. . . As far as the externals of these lessons are concerned, we are told that Beethoven, already very hard of hearing at this

---

[1] A pun on the name of Hauptmann (captain, literally: head man).

time (Hirsch says: already at that time one had to speak to him very loudly), used to keep his eyes fixed upon his pupil's hands and would break out into violent rages when a wrong note was struck, whereupon he would grow very red in the face while the veins on his temples and forehead began to swell; also, in his irritation or impatience he would pinch the artistic novice in a most ungentle manner; indeed, on one occasion he even bit his shoulder.

TO NEPOMUK HUMMEL

A happy journey, my dear Hummel; think at times of your friend,

Beethoven

Vienna, April 4th, 1816

TO COUNTESS ERDÖDY

Vienna, May 13th, 1816

My dear and worthy friend,

You have good reason to believe that I have quite forgotten you. Yet this is no more than the appearance: my brother's death caused me great sorrow and, later, great exertions on behalf of my dear nephew, whom I have been endeavouring to save from his corrupt mother. I succeeded in this, but until now I have not been able to do more than to place him in an institution, that is, far away from myself. And what is an institution compared to the immediate sympathy and care of a father for his child? For as such I regard myself now and rack my brain for a means of having this dear treasure nearer to me, so that I may influence him more quickly and more advantageously. Yet how difficult it is for me! Now for six weeks my health has been in a vacillating state, so that quite often I think of my death, but without fear. Only because of my dear Karl I shall be dying too soon. As I can see from your last letter to me, you, too, must be suffering greatly, my dear friend. It cannot be otherwise with us: even here we must prove our strength, that is, endure without knowing, feel our nothingness and yet perfect ourselves, for the Highest wishes to honour us with perfection in this way. Linke, I imagine, will now be with you: may he arouse pleasure in you on his cat-gut! As for Vogel, I hear that you are not satisfied with him: I don't know for what reason. I am told that you are looking for another tutor; please do not act too hastily and acquaint me with your opinions and projects. Perhaps I can give you good recommendations, but perhaps, too, you are doing the poor caged sparrow[1] an injustice? I embrace your children and express this in a trio; I am sure that they are progressing and perfecting themselves daily. Let me know soon, very soon, how you are keeping on that little foggy patch of earth[2] where you are now. Do not doubt my concern for you in your sufferings and in your joys, even if I do not always show or express it at once. How long are you staying? Where will you live in future? The dedication of the sonatas for violoncello[3] will have to undergo an alteration which, however, will not alter you or me.

Dear, esteemed Countess,

in haste, your friend

Beethoven

---

[1] An allusion to the tutor's name, Vogel (bird).   [2] Padua.

[3] The 'cello sonatas in C major and D major, Op. 102, the second edition of which contained a dedication to countess Erdödy.

TO COUNTESS ERDÖDY

Vienna, May 15th, 1816

Dear and honoured friend,

This letter had already been written when I met Linke to-day and learned of your deplorable misfortune, the sudden loss of your dear son. What consolation can I offer you at such a time? Nothing pains me more than the speedy, unforeseen passing on of those who are near to us; for this reason, too, I cannot forget the death of my poor brother. Not but that we have reason to believe that those who pass away swiftly suffer less than the others. Yet I feel the most sincere condolence with you in your irreparable loss.

Perhaps I have not yet told you that I, too, have not been at all well for a long time. Another reason for my long silence was my solicitude for my Karl, whom in my thoughts I had often associated with your dear son. I am seized with grief on your account and on mine, for I loved your son. Heaven watches over you and surely does not desire to add to your already grievous sufferings, even if your state of health should now deteriorate even further. Imagine that your son had been forced to go to war and like millions of others had met his death there. And you are still the mother of two dear, hopeful children.

I hope to have news of you soon, weep with you now. Do not, by the way, take any notice of all the chatter as to why I have not written to you, not even of whatever Linke may tell you, for though attached to you, he is very fond of chattering. And I believe that between you, dear Countess, and myself there is no need of intermediaries.

In haste, with respect,

Your friend

Beethoven

FROM NOTEBOOKS AND CALENDARS

1816

With all your works, as with the sonata for violoncello now, you will insist on appointing the day of publication to the publisher, so that the publishers in London and Germany will not know what the others are doing, for otherwise they will pay less, and there is no need for them to know; you can make it a pretext that someone else has ordered this composition from you.

Fate, show your power! We have no mastery over ourselves: whatever has been determined, must be, and so be it, then!

Endurance—Resignation—Resignation! Thus we may yet gain by the utmost misery and become worthy of God's forgiveness for our faults.

You will regard K. as your own child. Ignore all gossip, all pettiness for the sake of this holy cause. Now these circumstances are very hard for you, but He who is above exists; without Him there is nothing. In any case, the token has been accepted.

Leave operas and everything else, write only for your orphan! and then a hovel in which you may conclude this unhappy life!

Live only in your art! Restricted as you are now because of your (defective) senses, this is yet the only possible form of existence for you.

DR. KARL VON BURSY ON HIS VISIT TO BEETHOVEN

Vienna, June 1st, 1816

How could I fail to remark and distinguish the day on which I made the acquaintance of Beethoven? Already yesterday I looked for him and did not find him, for Herr Riedl had given me the wrong address. He lives at No. 1052 in the *Seilerstrasse*, not, as Mme Nanette Streicher wrote down for me, at No. 1056. I was quite convinced that Beethoven must reside at one of the ducal palaces and live under the aegis of one of those who patronize his exalted art. Consequently, I was most amazed when a neighbouring herring merchant directed me to the house next to his own with the words: "I believe that Herr von Beethoven lives somewhere in these parts, for I've often seen him go in there." I asked after him on the ground floor and was told that Beethoven lived on the third floor, up three flights of stairs. Once again, quite contrary to my expectations! Narrow stairs led up to the room in which a Beethoven lives and works. A small door, which was opened when I rang the bell, admitted me to a small hall, which also served as kitchen and nursery. There I was received by the manservant, who, together with his family, seemed to belong to Beethoven's household. He wished to admit me at once, but I gave him the letter from Amenda and now awaited the reply with great apprehension. "Be kind enough to enter!", at last the returning servant called out to me and through a thick, woollen curtain I entered the sanctum. Beethoven came out of the adjoining room to welcome me. It seemed difficult and unnatural to me to greet the Master of my art only with a remote and unfamiliar bow. I should have liked to seize his hand and imprint a kiss of the most heartfelt reverence upon it.

If Jean Paul quite contradicted my mental picture of him, Beethoven agreed with it very well. Short, somewhat stout, his hair swept back, much of it already grey, a rather ruddy complexion, fiery eyes, which, though small, are deep-set and full of extraordinary energy. Beethoven, especially when he laughs, bears a remarkable resemblance to Amenda. It was about the latter that he enquired first of all and expressed feelings of true friendship towards him. "He is an excellent fellow," he said, "it is my misfortune that all my friends are far away and that I am quite alone in this hateful city of Vienna." He begged me to speak loudly, as just at that time he was especially hard of hearing once again, for which reason he intended to spend the summer at Baden and in the country. Altogether, he has been unwell for a long time and has composed nothing new. I asked him about the libretto by Berge, and he said it was quite good and, with a few alterations, would be suitable for composition. Until now his illness had not permitted such a task and he would write to Amenda himself about it. I yelled into his ear that for such a work, I supposed, one needed complete leisure and calm. "No," he said, "I never do anything straight off and without interrupting it. I always work at several things at once, now at this, now at that." He often misunderstood me and had to apply the greatest concentration in order to understand what I was saying. Naturally, this disturbed and embarrassed me greatly. He too is aware of the tension and talks all the more himself, and very loudly. He told me much about Vienna and his life here. Gall and venom rage in him. He scorns everyone, is dissatisfied with everyone and everything, and curses a great deal, especially about Austria and more especially about Vienna. He speaks quickly and with the greatest vivacity. Often he struck the piano so violently with his fist that the whole room resounded with the blow. He is not reticent, for it did not take him long to acquaint me with his personal circumstances and to tell me a great deal about himself and his family.

"Why do you remain in Vienna, when every foreign ruler would allot you a place at his court, next to his throne?" "I am bound to this place by my circumstances," he said, "but things are done in a rascally and dirty fashion here. It could hardly be worse. From the top to the bottom, everyone is a scoundrel. One can trust no one. No one keeps his word unless he's put it in writing. They expect a man to work, but pay him as if they were beggars, not even as much as was agreed upon. Besides, they haven't got anything in Austria, as everything is nothing, i.e. paper." Beethoven had composed a special cantata at the time of the Congress. "The text had been pruned and cut like a French garden", he said. And, even then, it was not performed at the proper time. After many intrigues he gave a concert in the *Redoutensaal*. The King of Prussia paid him an extra entrance fee of ten ducats: very paltry! Only the Emperor of Russia paid the decent sum of 200 ducats for his ticket. He was very pleased that the General Director of the Imperial Theatres, Count Palffy, had received a good wigging on this occasion. He bears him a special grudge. Beethoven seems very interested in money and I must confess that this makes him more human, that is, lessens the distance between him and others.

Beethoven's brother died recently and he has undertaken the education of his orphaned nephew. He talked at great length about this, criticized the Viennese schools to which he had sent the young boy and from which he had promptly removed him. "The boy must become an artist or a scholar in order to live a higher life and not sink down completely into vulgarity. Only the artist and the independent scholar carry their happiness within them." He now expressed the most striking opinions about life in general. As soon as he was quiet, he wrinkled his brow and took on a sinister appearance, so that one could easily become afraid of him if one did not know that such an exalted artist's soul must be fundamentally good. Entirely winning my confidence, he permitted me to look him up very often, as he would only pay short visits to Baden from time to time; he asked me to turn to him if he could be of service to me. He noted my address and, when we parted, uttered these cordial words: "Don't be afraid, I shall send for you one fine day!"

His apartment is cheerful, faces the green Bastions and is quite tidy and clean. The ante-room leads to his bedroom on one side, his music-room on the other; this contains a grand piano, which is kept locked. I saw only little music, but a few scraps of music paper lay on his desk. Two good portraits in oil hang on the wall, one of a woman, the other of a man.

Beethoven himself was not clothed in rags like Jean Paul, but in full gala dress. This confirms what I had already heard about him, that he is vain and that for this reason his deafness is especially troublesome to him. This may account for his excuses to me to the effect that his hearing is usually better than at present. Incidentally, I see no justification for the rumour that he is mad at times, for I have made enquiries in this connection. Herr Riedl assures me that he is not mad at all and only suffers from the so-called artist's spleen. This means something different to every person. For example Riedl, as an art dealer and the publisher of several of Beethoven's works, probably regards as such spleen the high price which Beethoven demands for his manuscripts; for in effect he told me that Beethoven is incredibly expensive.

On July 27th I called on Beethoven at seven o'clock in the morning. I found him at home and spent a good half-hour in pleasant conversation with him. Above all, he spoke at length about Vienna, with the greatest indignation and bitterness. He wished that he were away from Vienna, yet partly he is also tied to this place by his brother's son, a boy aged ten, whom he would like to turn into a musician if only some kind of distinction is to be expected of him. He is said to be quite a good pianist already. Now Beethoven is about to take him into his home and appoint a tutor for him. Beethoven was very cordial and the pressure of his hand at parting gave me a better opinion of myself, raised me from the common sphere of daily life.

I found Beethoven at his writing-desk with a piece of music paper in front of him and, beyond it, a glass bowl in which he was making his coffee. I never saw his two pianos unlocked. I asked him about the libretto by Berge. "It isn't worth while to compose operas here; for the theatre management doesn't pay us anything." He cursed the music dealers for having defaced his works by pirating them. They put down opus numbers arbitrarily. Thus Mollo had lately pirated the Trio Variations in E major and prefaced them with the opus number 82, when this number belongs to four songs and these variations have a much earlier opus number. It is really a very vulgar sort of dishonesty, and everything appertaining to the book trade here is characterized by utter baseness. No one takes this trade seriously.

149

TO ZMESKALL

My sincere thanks, my dear Zmeskall, for the information you have given me. As far as the fortifications are concerned, I thought that you knew me well enough not to wish to accommodate me in swampy places. Incidentally, it is more difficult for me than for anyone else to set up a household, for I know nothing at all about such things, nothing whatsoever. I suppose I shall always be liable to blunder in this respect. Well, as for your latest letter, what am I to say to it? Ever since my childhood I have always been glad to recollect all the good deeds of others and have always kept them present in my mind. Then, too, came the time when, especially in an effeminate age such as ours, it was even pardonable in a young man to be somewhat intolerant. But now our strength as a nation is restored, and, quite apart from this, I have tried to acquire the habit of not condemning the whole man on account of specific weaknesses, but to be just and fair, to bear in mind what is good in men, and whenever this affected me personally and I was able to put these principles into practice, I have not only shown myself to be a friend of the whole human race, but have always considered individual members of it as my friends and called them by this name. In this sense, then, you also can be called my friend: even if in some respects we act and think differently, we have yet managed to agree in others. There! now I can stop counting. May you only put my friendly attachment to the test as often as possible!

As ever your friend,

Beethoven

TO GIANNATASIO DEL RIO

Vienna, November 14th, 1816

Worthy friend,

I wish to have Karl with me to-morrow, as it's the anniversary of his father's death and we intend to visit his grave. Perhaps I shall come at about twelve or one o'clock to fetch him. I should like to know what kind of effect my treatment of Karl has had on him after your recent complaints. Meanwhile I have been very moved to see how sensible he is to matters that involve his honour. Already when I was at your house I made allusions to his lack of industry; more gravely than usual we walked about together, fearfully he pressed my hand, yet all this found no response. At table he ate next to nothing and told me that he felt very sad; as yet, I was unable to discover the reason why. At last, while we were taking a walk, he declared that he felt so sad because he had been unable to be as industrious as usual. I now responded duly on my part and was kinder than before. Sensibility is certainly evident in this, and this very trait gives me cause to entertain the very highest hopes for him. Should I not come in person to-morrow, be kind enough to send me a few words in writing about the success of my dealings with Karl. Once again I request you to let me have the bill, now due, for the past quarter; it did occur to me that you might have misunderstood my letter, and perhaps it was even more serious than I thought. I recommend my dear orphan to your special attention and, as always, send my regards to you all.

Your friend,
Beethoven

FROM FANNY DEL RIO'S REMINISCENCES OF BEETHOVEN

Once he came during the spring and brought us violets with the words: "I am bringing you the spring." He had been very ill for a time (he often suffered from colics) and said: "One day this will be the end of me!" Then I called out to him: "As for that, we'll put it off for a long time yet!" to which he replied: "It's a bad man who doesn't know how to die! Ever since I was a boy of fifteen I have known how to die. However, it's true that as yet I've done little for Art!" "Oh, as far as that's concerned, you can go ahead and die!" I said. Thereupon he replied, as if talking to himself: "I've got some very different things in mind."

Once, in a cheerful, communicative mood, Beethoven told us about the time which he spent at Prince Lichnowsky's. Of the Princess he spoke with great respect. He told us how once the Prince, in whose house there were several guests during the French invasion, repeatedly tried to persuade him to play something for them on the piano, but how he had refused obstinately, which led to a scene between him and the Prince, whereupon Beethoven left the house immediately, without regard for anyone. Once he said: "It's easy enough to deal with the aristocracy", but it was necessary to have something with which to impress them.

About actors, he once said that this life, this play-acting in life, displeased and irritated him.

At that time Beethoven was giving lessons to the brother of the Emperor Francis, Archduke Rudolph. I once asked him whether his pupil played well. "Yes, when he's in full command of his faculties", was the reply, accompanied by laughter. Also, he once mentioned with a smile that he slapped the Archduke's fingers and once, when the exalted prince tried to put him in his place, he had pointed out a passage by a poet, Goethe, if I am not mistaken, which proved that he was justified.

Beethoven always showed us a feeling of profound gratitude and called our care for his nephew, and our exertions on his nephew's behalf, "invaluable". Once he told us that he himself had been brought up on proverbs and, later, had been taught by a Jesuit. Of his parents he spoke with great love and reverence, but especially liked to speak of his grandfather, whom he called "a man of honour". Often he would discuss political institutions with great bitterness and indignation; also, he was always about to undertake a great journey, perhaps to England. Once, too, he told us that he had received English visitors; laughing, he said: "They've taken my pen away from me!"

TO SIEGMUND ANTON STEINER

... The title should first be shown to an expert in languages. "Hammerklavier" is certainly German and, besides, the invention is German too; honour where honour is due.

To the Honourable Lieutenant-General von Steiner, for his own hands.

PUBLICANDUM

After an examination conducted by ourselves and after consulting with our council, we have decided and determined that henceforth on all such of our works as bear a German title the word "Hammerklavier" be substituted for "pianoforte", which decision our good Lieutenant-General as well as Adjutants and all others whom it may concern will immediately proceed to observe and carry into effect.

Instead of "pianoforte", "Hammerklavier"! wherewith the matter is settled once and for all.

Given, etc., etc., on the 23rd of January, 1817 by

Generalissimo—m.p.

TO KARL CZERNY

Vienna, 1817

My dear Czerny,

I beg you to be as patient as possible with Karl,[1] even if until now he is not doing as well as you and I should wish; otherwise he will achieve even less, for (but he must not be told of this) the bad arrangement and timing of his lessons is making too great a demand on him; unfortunately this cannot be put right at once, and you must, therefore, practise kindness wherever possible, but not without seriousness, and we shall soon have more success with K. in his present, really unfavourable circumstances. With regard to his playing when he is with you, I beg you that once he uses the right fingers, keeps

[1] Karl van Beethoven, the composer's nephew and adopted son.

the right time and plays the notes more or less correctly, that only then you will criticize his rendering and, once he has got so far, you will not interrupt his playing because of small mistakes, but will point these out only when he has ended the piece. Although I have given few lessons, I have always followed this method, for it soon forms musicians and this, after all, is one of the foremost aims of art, and is less tiring for both master and pupil—for certain passages, such as:

I also wish all the fingers to be used at times, also for passages like the following:

so that they may be played in a gliding manner; it is true, such passages sound "pearly", as the phrase goes, "played with few fingers or like a pearl", but there are times, too, when other jewels are more desirable. More at another time. I hope that you will receive all this in the same spirit of love in which I have expressed and conceived it; in any case, I am and still remain your debtor. May my sincerity always serve you as a security for the payment of this debt.

Your true friend,

Beethoven

TO BARONESS DOROTHEA VON ERTMANN

Vienna, February 23rd, 1817?

My dear, worthy Dorothea-Cecilia,

Often you have been forced to misjudge me, as I was forced to appear to you in a light that must have been repugnant to you. Much of it was due to the circumstances, especially in earlier days, when my manner received less acknowledgment than it does now. You know the interpretations of the false apostles, who resort to means very different from the holy gospel; I did not wish to be included in their number. Now accept something[1] which has long been intended for you and which should serve to prove my devotion to your artistic talent as well as to your person. If recently I could not hear you play at Czerny's, the fault lies with my illness, which at last seems about to give way. I hope to hear from you soon, especially how . . . is faring in St. Pölten and whether you think anything of your

Admirer and friend

L. v. Beethoven

FROM NOTEBOOKS AND CALENDARS

1817

During the summer work for your travels! Only in this way can you accomplish the great work for your poor nephew. Later, wander through Italy, Sicily with a few artists! Make plans and be untroubled on account of . . .

Sensual enjoyment without the union of souls is and always will be bestial: after it there is no trace of an exalted sentiment, rather one feels remorse.

A thousand lovely moments are lost when children are placed in wooden institutions, when good parents could give them the most soulful impressions that last until extreme old age.

Calm and liberty are the most precious of all possessions.

All evils (and afflictions) are mysterious and all the greater, indeed, more popular, the more one discusses them with others;

---

[1] The dedication of the piano sonata in A major, Op. 101.

155

far easier to endure only inasmuch as that which we fear becomes common property—then it seems as if some great evil had been overcome.

Your solitary life is like poison to you in your deaf condition: a base person will always harbour suspicions of you.

The frailties of nature have been given to us by Nature herself, and Reason, the ruler, should be able to guide and diminish them by applying her strength.

TO XAVER SCHNYDER VON WARTENSEE

Honourable Sir,

You once remembered your sojourn in Vienna and your visits to me and gave me written proof of your remembrance; to receive such a communication from one distinguished by goodness and nobility is most gratifying to me. Continue your ascent towards the firmament of Art: no joy is more constant, unmingled and pure than that afforded by Art.

You say that one day you would like to see me engrossed in admiring the majestic scenery of Switzerland; I, too, should like to see myself thus occupied. Should God restore my health, which for some years now has been deteriorating, I hope that I may yet see this wish fulfilled. The bearer of this letter, Hr. v. Bihler, who is engaged in travelling with his pupil v. Puthon, would doubtless be well received by you even without my recommendation. Yet I shall imagine that you attach great weight to my recommendation and entreat you most earnestly to bestow your favours upon him as generously as possible.

Your friend and servant,

L. v. Beethoven

Vienna, August 19th, 1817

When I caught an unusually large butterfly I brought it to him and asked him what it was called. Sometimes he told me the name, at other times he said crossly: "Leave me alone, little murderer, tormenting spirit!" and muttered to himself. If at that time I had even faintly guessed how great a man was Beethoven, I could certainly have collected hundreds of autographs without his being aware of it. Once he gave me a *groschen*[1] for returning a sheet of manuscript paper that he had lost, but I would not accept it under any circumstances. Thereupon he said: "You're a pig-headed little fellow, like all those called Louis." However, when he offered me the same coin in my mother's presence, when I looked at her questioningly to discover whether I might accept it and she nodded her consent, I offered Beethoven my hand to thank him and, embracing me, he said: "You see, rascal, that's the way to catch you. But I'm pleased with your continence, I was just the same myself, you little shrimp."

One day Beethoven was visited by a certain Count Montecuccoli, who was very musical and is said to have played the oboe with virtuosity. Beethoven was very ill-tempered and did not wish to receive Montecuccoli at all. The Count, however, persisted in his intention and went into the garden where Beethoven was sitting in loud conversation with the maid. Montecuccoli spoke at great length about some composition of Beethoven's, saying that the passage in question could not be played by any oboist as it stood. Beethoven would have to alter it. Beethoven replied sharply: "You, Count, are probably incapable of playing it, but a competent oboist could certainly do so; I therefore advise you to take some lessons—I haven't time to listen to you any longer." Montecuccoli called Beethoven a boor, but in such a way that he could not hear it, and walked away. My mother, who had overheard the whole conversation in a nearby bower, went up to Beethoven and said: "You should be ashamed of yourself, Herr von Beethoven,

[1] About a penny.

to receive such a fine gentleman and let him see you in a torn shirt collar and torn cuffs and to treat people so roughly." Beethoven asked her: "Was I really rough with that troublesome ass? I'm delighted to know it. In that case, perhaps, he'll leave me alone in future. But as far as my torn linen is concerned, I beg you to do me the favour of having half a dozen shirts made for me. I'm always forgetting about it, and so is my sister-in-law."

My mother obeyed his wish and whenever he wore one of the new shirts he would say to her: "Well, Frau von Cramolini, I suppose that now you're satisfied with my appearance?" Soon afterwards my mother moved to Vienna and never again, unfortunately, came into contact with Beethoven. She was very indignant that Beethoven never visited her in Vienna to thank her for all those little services. "He is and always will be a grumpy old bear, and yet one can't really be angry with him. For it's all due to his deafness."

TO MARIE PACHLER-KOSCHAK

Vienna, Autumn, 1817

I am very glad that you are adding another day. Let us make a great deal of music yet. You are playing the sonatas in F major and C minor for me, are you not?

I have never yet found anyone who plays my compositions as well as you do, not excepting the great pianists: all they have is mechanical skill or affectation, but you are the true foster-mother of my spiritual children.

CIPRIANI POTTER'S ACCOUNT OF HIS VISITS TO BEETHOVEN (*as given to Thayer*)

He heard so much of Beethoven's rudeness of manners and moroseness of disposition, and so often noticed how people shook their heads when he or his music was mentioned, that he hesitated to visit him. Two weeks had thus passed when one day, at Streicher's, he was asked if he had seen Beethoven and if he had letters to him. He therefore explained why he had not seen him. He was told this was all nonsense; Beethoven would receive him kindly. He exclaimed: "I will go out at once!" which he did, namely, to Mödling. He presented a letter or two, one of the first being that of Dragonetti. Upon opening that, Beethoven also opened his heart to his visitor and demanded immediately to see some of his compositions. Potter showed him an overture—probably one that had been commissioned and played by the London Philharmonic Society in 1816. Beethoven looked through it so hurriedly that Potter thought he had only glanced at it out of politeness and was greatly astonished when Beethoven pointed to a deep F sharp in the bassoon part and said it was not practicable. He made other observations of a similar nature and advised him to go to a teacher; he himself gave no lessons but would look through all his compositions. In answer to Potter's question as to whom he would recommend Beethoven replied: "I have lost my Albrechtsberger and have no confidence in anybody else"; nevertheless, on Beethoven's recommendation Potter became a pupil of Aloys Förster, with whom he studied a long time until one day the teacher said to him that he had now studied sufficiently and needed only to practise himself in composition. This brought out the remark from Beethoven that no one ought ever to stop studying; he himself had not studied enough: "Tell Förster that he is an old flatterer!" Potter did so, but Förster only laughed. Beethoven never complimented Potter to his face: he would say: "Very good, very good", but never give unequivocal praise. Yet at Streicher's he praised him and expressed his surprise that Potter did not visit him at Mödling. Once Beethoven advised him never to compose sitting in a room in which there was a pianoforte, in order not to be tempted to consult the instrument; after a work was finished he might try it over on the instrument, because an orchestra was not always to be had.

Beethoven used to walk across the fields to Vienna very often and sometimes Potter took the walk with him. Beethoven would stop, look around and give vent to his love for nature. One day Potter asked: "Who is the greatest living composer, yourself excepted?" Beethoven seemed puzzled for a moment, then exclaimed "Cherubini". Potter went on: "And of dead authors?" Beethoven answered that he had always considered Mozart as such, but since he had been made acquainted with Händel he had put him at the head. The first day that Potter was with Beethoven the latter rushed into politics and called the Austrian government all sorts of names. He was full of going to England and said his desire was to see the House of Commons. "You have heads upon your shoulders in England", he remarked. One day Potter asked him his opinion of one of the principal pianists then in Vienna (Moscheles). "Don't ever talk to me again about mere passage players", came the answer. At another time Beethoven declared that John Cramer had given him more satisfaction than anybody else. According to the same informant, Beethoven spoke Italian fluently but French with less ease. It was in Italian that Potter conversed with him, making himself heard by using his hands as a speaking-trumpet; Beethoven did not always hear everything, but was content when he caught the meaning. Potter considered "Fidelio" the greatest of all operas and once remarked to Beethoven that he had heard it in Vienna, which brought out the remark that he had *not* heard it, as the singers then at the opera-house were not able to sing it. He was asked if he did not intend to write another opera. "Yes," replied Beethoven, "I am now composing 'Romulus'; but the poets are all such fools; I will not compose silly rubbish." Potter told him of the deep impression made upon him by the Septet when first he heard it; Beethoven replied in effect that when he wrote the piece he did not know how to compose; he knew now, he thought, and, either then or at another time, he said, "I am writing something better now". Soon after, the Pianoforte Sonata in B flat (Op. 106) was published.

TO IGNAZ VON MOSEL

Vienna, 1817

Honourable Sir,

I am delighted to know that you share my opinion of those headings, inherited from times of musical barbarism, by which we describe the tempo of a movement. For example, what can be more absurd than Allegro, which once and for all means cheerful, and how far removed we are often from the true meaning of this description, so that the piece of music itself expresses the very opposite of the heading! As far as these four main connotations are concerned, which, however, are far from being as right or as true as the four main winds, we would do well to dispense with them. Those words which describe the character of the piece are a very different matter: these we could not give up, as the tempo is really no more than the body, while these refer rather to the spirit of the piece. For myself, I have often thought of giving up these absurd terms Allegro, Andante, Adagio, Presto. Maelzel's metronome gives us an excellent opportunity to do so. I give you my word for it here, in my future compositions I shall not use those terms.

It is altogether a different question whether, by doing so, we shall encourage the general use of a metronome, necessary as it is; I hardly think so. But I do not doubt for a moment that we shall be decried as violators of tradition. If this would serve to further our cause, it would still be preferable to being accused of feudalism. I therefore think that it would be best, especially for our countries, in which music has become a national need and in which every village schoolmaster must demand the use of a metronome, if Maelzel attempted to dispose of a certain number of metronomes by subscription, at higher prices; and as soon as this number covers his expenses, he will be able to offer the rest of the metronomes required for the national need at so cheap a price that we can surely expect the most general and extensive use of the instrument. It goes without saying that certain persons must take a prominent part in this enterprise, so as to arouse enthusiasm. As far as I am concerned, you can count on me with certainty and it is with pleasure that I await the part which you will assign to me in this undertaking.

I am, Sir,

Your most respectful and devoted

Ludwig van Beethoven

TO NANETTE STREICHER

I am pleased to know that you will continue to take an interest in my domestic affairs and that all your other work will not be in vain. Together with the kitchen book you will receive a letter which I wrote to you even before you left for Klosterneuburg. As for Nany, her behaviour has improved and I do not at all think that she is wilful in this. Perhaps it is possible that the other maid would have a better effect on our household; yet you must not cease to supervise it. You can easily see from the kitchen book whether I have dined alone, in company or other than at home. I do not regard Nany as wholly honest, quite apart from the fact that, on top of everything, she is a frightful beast. Not kindness, but fear, is the only means of dealing with such people; I now see this quite clearly. It goes without saying that the maidservant can begin her duties on Saturday morning; only I beg you kindly to let me know whether Baberl must leave on Friday morning or after lunch.

The kitchen book alone will not give an adequate idea of everything; you will have to appear unexpectedly from time to time during mealtimes, as a guardian angel, in order to see for yourself how we are faring. At present I never eat at home except when there are guests; for I do not wish to spend as much on myself as would suffice to feed three or four persons. My dear son Karl will now soon be with me, so that there is all the more need for economy.

I cannot well prevail upon myself to visit you; I am sure that you will excuse me, I am very susceptible and not accustomed to such things; even less do I wish to expose myself. As soon as you can, come to see me; but let me know in advance. I have a great deal to discuss with you. Send this little book back to me in the same way towards the evening. Until the other person arrives, we shall make good progress and your kind and friendly helpfulness should make it possible to continue in this way. Nany, besides her twelve kreutzers of bread money, receives one roll in the morning: is this also the case with the kitchen maid? One roll a day amounts to eighteen guilders a year.

May you prosper and thrive! Miss Nany is quite changed since I threw half a dozen books at her head. Probably something of it chanced to penetrate into her brain or her evil heart. At least we have a full-bosomed swindler!!!

In haste, your

L. v. Beethoven

1818

I can only tell you that I am better; it is true that in the past night I often thought of my death, yet such thoughts are no less familiar to me in the daytime. About the future housekeeper I should like to know whether she has a bed and a chest of drawers. By bed I mean partly the frame, partly the bedding, mattress, etc., themselves. You won't forget to talk to me about the linen, will you? so that we may be quite certain about everything; she will want earnest money, too, which I shall give her in due course. About everything else, to-morrow or the day after, my music. and unmusic. papers are almost in order; that was one of the 7 labours of Hercules.

In haste, your friend

Beethoven

Write a national song for the Leipzig October[1] and have this performed every year! N.B. every nation its own march and the *Te deum laudamus.*

Karl's mother sought the comparison herself, only . . ., my scruples, then, must end, and I am surely entitled to think that the widow has made adequate provision for herself, as I sincerely wish her. I have done my part, O Lord! It might have been possible without offending the widow, but it was not. Only thou, Almighty God, canst see into my heart, knowest that I have sacrificed my very best for the sake of my dear Karl: bless my work, bless the widow! Why cannot I obey all the prompting of my heart and help the widow?

God, God! my refuge, my rock, O my all! Thou seest my inmost thoughts, thou knowest how it hurts me to be compelled to make others suffer in my good works for my dear Karl!!! O hear me, Ineffable One, hear me, thy unhappy, unhappiest of all mortals!

Write a . . ., in which some melodrama, too, occurs, briefly, a cantata with chorus and mimes, so that one may show oneself from every angle.

In order to write true church music, look through all the church chorales of the monks, etc., to find out the most accurate translations of all the sections, also the perfect prosody of all the Christian and Catholic psalms and canticles generally.

Once again sacrifice all the trivialities of social life to your art! O God over all!

For eternal Providence,

All-knowing, guides the fortune and the misfortune of mortals. (Homer)

[1] The Leipziger Messe, an annual fair.

Only love, yes, only love is capable of granting you a happy life. O God, let me find her at last, the woman who may strengthen me in virtue, who is permitted to be mine.

Baden, July 27th, when M. drove past and it seemed as if she were looking at me.

A small house in that place, so small that one has just a little room for oneself! Only a few days in this divine Brühl! Longing or desire, liberation or fulfilment!

Adagio Cantique

Pious song in a symphony in the ancient modes. Lord God, we praise thee—allelujah—either by itself or as the introduction to a fugue. Perhaps the whole of the second symphony may be characterized thus, in which case voices will enter in the last movement or already in the *adagio*. The violins of the orchestra will be increased tenfold in the last movement. Or the *adagio* will be repeated in a certain fashion in the last movement, whereupon the voices will enter one after the other. In the *adagio*, text of a Greek myth—*Cantique ecclésiastique*—in the *allegro*, feast of Bacchus.

TO VINZENZ HAUSCHKA

Mödling, June, 1818

Dearest Member of the Society of the Enemies of Music of the Austrian Empire,[1]

(*Follows music to the words:*

   I am prepared
   I am prepared, and so on)

I have no theme but a religious one, while you ask me for an heroic one; I've no objection but believe that to mix in some

[1] A reference, of course, to the Vienna Society of the Friends of Music, of which Hauschka was the Director.

religious ingredients, too, would have an excellent effect on such a crowd.

(*Follows music to the words:* Amen)

Herr von Bernhard[1] would suit me very well, only don't forget to pay him! I don't mention myself in this connection; as you go so far as to call yourselves friends of music, it follows that you intend to enter many an item under this heading!!!

Now farewell, dearest Hauschkerl.[2] I wish you a regular movement of the bowels and the most beautiful of privies. As for me, in these parts I wander about the mountains, crevices and valleys with a sheet of manuscript paper, scribbling down many things for the sake of my daily bread. For in this almighty, once Phaeacian land I have reached such a height that always, in order to gain some time for a great work, I must previously scribble as much for the sake of money as is necessary to support me during the writing of that same great work. However, my health is much improved and if the matter is urgent, I shall be able to oblige you. Well

(*Follows music to the words as above:* I am prepared)

If you think it necessary to speak to me about this, write to me, whereupon I shall make all the arrangements needed for this purpose. My compliments to the Society of the Enemies of Music.

Your friend in haste

Beethoven

TO THE VIENNA MAGISTRACY

Vienna, February 1st, 1819

Honourable Magistrate,

As I am to speak of future education it seems most fitting to me to begin with such as already exists, from which it will

---

[1] Joseph Karl Bernhard (1780–1850), Editor of the *Wiener Zeitung*, was to write the text of the Oratorio here in question.
[2] The diminutive, used as a form of endearment.

become clear that any other can only be detrimental to my nephew. I have already informed you that he has a tutor, whose services he will continue to enjoy. However, so that his zeal may be further aroused, I am letting him continue his studies with Herr von Kudlich, the principal of an institute in my vicinity, near the *Landstrasse*, in the presence of his tutor. Here he is in the company only of a single boy, the son of a certain Baron Lang, and under perpetual supervision during all the time that he spends there. Another advantage, and a very special one, is that Herr von Kudlich teaches entirely according to the thorough method employed at the university, and adheres to this method which all experts, and I, too, regard as the best and which often not every tutor practises, so that often the pupil experiences difficulties in his examinations. To this is added the special instruction in French and drawing, in music, and thus not only is he usefully and pleasantly occupied all day long, but also under perpetual, and very necessary, supervision. Furthermore, I have found a Reverend Father who gives him special instruction in his duties as a Christian, as a human being; for only upon this foundation can true men be educated. Later, towards the summer, he will also begin his acquaintance with ancient Greek. It must be apparent that I am not sparing any expenses, so that I may achieve the fine purpose of presenting the State with a useful and moral citizen. The present arrangement leaves nothing to be desired: therefore no change is needed. However, should I become aware of such a need, I shall propose and carry out that which is even better in the most conscientious fashion. Every man who is not intended for manual work, whatever profession he may adopt, must have studied at least five or six schools. After this it should be possible to discern what he is fitted for by nature, and inclination. Whether he will become a civil servant or a scholar, never can the foundation be laid in any other manner. His exceptional capacity, and also partly his peculiarities, call for exceptional measures; and never have I acted more beneficially or more magnanimously than when I adopted my nephew and took charge of his education. If (according to Plutarch) a Philip did not disdain personally to direct the education of his son Alexander, and to give him the great Aristotle as a teacher, because he did not regard the ordinary teachers as adequate, if a Laudon personally directed the education of his son, why should not such great and exalted examples be emulated in our time? Already in his father's lifetime my nephew was entrusted to me by him, and I confess that I feel better suited than anyone to inspire my nephew with virtue and industry by my own example. Boarding-schools and institutes do not provide sufficient supervision for him and all the learned authorities, among them a Professor Stein, a Professor (of Pedagogy) Simmerdinger, agree with me that such places are not at all suitable for him; indeed, they declare that the greater part of our youth is corrupted by such places and that some even enter them as moral persons and leave as immoral ones. Unhappily I must support the experiences and opinions of these men and of many parents. Had the boy's mother been able to control her malice and permitted my plans to develop undisturbed, even now some very favourable results would reward my past endeavours. Yet when a mother of this sort attempts to involve her child in the secrecies of her common and evil surroundings, induces him to practise deception in his tender years (a plague for children!!!), bribery of my servants, untruthfulness, while she laughs at him when he tells the truth and even gives him money so as to arouse in him lusts and desires which are harmful to him, when she tells him that all these are mere trifles, while others and myself consider them grave faults, this business, difficult enough in itself, becomes even more difficult and more dangerous. Let no one believe, however, that she behaved differently when my nephew was in the institution. Yet for this purpose, too, I have constructed a new dam: besides the tutor, a woman of good social standing will enter my household, which she will conduct; under no circumstances will this woman accept bribes from her and thus the supervision of my nephew will become even stricter. Secret meetings of the mother with her son always have detrimental consequences; yet this precisely is what she desires, as she seems to feel most uncomfortable in the presence of persons whose morals and natural disposition are truly good. So many accusations dishonouring to me have been made, and from such quarters, that I should not even speak about them, for not only is my moral character generally and publicly recognized, but even such distinguished authors as Weissenbach and others have taken the trouble to write about it, so that no one who is impartial has any reason to ascribe base thoughts or actions to me. In spite of all this, I consider myself obliged to clarify certain matters in this connection. . . . In any case, I have always borne his spiritual welfare in mind, i.e. to remove him from his mother's influence. Gifts of fortune can be acquired, but morality must be inculcated early (especially when a child has already had the misfortune to suck in such mother's milk, has even spent several years in her charge, has been utterly misused during this time and was even obliged to help deceive his father), and in any case he is my heir. Even now I should leave him enough for him to live without stint until he concludes his studies and is ready to accept employment. All we need is quiet and no further interference from the mother; certainly we should soon attain the fine goal which I have fixed. I could end by becoming light-headed and weary with all these intrigues and slanders, but no! I shall prove that whoever acts nobly and well can even endure maltreatment in return for this, without ever being compelled to lose sight of his fine, self-chosen goal. I have vowed to represent his best interests until the end of my life, and even apart from this, only that which is most advantageous to my nephew in all circumstances is to be expected of my character and my convictions.

Should I now reply to the intrigues of a Mr. Court Scrivener Hotschova against me, or to the priest of Mödling who is despised by his own congregation and is reputed to practise illicit intercourse, who in the military fashion has his pupils laid on a bench to be flogged and who could not forgive me for keeping watch on him and for insisting that my nephew should not be flogged like a beast? Should I? No! the association of both these men with Frau van Beethoven is sufficient evidence against them, and only men of this kind could have made common cause with her against me. . . . May it be clear from all this that, just as I was already the benefactor of my nephew's father, I deserve to be called an even greater benefactor of his son, indeed, that I may rightly be called his father! No motive, public or private, can be ascribed to me, other than the love of virtue; indeed, the law courts themselves have admitted as much and thanked me for my paternal care.

Ludwig van Beethoven,
Guardian of my nephew Karl van Beethoven

TO ARCHDUKE RUDOLPH

1819

Your Imperial Highness, On the day when Your Imperial Highness were gracious enough to send for me I was not at home and immediately afterwards I succumbed to a strong catarrh, so that I now approach Your Imperial Highness in writing from my bed—however great a flood of congratulations may have reached you, my most gracious Sir, I know only too well that this new dignity[1] cannot be accepted by Your Imperial Highness without sacrifices on your part, but when I reflect how great an opening it will present to you and to your noble and generous sentiments I cannot refrain from adding my congratulations to the rest. There is scarcely any goodness—without sacrifices and it seems that the more virtuous and noble of men are intended to make such sacrifices, rather than other men, so that their virtues may be put to the test.

con fuoco

Ful – fil – ment   Ful – fil – ment

---

[1] The Archduke's installation as Archbishop of Olmütz; on August 30th, 1819, the Archduke was also awarded the Grand Cross of the Order of St. Stephen.

How gladly I would sing this now, if only Your Imperial Highness were wholly recovered, but the new field of activity, the change, later the need to travel will doubtless very soon restore Your Imperial Highness' invaluable health to a most satisfactory state, and then I shall execute the above theme with a mighty A-men or Alleluja—as for the masterly Variations[1] by Your Imperial Highness, I have recently sent these away for copying, not without first attending to several small errors, yet I must exclaim to my exalted pupil: *"La Musica merita d'esser studiata"*[2]—with so fine a disposition and so rich a gift of invention on Your Imperial Highness' part it would be a pity not to penetrate right to the Castalian spring, for which expedition I offer myself as companion, as soon as Your Imperial Highness' time permits. Your Imperial Highness can become a creative artist in two respects, both to the joy and well-being of many a person and for your own sake. Until now creative musicians and dispensers of happiness to mankind are not to be found in the world of monarchs. And now about myself—I must crave your gracious indulgence—I now enclose two pieces on which is written that I wrote them already before Your Imperial Highness' name-day last year, but depression and many an unhappy circumstance, my very poor health at the time had so discouraged me that I could approach Your Imperial Highness only with the greatest timidity and diffidence, and, while my health improved after Mödling and till the end of my sojourn here, yet how many other sufferings afflicted me, meanwhile much remains in my writing-desk which would prove my remembrance of Your Imperial Highness, and I hope to execute all this when I am in a better position—Your Imperial Highness' writ to the effect that I should come and, again, that you would inform me of this, when? I did not know how to interpret, for a courtier I have never been, nor am one, nor shall ever be able to be one and feel exactly like Sir Davison[3] in Maria Stuart, when Queen E. delivers the death sentence into

[1] The Archduke's Variations on a theme of Beethoven, published by Steiner in 1819.
[2] "Music deserves to be studied."
[3] William Davison in Schiller's *Maria Stuart*.

his hands, I wish that I could visit my most gracious lord as before. God knows my inmost thoughts and though appearances may be against me, one day everything will be clarified in my favour. The day on which a High Mass composed by myself will be performed at the ceremonies for Y.I.H. will be the greatest day of my life, and God will grant me illumination so that my poor faculties may contribute to the glorification of that solemn day. Together with my deep gratitude, the sonatas will follow, only the 'cello part is still missing, I think, as I could not find it immediately. As the engraving is excellent, I have taken the liberty of adding an engraved copy, as well as a string quintet.[1] Two other pieces have been added to those written by my own hand on Y.I.H.'s name-day, of which the latter is a grand Fugato, so that together they make a grand sonata[2] which will now be appearing soon and for a long time already has been destined in my heart for Y.I.H.; this has nothing at all to do with the latest event in Y.I.H.'s life. While craving pardon for my letter, I implore the Lord that His blessings may flow freely upon the head of Y.I.H., the new vocation of Y.I.H., which so widely embraces the love of all men, is surely one of the finest, and in this Y.I.H. will always be the best of all models both in your worldly and your spiritual capacity.

Your Imperial Highness'
most obedient and faithful servant

AN ACCOUNT BY MORITZ SCHLESINGER
(*from the biography by A. B. Marx*)

His housekeeper told me that I should probably not be able to speak to him, as he had come home in a fury. I gave her my visiting card, which she took to him, and to my great amazement she returned after a few minutes, asking me to enter. I found the great man at his writing-desk. I wrote down at once that I

[1] Quintet in C minor, Op. 104, arranged from the Trio, Op. 1, No. 3.
[2] Piano Sonata in B flat, Op. 106.

was happy to make his acquaintance. This (the fact that I wrote) made a favourable impression upon him. He at once let himself go and told me that he was the most unfortunate person in the world; he had just come from the inn, where he had asked for a piece of veal, for which he felt a special appetite; but none had been available—all this with a very serious, gloomy expression. I consoled him, we spoke of other things (myself always writing) and in this way he must have kept me there for about two hours; for, afraid of boring or disturbing him, I was often about to get up, but every time he begged me to stay. When I had left him, I hurried back to Vienna in my carriage, at once asked the son of my landlord whether a joint of veal was to be had and, when he said yes, had this placed upon a dish, well covered, and, without a word in writing, at once sent a man to Baden in the same carriage to deliver it to Beethoven in my name. On the following morning, I was still in bed when Beethoven entered my room, kissed and caressed me, saying that I was the best fellow he had ever met; never had anything made him so happy as this piece of veal at the moment when he had felt such a craving for it.

TO ARTARIA, MUSIC PUBLISHERS, IN VIENNA

On October 1st, 1819

Excellent *Virtuosi senza Cujoni*,

Whereas we are informing you of this, that and the other, from which you are to draw the most favourable conclusions, we entreat you to send us by way of author's copies six, I say 6 copies of the Sonata in B flat, as well as 6 copies of the Variations on Scottish Songs. We beg you to send same to Steiner in Paternoster Mews, to which address other things, too, will be sent to me.

In the hope that you are conducting yourselves in an orderly and lawful manner, I am your, etc.

Devoted B.

TO ERNST THEODOR AMADEUS HOFFMANN

Vienna, March 23rd, 1820

Honourable Sir,

I take this opportunity of approaching so brilliant a man as yourself by means of Herr Neberich. You have written even about my little person. Our feeble Herr Starke,[1] too, showed me some lines in his album written by you about myself. I therefore have reason to believe that you take some interest in me.[2] Permit me to say that from a man endowed with such excellent qualities as your own this interest is most gratifying to me. I wish you all that is beautiful and good and am, Sir,

Your most respectful and devoted

Beethoven

FROM ANTON SCHINDLER'S BIOGRAPHY[3]

Towards the end of August I arrived at the Master's house in Mödling, accompanied by the musician Johann Horzalka, who is still living in Vienna. It was four o'clock in the afternoon. As soon as we entered we were told that during the same morning both of Beethoven's maidservants had run away and that at some time after midnight there had been a scene which disturbed all the inmates of the house, because, tired of waiting for their master, both the maidservants had fallen asleep and the meal prepared for him had become inedible. In his draw-ing-room, behind a locked door, we heard the Master singing, howling and stamping over the fugue for the *Credo* (of the Mass

[1] A pun on the name of Starke; "*stark*" is German for "strong".

[2] E. T. A. Hoffmann had written excellent reviews of the following works by Beethoven: The Fifth Symphony (1810); The Sixth Symphony (1810); "Christ on the Mount of Olives" (1812); The Coriolan Overture (1812); Fantasia for Pianoforte, Chorus and Orchestra (1812); the two Trios, Op. 70 (1813); the music to Egmont (1813); and the Mass in C (1813). Already in the first of these articles, that on the Fifth Symphony, he compared Beethoven to Mozart and Haydn, and placed him in the first rank of instrumental composers. Hoffmann, who was a composer as well as the writer of those fantastic tales to which he owes his fame, was well qualified to be a music critic; the reviews mentioned above can still be read with interest and pleasure.

[3] *Biographie von Ludwig van Beethoven*, 1840 and 1860.

in D). After listening to this almost gruesome sound for some time, we were just about to leave when the door opened and Beethoven stood before us, a wild look on his face, which was almost terrifying. He looked as if he had just emerged victorious from a life and death struggle with the entire host of contrapuntists, his constant antagonists. His first remarks were confused, as if he felt unpleasantly surprised by our eavesdropping. Soon, however, he began to speak of the past day and, with evident self-control, said: "A fine household, they've all run away and I've had nothing to eat since yesterday noon." I tried to soothe him and helped him to dress. My companion, however, hurried away to the restaurant of the spa pavilion to order a meal for the starving Master.

TO ARTARIA

Honourable Messrs. Artaria, Falstaff [1] & Co.

I entreat you most courteously to hand over to Hr. von Oliva the sum of 300 fl., all which should already be here; just in the process of moving in, I was unable to have the honour of conveying my gratitude to you and to Sir John Falstaff.

Vienna, October 26th, 1820.

Your most devoted servant, Beethoven

FROM A LETTER OF WILHELM CHRISTIAN MÜLLER

Vienna, October 26th, 1820

After some days we discovered that he had moved to the city and hurried to his house. He excused himself for having moved house, spoke about all that was wrong in the world, about the lack of good taste in music and about politics, in the last instance with caustic wit. At my enquiring about his pension,

---

[1] Beethoven's nickname for Ignaz Schuppanzigh.

he told me that when he had been offered the post of *Kapellmeister* at Kassel, three great noblemen had promised him 2000 guilders if he would remain in Vienna. One of them, however, had been declared bankrupt, the second had broken his neck—the third, Archduke Rudolph, his pupil, had been paying his third until that time. He had lost his savings because of his brother; in spite of it, he had adopted his brother's son and brings him up like a father.

A cold had deprived him of his hearing, probably because endless use had made it the most sensitive, and therefore the weakest part of his system. He believed that his ear-trumpets had completely destroyed what remained of his hearing.

He took us to his splendid fortepiano, exulting in the fact that the Philharmonic Society in London had made him a present of it. The English, he said, were an honourable people, who knew not only how to value art, but how to reward it and, furthermore, had instituted freedom of speech and writing, even in opposition to the King and the most powerful ministers of state, tolerating neither censors nor tax-collectors. He called himself a fool for not accepting the invitation of the English lovers of art out of loyalty to Vienna, where art was cultivated madly as a fashion without any understanding of true art, nor any respect for it, nor yet any desire to reward the artist. "From time to time", he said, "a rash, disrespectful word escapes me; for that reason they think me mad." In order to distract him from this gloomy topic, we asked him to improvise for us. However, it was impossible to persuade him, probably because he cannot hear the expression of his playing and therefore thought he might lose our great admiration for him in this way. Elise had to play something. He asked her whether she composed. When she replied that she lacked a teacher of composition, he retorted: "But you have Riem, a very capable fellow."

TO TOBIAS HASLINGER

Baden, September 10th, 1821

Best of friends,

When I was in my carriage yesterday, on the way to Vienna, sleep overpowered me, the more so as I had scarcely ever had a good night's sleep (because of my early rising here). Now, as I was slumbering, I dreamed that I was travelling far away, no less far than Syria, no less far than India and back again, to Arabia, too, and at last I came even to Jerusalem. The Holy City reminded me of the Holy Scriptures; no wonder, then, that I thought of the man Tobias, too, and naturally this led to my thinking also of our little Tobias and of the *pertobiasser*; now, during my dream journey, the following canon occurred to me:

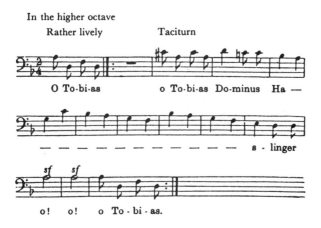

Yet I had hardly awoken when the canon was gone and I could not recall a single note or word of it to my mind. However, when on the next day I returned here, in the same carriage (that of a poor Austrian musician) and continued my dream journey, though now awake, lo and behold, in accordance with the law of the association of ideas, the same canon occurred to me; now, waking, I held it fast, as once Menelaus held

Proteus, and only granted it one last favour, that of allowing it
to transform itself into three voices:

Farewell! Soon I shall send in something about Steiner, too,
just to prove that he hasn't a heart of stone.[1] Farewell, very
dearest of friends, we wish you continually that you may never

[1] A pun: the German has "*steinernes Herz*".

178

be true to the name of publisher and may never be publicly humiliated,[1] but a publisher who is never humiliated either in public or in private, neither in taking nor in giving. Never fail to sing the epistles of St. Paul every day, go to see Father Werner[2] every day, for he will show you the book whereby you will go to Heaven forthwith; you see my solicitude for your spiritual health, and I remain always with the greatest pleasure from eternity to eternity.

Your most faithful debtor
Beethoven

A CONVERSATION AT A MUSIC PUBLISHER'S, probably Steiner and Haslinger (according to Seyfried)

Beethoven. Is it true that Weber, the Director of the Prague Conservatoire, has arrived here with Pixis?

X. Yes, and both of them desire permission to visit you.

Beethoven. They shouldn't trouble. They'd hardly find me at home. They say that the pupils there are rather good?

X. That, at least, is the testimony of all those who have heard them.

Beethoven. Quite plausible; for the Bohemian is a born musician. The Italians should take example by this. What, in the end, have they got to show for all their celebrated conservatoires? Now, take their idol, Rossini, if Fortuna had not endowed him with a fine talent and love-sick melodies by the score—the sum of what he took away with him from school would have enabled him to stuff his paunch with potatoes at the very most. Ha, ha, ha!

---

[1] The pun on "*Verleger*" (publisher) and "*verlegen*" (embarrassed, at a loss) was one of which Beethoven was especially fond.

[2] The dramatic poet Zacharias Werner, who had become a convert to Roman Catholicism.

TO FRANZ GRILLPARZER

Vienna, End of April, 1822

Honourable Sir,

I am the innocent cause of your having been pestered and harassed, for I gave no other order than that the truth of the rumour, to the effect that you have written a libretto for me, should be ascertained. How heartily I must thank you for being kind enough even to send this beautiful poem[1] to me in order to convince me that you really thought it worth your while to sacrifice your exalted Muse for my sake. I hope that your health will soon improve; mine, too, is poor and only country life can give me any relief, as, I hope, it will do within the next few days. And it is there precisely that I hope to receive your visit, so that we may discuss all the necessary points. Partly overworked, unduly pressed, partly, as already touched upon, in poor health, I am prevented from going to see you at this very moment and from expressing to you more vividly than is possible in mere words the pleasure that your splendid poem has given me. I might almost say that I am prouder of this event than of any of the greatest honours and awards that I could receive.

With the greatest respect,

Your most devoted

Beethoven

TO C. F. PETERS, MUSIC PUBLISHER IN LEIPZIG

Vienna, June 5th, 1822

Honourable Sir,

As you have honoured me with a letter and as I am very busy at this moment and have been sickly for the last five months, I confine myself to essentials in my reply. Although I was with Steiner some days ago and asked him in jest what he had brought me from Leipzig, he did not say a word about your

[1] Grillparzer wrote the dramatic poem *Melusine* for Beethoven; but the music, if composed, was never written down.

message to me, nor mentioned you at all, but pressed me most insistently to give him an assurance that I should offer all my present, as well as all my future, works to none other than himself, and this by contract. I refused to do so. This occurrence proves clearly enough why often I give precedence to other foreign, or even local, publishers. I am fond of rectitude and honesty and am of the opinion that one should not exploit an artist unfairly; for, alas, bright as the exterior of fame may seem, it is yet not granted to him to be Jupiter's guest on Olympus every day. Unhappily, all too often and all too repulsively, vulgar humanity drags him down from those pure aetherial heights. . . .

More than all this, I treasure the hope that my complete works may soon be published, for I wish to prepare such an edition in my lifetime. True, I have had several offers to this effect, but there were conditions which I could scarcely overcome and was neither able nor willing to fulfil. I could complete the whole edition in two, or possibly one or one-and-a-half years, given the necessary assistance, could entirely revise all my works and add one new work in every *genre* of composition, for example, a new set of Variations to the Variations, a new Sonata to the Sonatas and so forth, a new product for every *genre* to which I have contributed in the past, and for all this together I would demand ten thousand guilders in convention coin.

I am no merchant and rather wish that I were different in this respect; however, it is competition that guides and determines me here, as one cannot ignore it. I beg you to maintain the greatest discretion, for, as you can see even from the actions of these gentlemen, I am much exposed to intrigues and troubles of many kinds. As soon as something of mine is published by your firm, it will no longer be possible to plague me. I should be most gratified if a connection could be established between us, for I have heard much good spoken of you. You would then find also that I should prefer to deal with someone of your kind, rather than with many a representative of the common species.

I beg you for a speedy reply, as I am just in the process of having to decide about the publication of various works. How regrettable that Steiner, who has some estimable qualities, has once again shown himself to be a common merchant! If you think it important enough, kindly send me a copy of the list that you entrusted to him. Awaiting a speedy reply, your respectful and devoted

Beethoven

TO C. F. PETERS

Vienna, June 26th, 1822

Honourable Sir,

This is merely to confirm that I shall let you have the mass,[1] as well as the piano score, for the sum of 1000 fl., convention coin in 20-florin pieces. You should receive the score in copy by the end of July, perhaps a few days earlier or later. As I am still very busy and have been sickly for the last five months and such works must be very carefully revised before they can be sent to distant places, this matter cannot be dealt with in a hurry. On no account will Schlesinger receive any more of my works, as he, too, has played a Jewish trick on me; in any case, he is not among those to whom I might have given the Mass. However at present the competition for my works is most intense, for which I thank the Almighty; for I have also suffered great losses. Moreover I am acting as foster-father to the son of my brother, who died in penury. As this boy, at the age of fifteen, shows so much aptitude for the sciences, not only do his education and maintenance cost me a great deal of money now, but provision must be made for his future, too, as we are neither Red Indians nor Iroquois, who, as is well known, leave everything to God, and as a pauper's life is never exactly a happy one. I shall not breathe a word of anything that passes between us, by personal preference if for no other reason, and

[1] Beethoven promised "a Mass" to at least five publishers: Peters, Simrock, Schlesinger, Artaria and Probst. In March, 1823, he informed Peters that he intended to write "three masses at least", but completed only one of these, the Missa Solemnis in D, Op. 123, which was published by Schott & Sons.

beg you to keep equally silent about my [*sic*] present connection with me. I shall not fail to let you know when it is time to speak, which now is not at all necessary. In order to give you at least partial proof of my truthfulness, I enclose this declaration by Steiner, whose hand you will recognize; it is somewhat difficult to decipher. I assure you on my honour, which next to God I value highest, that I never asked Steiner to accept commissions on my behalf. It has always been my foremost principle never to approach a publisher, not out of pride, but because it gave me pleasure to observe how far the territory of my small fame had extended. I suspect that Steiner made this offer to you out of cunning; for I remember that you were kind enough to entrust him with English musical publications intended for me. Who knows whether he did not play me this trick because he suspected that you would make an offer. As for the songs,[1] I have already given you my opinion about them. I think that a payment of 40 duc. for the three songs and the four marches would not be excessive. You can write to me about this. As soon as the Mass has been prepared, I shall let you know and ask you to have the payment remitted to a house here, to whom I shall deliver the work as soon as I receive your remittance, but shall make sure that I am present when the work is handed over to the post and that the freight charge is not too great. I should like to be acquainted soon with your plans regarding the edition of my complete works, for I am bound to feel that this enterprise concerns me deeply.

I must conclude for to-day and wish you all that is agreeable and am respectfully

Your most devoted

L. v. Beethoven

AN ACCOUNT BY FRIEDRICH ROCHLITZ

. . . I was just about to begin my dinner, when I met the young composer Franz Schubert, an enthusiastic admirer of Beethoven, who had spoken to him about me. "If you wish to

---

[1] *"Opferlied"*, Op. 121 b; *"Bundeslied"*, Op. 122; and *"Der Kuss"*, Op. 128. These three songs were not published by Peters, but by Schott.

see him less constrained and in a cheerful mood," Schubert said, "you have only to dine at this moment at the inn where he has just gone with the same intention." He took me there. Most of the seats were occupied: Beethoven was surrounded by several of his acquaintances, all of them strangers to me. He really seemed to be cheerful. Thus he returned my salutation: but I did not join him, intentionally. Yet I found a place from which I could observe him and, as he was talking loudly enough, understand most of what he said. It was not really a conversation that took place at his table, for he spoke while the others listened, most of the time rather lengthily and, it seemed, into the blue. Those who surrounded him contributed very little, only laughed or nodded their approval. He was philosophizing, politicizing, too, in his fashion. He spoke of England and the English, to whom he attributed incomparable splendour, which made some of his utterances somewhat bizarre. Then he told several stories about Frenchmen, dating from the time of the two occupations of Vienna: he was not at all well disposed towards these. All his conversation flowed quite spontaneously and he seemed to hold nothing back, and all of it, too, was spiced with highly original, but ingenuous, opinions and charming conceits. . . . Now he had finished his meal, got up and joined me. "Well, how does old Vienna agree with you?" he said cordially. I intimated by signs that I was well, drank to his health and invited him to reciprocate. He accepted, but directed me to a small adjoining room. This suited me very well. I took the bottle and followed him. Here we were alone, except for an occasional intruder, who gaped at us but soon trundled off again. He offered me a little slate on which I was to write down whatever my signs did not convey. He began by praising Leipzig and its music, that is, of the music chosen to be played in churches, concert-rooms and theatres: apart from this, he does not know Leipzig and only passed through it in his youth, on his way to Vienna. "And even if nothing appeared about it in print apart from those dry registers, I should read them with pleasure," he said, "for one can see even from these that there's judgment in them, and good will towards all. Here, on the other hand . . ." Now he was off, and he did not mince his words, nor was there any stopping him. He mentioned himself: "You'll hear nothing of mine." "Now in summer!" I wrote. "No," he exclaimed, "not in the winter either. What should you hear? 'Fidelio'? This they can't perform, nor have they any wish to hear it. The symphonies? For these they haven't time. The concertos? You'll only hear every man grinding away at what he's produced himself. The solo stuff? All this went out of fashion here long ago, and fashion is all. At the very most, Schuppanzigh digs up a quartet from time to time," etc.

At last he had finished unburdening himself and reverted to the subject of Leipzig. "But," he said, "I suppose you really live in Weimar?" He may have got this idea from seeing my address. I shook my head. "In that case, you don't know the great Goethe either?" I nodded, and vehemently. "I know him too," he continued, drawing himself up and with an expression of radiant joy in all his features. "I made his acquaintance at Karlsbad—God knows how long ago. At that time I wasn't as deaf as I am now: but I was already hard of hearing. What patience the great man had with me! How much he has done for me!" He told me many little anecdotes and some most entertaining details. "How happy our meeting made me at that time! I would willingly have died for him, ten times if necessary! At that time, too, when I was truly kindled, I thought out my music for his 'Egmont', and it's successful, isn't it?" I now made whatever gestures, expressive of joy, I could muster. Then I wrote down for him that we perform this music not only with every performance of "Egmont", but at concerts almost regularly once a year together with a kind of commentary, usually consisting of extracts from those scenes of the drama to which the music refers. "I know, I know," he exclaimed. "Since that summer at Karlsbad, I have been reading Goethe every day—that is, when I read at all. He has killed Klopstock for me. That astonishes you? And now you're laughing? Oh, I see, it's because I've read Klopstock at all! For years I was preoccupied

185

with him, when walking and at other times. True enough, I didn't always understand him! He jumps about so, and he always begins right up at the top, always *maestoso*! D flat! Isn't that so? Yet he's great in spite of it and elevates the soul. Where I didn't understand him, I guessed his meaning all the same—just about. If only he were not always just on the point of dying. I should have said that death comes soon enough in any case. Still, at least it always sounds well enough, etc. But as for Goethe, he's alive, and he wants all of us to be alive with him. That's why he can be set to music. No one is so suitable for composition. Only, I am not keen on writing songs." At this point, dear Härtel, I had the finest opportunity to mention your idea and your message. I wrote down the proposition and your acceptance, while I put on as grave an expression as I could. He read. "Ha," he exclaimed, and thrust out one of his arms. "That would be a fine piece of work! This is worth talking about!" He continued in this vein for a while, at once examined every aspect of the idea, very soundly, I think, and gazed fixedly at the ceiling, his head thrown back. Then he began: "But for some time I have been thinking about three other great works. Much of it has already been sketched out, in my head, that is. First of all I must get these off my chest: two great symphonies and each of them different, different, too, from my others, and an oratorio. And these will take long; for, you see, lately it hasn't been easy for me to write. I sit and think and think: I've had it for a long time, but it refuses to be put down on paper. I am terrified of beginning such great works. Once I've started, it goes well enough . . ." And so he continued for a long time.

TO FERDINAND RIES

Vienna, December 20th, 1822

My dear Ries,

Overwhelmed with work, I could not answer your letter of November 15th until now. . . . With pleasure I accept the offer to write a new symphony for the Philharmonic Society. If the payment made by Englishmen cannot be related to that made by all the other nations, I should yet write for the foremost artists in Europe even without any payment at all, if only I were not still poor Beethoven. If only I were in London, what would I not write for the Philharmonic Society! For Beethoven can write, thank God, although, it is true, he can do nothing else at all. If only God restores my health, which has, at least, improved a little, I shall be able to satisfy all the demands from every part of Europe, indeed, even from North America,[1] and my branch may yet be green. . . .

FOR COUNTESS WIMPFFEN, January 20th, 1823

Somewhat slow

[1] The Music Society of Boston, Mass., had asked Beethoven to compose an oratorio for them.

TO FERDINAND RIES

Vienna, February 5th, 1823

My dear, good Ries,

Until now I have no further news of the symphony,[1] but you may count upon it with certainty. As I have made the acquaintance here of a very amiable, accomplished man who is employed in our Imperial Embassy in London, this man will undertake later to help me convey the symphony to you in London, so that it will not take long to reach you. If I were not so poor that I must live by my pen, I should accept nothing at all from the Philharmonic Society. As it is, I must certainly wait till the payment for the symphony has been remitted here. However, in order to give this Society some proof of my love and confidence, I have already given the overture[2] touched upon in my last letter to the gentleman from the Imperial Embassy mentioned above. I imagine that your address will be known at Goldschmidt's; if not, leave it with them, so that this very obliging man need not spend much time in looking you up. I leave it to the Society to make the necessary arrangements with regard to the overture. Like the symphony, they may keep the overture for eighteen months—I should not publish it until this period has elapsed. Now one more request: my noble brother[3] here, who keeps a carriage, has been wishing to leave me behind, too, and so, without asking me, he has offered the

[1] The Ninth.
[2] *The Consecration of the House*, Op. 124.
[3] Johann van Beethoven, the elder of Beethoven's two brothers.

188

said overture to a London publisher by the name of Bosey.[1] Only let him know that for the time being we cannot be sure that he can have this overture; tell him that I shall write to him about it. Everything in this matter depends on the Philharmonic Society. Simply tell them that my brother is mistaken in the matter of the overture. As for the other works about which he has written to you, the publisher may have them. As I can now see, he (my brother) bought them from me in order to practise usury with them. *O frater!* I must beg you again especially, in the matter of the overture, to write to me as soon as you receive it, letting me know whether the Society intends to accept it, because otherwise I should publish it soon.

I have seen nothing of the symphony which you have dedicated to me. Did I not regard the dedication as a kind of challenge, to which I must respond, I should have dedicated some work to you long ago. As it is, I still believed that I must first see your work, and how gladly I would give you some token of my gratitude! For I am deeply indebted to you for all the attachment and helpfulness that you have shown me. If my health should improve as a result of a bath cure planned for next summer, in 1824 I shall kiss your wife in London.

Wholly yours,

Beethoven

TO GOETHE

Vienna, February 8th, 1823

Your Excellency,

Still, as in my boyhood years, absorbed in your immortal, never aging works and, as ever, remembering the hours once spent in your company, I have now occasion to recall myself to your memory. I hope, your Excellency, that you have received my dedication of "Meeresstille" and "Glückliche Fahrt",[2] set to music by me. Both, because of the contrast

---

[1] Boosey.

[2] The two songs "Calm Sea" and "Happy Voyage", Op. 112, were composed in 1815; the poems, as well as Beethoven's setting of them, were conceived as two parts of one work and are indeed a study in contrasts.

between them, seemed to me very suitable for a musical setting which might express this very contrast. How very pleased I should be to hear whether I have fittingly combined my harmony with yours! Instruction, too, which, so to speak, would be regarded as the truth, would be most welcome to me; for I love the truth more than anything, and never shall it be said of me: *veritas odium parit*. A number of your poems, unique as ever, should soon be appearing, set to music by me, among them "Rastlose Liebe". How highly I should value a general remark upon the composing or setting to music of your poems! Now a request to your Excellency. I have written a grand Mass, which, however, I do not wish to publish as yet, but which is intended only for the most prominent Courts. The cost amounts only to 50 ducats. For this purpose I have applied to the Grand-Ducal Weimar Embassy, who accepted my petition to his Highness the Grand Duke and promised to convey it to him. The Mass could also be performed in the manner of an oratorio and who knows that nowadays the charitable societies may not require such works! My request consists in this, that your Excellency draw the attention of his Highness the Grand Duke to this petition, so that his Highness may subscribe for the work. The Grand-Ducal Weimar Embassy also disclosed to me that it would be very advantageous if the Grand Duke were previously disposed in its favour. I have written so much, but earned—almost nothing. Now, however, I am no longer alone; already for six years I have been a father to the son of my late brother, a promising youth in his sixteenth year, wholly devoted to the humanities and already quite at home in the rich mines of Hellenism. However, in these parts such an education costs a great deal and with boys who are studying one must think not only of the present, but of the future, and much as in the past all my thoughts were directed above, I am now compelled to lower my gaze. My subsistence is without substance. My ailing condition in recent years did not permit me to go on tour in the interest of my art, nor, indeed, to take up anything that might be of profit to me. Should my health be entirely restored

to me, perhaps I may yet look forward to better things. You must not think, however, your Excellency, that I have now dedicated "Meeresstille" and "Glückliche Fahrt" to you on account of the service which I am asking of you. I did so already in May, 1822, and there was no question of circulating the Mass in this manner until some weeks ago. The reverence, love and esteem which, ever since my boyhood, I have felt for our unique, immortal Goethe have never changed. Such things cannot easily be expressed in words, especially not by a bungler of my sort who has never endeavoured to master anything but music. Yet a strange feeling always compels me to say so much to you, for I live in your writings. I know that you will not fail to do this one service to an artist who feels only too strongly how far mere money-making is from true art, when necessity constrains him to seek such aid, for others, as well as himself. The virtuous course is always clear to us, and so I know, your Excellency, that you will not refuse my request. A few words from you to me would envelop me in bliss.[1]
As ever your Excellency's

Sincerely, boundlessly devoted

Beethoven

TO KARL FRIEDRICH ZELTER

Vienna, February 8th, 1823

My excellent fellow artist, It is a request to you that makes me write as we are so far away from each other that we cannot meet, our correspondence, too, can only be infrequent. I have written a great Mass, which could also be performed as an oratorio (for the poor, by now a well-established tradition), yet did not wish to have it engraved and published in the usual way, but only to have it circulate among the foremost courts of Europe; the subscription rate is 50 duc. No copies except those subscribed for are available, so that the Mass is really no more

---

[1] Goethe did not reply to this letter; he received it on February 23rd, when he was dangerously ill, and seems to have forgotten about it after his recovery.

than in manuscript; yet even these copies must amount to a considerable number if the author is to get anything out of it. I have handed over to the Royal Prussian Embassy here a request that the King of Prussia might graciously consent to take a copy, have also written to Prince Radziwill, asking him to support my request. I beg you to do whatever you can in this matter. A work of this kind could also be of use to the Academy of Vocal Music,[1] for, with some small alterations, it could almost be performed by voices alone; yet the more these are doubled and multiplied by being combined with instruments, the more powerful the effect should be. As an oratorio, it should be fitting, too, since the charitable societies need works of this kind. In poor health for several years and, consequently, not in a very flourishing condition, I have resorted to this enterprise. Though I have written much—my writings have earned me almost O!—[once I] directed my gaze above; but a man is often compelled on his own account or on account of others, so must he lower himself, yet even this is part of human destiny. With true esteem I embrace you, my dear fellow artist.

Your friend Beethoven

TO ZELTER

Vienna, March 25th, 1823

Honourable Sir,

I avail myself of this opportunity to convey my very best wishes to you. The bearer of this letter begged me to recommend her to you. Her name is Cornega,[2] she has a fine mezzo-soprano voice and is altogether an accomplished singer, has appeared in several operas, too, and won applause.

I have been giving more thought to your proposal regarding your Academy of Vocal Music.[3] Should it (the Mass) ever

[1] The *Singakademie* in Berlin, of which Zelter was the director.

[2] Nina Cornega, a contralto, was a pupil of Salieri's.

[3] On February 22nd Zelter had replied to Beethoven's earlier letter, saying that he was prepared to take one copy of the Mass if Beethoven could adapt it for performance almost without instruments.

appear in print, I shall send you a copy, without accepting any payment. What is certain is that it could almost be performed simply *a la capella* yet for this the whole work would have to be radically revised, and perhaps you have the patience to do it. Besides, the work contains one piece which is entirely *a la capella* and I would go as far as to say that this style is the only true style for devotional music. Thank you for your readiness to oblige. I would never accept anything from such an artist as you so honourably are. I honour you and desire nothing so much as an opportunity of proving this to you in practice.

With high esteem,
Your friend and servant
Beethoven

AN ACCOUNT BY LOUIS SCHLÖSSER

. . . I endeavoured to divert his thoughts from these matters (his financial troubles), by reverting to the subject of the enthusiasm evoked by "Fidelio" in recent times and by remarking in this connection that the proper understanding of this work, lacking in the past, was now about to break through and that German art longed for a new dramatic work by him. "Yet where am I to find a good libretto, agreeable to me?" he replied. "Many poets have already offered me verses specially written for me, but they have no idea of the musical requirements and I shall never compose frivolous subjects. Grillparzer has promised me a libretto called 'Melusine', and I have more confidence in him than in any of the others—now we shall see what will come of it." Unfortunately, this hope, as we well know, was not realized. The Ninth Symphony filled his imagination, at home in the highest spheres, and the completion of this gigantic work displaced every other occupation at this time. Yet I was able to gather from his reply that in the near future he would publish several new quartets and sonatas, the manuscripts of which had already been sent off. These are the world-famous string quartets Op. 127, 130, 132 and 135[1] and the great sonatas Op. 109, 110 and 111. All of them are incomparable masterpieces. When the hour of parting approached and I expressed my gratitude for all that his noble hospitality had granted me both physically and mentally, he called after me when I had already left his apartment: "Good-bye, till we meet again!"

Some weeks later we met by chance in the *Kärtnerstrasse*. His sharp eyes had observed me before I saw him; coming towards me, he at once took my arm with the words: "If your time permits, accompany me to the *Paternostergassl*, to Steiner's, whom I must give a piece of my mind: these publishers are always ready with excuses and evasions. When it's a question of publishing my works, they would like to put this off Heaven knows how long, perhaps till after my death, because they think that these works will be more profitable to them later; however, I shall know how to deal with them" (literally). At this meeting I had at once been astonished to see Beethoven—usually so little concerned with his attire—dressed with extraordinary elegance: a blue tail coat with yellow buttons, trousers impeccably white, his waistcoat likewise and a new beaver hat, which, as usual, he wore on the back of his head. I left him at the entrance of the shop crowded with people while, thanking me for my company, he went off with Herr Steiner to the latter's office. . . .

One day I brought him a new, somewhat complicated composition of mine; after reading it carefully, he declared: "You have put too much into it, less would have been better; this is due to youth, always ready to take Heaven by storm, always afraid of not having done enough, but I'm sure that a riper age will remedy this, and I still prefer an excess of ideas to a lack of them." "How should one set about finding the right way, and —how did you yourself attain this great end?" I added shyly. "I carry my thoughts about with me for a long time, often for a very long time, before writing them down," he replied. "I

[1] Here Schlösser is being wise after the event; for several of the quartets had not been written, or even planned, at the time of his visit.

can rely upon my memory in doing so, and can be sure that once I have grasped a theme I shall not have forgotten it even years later. I change many things, discard others and try again and again until I am satisfied; then, in my head, I begin to elaborate the work in its breadth, its narrowness [*sic*], its height and its depth, and as I am aware of what I want to do, the underlying idea never deserts me. It rises, it grows up, I hear and see the image in front of me from every angle, as if it had been cast, and only the labour of writing it down remains, a labour which need not take long but varies according to the amount of time at my disposal, as very often I work at several things at the same time, but I can always be sure that I shall not confuse one with the other. You may ask me where I obtain my ideas. I cannot answer this with any certainty: they come unevoked, spontaneously or unspontaneously; I could grasp them with my hands in the open air, in the woods, while walking, in the stillness of night, at early morning, stimulated by those moods which with the poets turn into words, into tones with me, which resound, roar and rage until at last they stand before me in the form of notes. . . ."

When I seized my pen to thank him for the last time for all the infinite kindness he had shown to me, he immediately drew back my hand. "Let's have nothing about gratitude!" he called out, "there's no need for that between us: what I did came from my heart. And no more emotion, please! A man should be firm and courageous in all things. Come back to Vienna soon. When are you leaving?" "On the 26th or 27th," I replied. "Then you may permit me to burden you with letters and messages to Paris, and you may tell the publisher Schlesinger orally that I know the reason why he has delayed the publication of my works, but that I shall tolerate it no longer."

TO LUIGI CHERUBINI

(*Draft of a letter*)   *Vienna, March, 1823*

Most highly esteemed Sir,

   With the greatest pleasure I take this opportunity to approach you in writing. In spirit I am near you often enough, for I value your works more highly than other compositions for the theatre. Only, the world of Art has reason to regret that, in our Germany at least, no great theatrical work of yours has appeared in recent times. Highly as your other works are valued by true connoisseurs, it remains a real loss to Art not to possess a new product of your great spirit for the theatre. True art remains imperishable, and the true artist takes intense pleasure in the true, great products of genius, and thus I, too, am delighted whenever I hear a new work by yourself and feel more concern for it than for my own works. In short, I honour and love you. If only my chronic illness did not prevent me from seeing you in Paris, with what extraordinary pleasure I should discuss artistic matters with you! Now I must add further that I speak of you with enthusiasm to every artist and art-lover; otherwise you may assume that because I am now about to ask a favour of you, this is merely the overture to my request. Yet I hope that you do not think me capable of so base an attitude. My request consists in the following:

   I have just completed a great solemn Mass and wish to send this work to the European courts, as for the time being I do not wish to have it engraved and made public. By means of the French Embassy here, I have therefore despatched an invitation to His Majesty the King of France, among others, to subscribe to this work, and am convinced that on your recommendation the King will surely agree to do so. *Ma situation critique demande que je ne fixe pas seulement comme ordinaire mes pensées au ciel; au contraire, il faut les fixer aussi en bas pour les nécessaires de la vie.*

   However my request to you may fare, I shall still always love and honour you, *et vous resterez toujours celui de mes contemporains, que j'estime le plus. Si vous me voulez faire un extrême plaisir, c'était, si vous m'écrirez quelques lignes, ce que me soulagera bien. L'art unit tout le monde*, how much more true. artists, *et peut-être vous me daignez aussi de me mettre* to count me among this number.

Avec le plus haut estime

Votre ami et serviteur[1]

Beethoven

FRANZ LISZT'S ACCOUNT OF HIS VISIT TO BEETHOVEN

I was about eleven years old when my respected teacher Czerny took me to see Beethoven. Already a long time before, he had told Beethoven about me and asked him to give me a hearing some day. However, Beethoven had such an aversion to infant prodigies that he persistently refused to see me. At last Czerny, indefatigable, persuaded him, so that, impatiently, he said: "Well, bring the rascal to me, in God's name!" It was about ten o'clock in the morning when we entered the two small rooms in the *Schwarzspanierhaus*, where Beethoven was living at the time, myself very shy, Czerny kind and encouraging. Beethoven was sitting at a long, narrow table near the window, working. For a time he scrutinized us grimly, exchanged a few hurried words with Czerny and remained silent when my good teacher called me to the piano. The first thing I played was a short piece by Ries. When I had finished, Beethoven asked me whether I could play a fugue by Bach. I chose the Fugue in C minor from the Well-Tempered Clavichord. "Could you also transpose this fugue at once into another key?" Beethoven asked me. Fortunately, I could. After the final chord, I looked up. The Master's darkly glowing gaze was fixed upon me penetratingly. Yet suddenly a benevolent smile broke up his gloomy features, Beethoven came quite

---

[1] Beethoven's French has been corrected by the German editors of his letters. According to Thayer, Beethoven wrote "une estreme plaisir", "L'art unie touta le monde", etc.

Cherubini did not receive the letter for which the above is a draft, to his sincere regret in later years. King Louis XVIII, however, not only subscribed to the Mass, but sent Beethoven a gold medal weighing the equivalent of twenty-one louis d'or, and inscribed "Donnée par le Roi à Monsieur Beethoven".

close, bent over me, laid his hand on my head and repeatedly stroked my hair. "Devil of a fellow!" he whispered, "such a young rascal!" I suddenly plucked up courage. "May I play something of yours now?" I asked cheekily. Beethoven nodded with a smile. I played the first movement of the C major Concerto. When I had ended, Beethoven seized both my hands, kissed me on the forehead and said gently: "Off with you! You're a happy fellow, for you'll give happiness and joy to many other people. There is nothing better or greater than that!"

This event in my life has remained my greatest pride, the palladium for my whole artistic career. I speak of it only very rarely and only to my intimate friends.

TO ARCHDUKE RUDOLPH

Vienna, July 1st, 1823

... I give thanks to Him who is above, beyond the stars, that I am now beginning to be able to use my eyes again. I am now writing a new symphony for the Philharmonic Society in England and hope to complete it within the next fourteen days. Even now I cannot use my eyes for any length of time without excessive strain, I therefore beg Your Imperial Highness for further gracious forbearance in the matter of the Variations written by yourself, which seem most charming to me but do still require my more detailed attention. I hope that Your Imperial Highness will continue to acquire special practice in writing down your ideas straight away at the piano; for this purpose there should be a small table next to the piano. Not only is the imagination strengthened in this way, but one also learns to pin down the remotest ideas at once; it is likewise necessary to write without a piano. Nor should it give Yr. Imperial Highness a headache, but rather the considerable pleasure of finding yourself absorbed in this art, to elaborate a simple melody at times, a chorale, with simple and, then again, with more varied figurations in counterpoint and so forth to more difficult exercises. Gradually we develop the capacity to express just exactly what we wish to, what we feel within us, a need characteristic of all superior persons. . . .

FROM GRILLPARZER'S "RECOLLECTIONS OF BEETHOVEN"

. . . A few days later, Schindler, at that time Beethoven's agent—the same who in later years wrote Beethoven's biography—came to see me and, in the name of his lord and master, who was unwell, invited me to visit him. I got dressed and we set out at once for Beethoven's lodgings, which at that time were in the suburb Landstrasse. I found him lying on a disordered bed in dirty night attire, a book in his hand. At the head of the bed there was a small door which, as I discovered later, communicated with the larder and which Beethoven was, in a way, guarding. For when subsequently a maid emerged from it with butter and eggs he could not restrain himself, though in the middle of a spirited conversation, from casting an appraising glance at the quantity of the food that was being carried away—and this gave me a painful picture of his disordered household.

When we entered, Beethoven rose from his bed, gave me his hand, lavished expressions of his goodwill upon me and at once broached the subject of the opera. "Your work lives here," he said, pointing to his heart, "in a few days' time I shall be moving to the country and there I shall begin at once to compose it. Only the chorus of huntsmen at the beginning is troubling me. Weber used four horns; you can see that I should need to use eight of them: where will this lead to?" Although I was far from seeing the logical necessity for this argument, I yet declared to him that the huntsmen's chorus could simply be omitted without damage to the whole, with which admission he seemed very satisfied; neither at that time, nor later, did he make any other objection to the text or demand any alteration. Indeed, he insisted that we should draw up a contract on the spot. The profits of the opera were to be evenly divided between us, etc. I told him, quite truthfully, that in writing my works I had never given a thought to remuneration of any kind (this was the reason, too, why these works which— with the exception of Uhland—I regard as the best produced in Germany since the death of her great poets, have hardly earned me as much as a single volume of travel sketches or pictorial fantasies has invariably earned its dead, living or half-dead author). Least of all was this matter to arise between us. He was to do whatever he liked with the libretto, for I would never draw up a contract with him. After a good deal of inconclusive talk—or rather writing, as Beethoven could no longer hear the spoken word—I left, after promising to visit him in Hetzendorf as soon as he had settled there. . . .

In the course of the summer I visited Beethoven, who had invited me, at Hetzendorf in the company of Herr Schindler. I do not know whether Schindler told me on the way or whether somebody else had told me previously that until now urgent commissions had prevented Beethoven from beginning to compose the opera. I therefore avoided all reference to it. We went for a walk and conversed as well as it is possible to converse half in writing, half in speaking and without ceasing to walk. I am still moved when I remember that when we sat down to eat Beethoven went into the adjoining room and returned with five bottles. He placed one in front of Schindler's plate, one in front of his own and three in a row in front of mine, probably in order to make it clear to me in his wild and naïve, yet good-natured manner that I was free to drink as much as I liked. When I drove back to town, now without Schindler, who remained at Hetzendorf, Beethoven insisted on accompanying me. He sat down next to me in the open carriage but instead of going only as far as the outskirts of the village he drove with me as far as the city, getting out at the city gates and, after a cordial handshake, setting out alone on the homeward journey of an hour and a half. As he was alighting from the carriage I saw a piece of paper at the place where he had been sitting. I thought he had left it behind and beckoned to him to return. However, he shook his head and, laughing loudly, as after some successful ruse, he ran all the faster in the opposite direction. I unfolded the paper and found that it contained the exact amount of the fare upon which I had agreed with the coachman. His way of life had so estranged him from all the customs and usages of the world that it never occurred to him that, in all other circumstances, his conduct would have been interpreted as a gross insult. Needless to say, I took the matter as it was intended and, laughing to myself, paid the coachman with the money given to me.

TO C. F. PETERS

Hetzendorf, July 7th, 1823

Honourable Sir,

As soon as the work intended for you or for your children is completed, I shall immediately hand it over to Meissel Brothers.[1] Should it be necessary to increase the payment, you will be informed of this. Spare me any further letters, for you never know your own mind. Not a word about your—conduct towards me! Only of one thing I must complain, that you accuse me of having accepted money in advance. It is clear from your letters that you thrust it upon me without my asking for it, as you say that you always make an advance payment to composers. Here people stopped me in the street to remind me to fetch the money, and my circumstances at that time demanded the utmost secrecy, so that I took the money only because of such gossip; and if this business has now suffered delay, whose fault is it but your own? Besides, some very much greater sums of money are ready for me elsewhere, and others are content to wait, as they have some consideration for my art and, again, for my poor health. Be assured that I have seen through you morally, or rather commercially and musically. Nevertheless I shall make allowances because of the sum of

---

[1] A firm of bankers in Vienna.

money placed at my disposal, for I am a man in full command of his faculties, and I do not need to be reminded of my honour.

Beethoven

TO FERDINAND RIES

Hetzendorf, July 16th, 1823

My dear Ries,

It was with great pleasure that I received your letter the day before yesterday. . . . The variations,[1] I suppose, will have arrived by now. I could not write the dedication to your wife myself, as I don't know her name. So please write it in yourself in the name of your friend and your wife's friend: keep it for her as a surprise: the fair sex likes it best in that way. Between ourselves, together with beauty, surprises are the best thing of all! . . . As for the *allegri di bravura*, I must have a look at yours. Frankly, I am not keen on things of that kind, as they are all too conducive to mechanical effects; at least, those which I know. I don't know yours yet, but will inquire for them at Peters', with whom I beg you to deal only with the greatest caution. Is there not something which I could do for you here? These publishers, whom one should always publicly humiliate so that they may be worthy of their names,[2] pirate your works and you get nothing out of them; perhaps something could be done about this. I shall surely send you some choruses, even compose some new ones, if necessary; they are among my favourite forms.

Many thanks for the payment for the bagatelles![3] I am well satisfied. Don't give anything to the King of England.[4] Accept whatever you can get for the variations; I shall be satisfied with anything; only I must insist on one condition, that for the dedication to your wife I shall accept no payment other than a kiss, which I am to receive in London. You sometimes write

[1] The Diabelli Variations, Op. 120.
[2] The usual pun (see page 179).   [3] Op. 119.
[4] Beethoven had sent his "Wellington's Battle and Victory at Vittoria" to King George IV, but had received no acknowledgment; Beethoven was deeply offended by this incident, to which the above remark may well be referred.

guineas and I receive only sterling; yet I hear that there is a difference between them. Don't be angry with a *pauvre musicien autrichien* on this account; really my position is still precarious. I am also writing a new string quartet.[1] Could one offer this to the musical or unmusical Jews in London? *En vrai juif?*

With a most hearty embrace, your old friend

Beethoven

TO ARCHDUKE RUDOLPH

Baden, August, 1823

Your Imperial Highness,

I was deeply moved to receive your gracious communication yesterday. To be allowed to thrive in the shade of an equally thriving tree splendidly laden with fruit is a comfort for those men who are capable of the higher thoughts and feelings. So, too, it is with me under the aegis of Your Imperial Highness.

My physician assured me yesterday that my health was improving; yet I am still obliged to empty a whole (bottle of) mixture within twenty-four hours and, since this mixture is a laxative, it leaves me extremely feeble, while at the same time, as Your Imperial Highness can see from the enclosed rules of conduct prescribed by my physician, I am forced to take a great deal of exercise every day. Nevertheless, there is some hope that soon I may yet attend frequently upon Your Imperial Highness during your sojourn here, even if my health should remain imperfect. As long as I live in this hope, my health will surely improve more promptly than it would otherwise do.

May Heaven bless me through Your Imperial Highness, and may the Lord Himself always be above and with Your Imperial Highness. There is nothing higher on earth than to come nearer to godhead than other men and thus to convey the divine radiance to mankind. Deeply aware of Your Imperial Highness' gracious disposition towards me, I hope to be able to approach you in person with the least possible delay.

Your Imperial Highness' most obedient, faithful servant,

Beethoven

[1] String Quartet in E flat, Op. 127.

TO KARL VAN BEETHOVEN

Baden, August 16th, 1823

Dear boy,

It was my intention not to say anything to you until I should feel better in this place, but this is not yet wholly the case. I came here with a cold and a catarrh, both of them most unpleasant for me, as my chronic condition is catarrhal in any case and I very much fear that this will soon cut my thread of life or, what would be worse, gnaw through it gradually. My ruined abdomen, also, calls for medicine and a diet, and this is what one owes to faithful servants! You can imagine in what a state I run about, for not until to-day could I properly (or rather not properly, for my own will is not involved) resume my service to the Muses. I must, but no one may know of it— for the baths make the enjoyment of lovely scenery even more attractive, at least to me, but *nous sommes trop pauvres et il faut écrire ou de n'avoir pas de quoi.* See to it that all the necessary preparations are made for your examination, and be very modest, so that you will prove to be better and more advanced than they expect. Don't hesitate to send your washing here; your grey trousers can still be worn, certainly in the house. For, dear son, you are indeed very dear! My address: "At the copper-beater's", etc. Write to me at once to say that you have received this letter. As for Schindler, that despicable object, I shall send you a few lines to him, as I do not like to be in direct communication with the wretched fellow. If only everything could be written down as fast as one thinks, feels, I should certainly be able to tell you much that is not unremarkable. For to-day I will only add the wish that a certain Karl may be wholly worthy of my love, of my great concern for him and may duly appreciate all this one day. Although, as you know, I do not ask for much, there are still many ways in which one can show to persons distinguished by virtue and noble minds that one can recognize these attributes in them and is conscious of them.

I embrace you cordially,

Your faithful, veritable father

FROM AN ACCOUNT BY EDWARD SCHULZ
(published in the English review, "Harmonicon", January, 1824)

. . . In the whole course of our table-talk there was nothing so interesting as what he said about Handel. I sat close by him and heard him assert very distinctly in German: "Handel is the greatest composer that ever lived." I cannot describe to you with what pathos, and I am inclined to say, with what sublimity of language, he spoke of the "Messiah" of this immortal genius. Every one of us was moved when he said: "I would uncover my head, and kneel down at his tomb!" H. and I tried repeatedly to turn the conversation to Mozart, but without effect. I only heard him say: "In a monarchy we know who is the first"; which might or might not apply to the subject. . . . He is engaged in writing a new opera called "Melusine", the words by the famous but unfortunate poet Grillparzer. He concerns himself but very little about the newest productions of living composers insomuch that when I asked about the "Freischütz", he replied: "I believe *one* Weber has written it." . . . He appears uniformly to entertain the most favourable opinion of the British nation. "I like", said he, "the noble simplicity of the English manners", and added other praises. It seemed to me as if he had yet some hopes of visiting this country with his nephew. I should not forget to mention that I heard a MS. trio[1] of his for the pianoforte, violin and violincello, which I thought very beautiful, and is, I understood, to appear shortly in London.

FROM SIR JULIUS BENEDICT'S REMINISCENCES
(as reported by Thayer)

Herr Steiner introduced me to the great man as a pupil of Weber. The other persons present were the aged Abbé Stadler and Seyfried. Beethoven said to Steiner: "I am glad to hear

[1] The Trio in B flat, Op. 97.

that once again you are publishing a German work. I have heard many favourable things about Weber's opera and hope that it will earn both him and you a great deal of fame and money!" Steiner took this opportunity to say: "This is a pupil of Weber's", whereupon Beethoven offered me his hand in a most kindly manner and said: "Please tell Herr von Weber how happy I should be to see him at Baden, as I shall not be in Vienna before next month." . . .

A few days later I had the pleasure of accompanying Weber, Haslinger and a third friend[1] to Baden; they accorded me the great privilege of visiting Beethoven in their company. Nothing could be more cordial than his manner of welcoming my teacher. He wished to take us to Helenenthal and show us all the surroundings; but the weather was unfavourable and we were forced to give up this outing; we all lunched at one table at the inn; I sat at the opposite end to them and had the pleasure of listening to their conversation.

On the morning after the first performance of "Euryanthe",[2] when the shop[3] was crowded with musical experts, Beethoven is said to have put in an appearance and asked Haslinger: "Well, how did the opera go last night?" The reply was: "A great triumph." Thereupon he exclaimed: "I'm delighted, delighted!" and when he noticed Benedict, he said: "I would gladly have attended the performance but"—and he pointed at his ears—"I no longer go to the theatre." Then he asked Gottdank, the producer: "What sort of progress has little Sontag[4] made? I take a very great interest in her. And how is the libretto? Good or bad?" G. gave a positive answer to the first question, while in reply to the second he shrugged his shoulders and made a negative gesture. Then Beethoven said: "It's always the same story! The Germans cannot write a good libretto." Benedict took the conversation book and wrote: "And Fidelio?" Whereupon Beethoven replied: "That's a

---

[1] Piringer.   [2] October 25th, 1823.
[3] The shop in question was Steiner's and Haslinger's music shop, which seems to have served as a kind of club.
[4] Henriette Sontag, soprano, who sang the solo part in the first performance of the Ninth Symphony. She visited Beethoven on September 8th, 1822.

French and Italian libretto." And when Benedict asked him:
"Which do you regard as the best libretti?" he mentioned the
"Water-Carrier"[1] and "The Vestal".[2]

FROM MAX MARIA VON WEBER'S BIOGRAPHY OF HIS FATHER

Now that Weber's "Freischütz" made such a great stir in the
world and Beethoven read so much about it, in letters written
to him and elsewhere, he, too, took the score home with him
and studied it very thoroughly, although previously he had
felt little respect for Weber's compositions. Its deep originality,
which, naturally, did not escape him, impressed him pro-
foundly and in the presence of his friends, striking the score, he
exclaimed: "This little man, usually so soft, why, I'd never
thought him capable of it! Now this Weber must write operas,
nothing but operas, one after the other, without any pre-
liminary nibbling! Kaspar, that monster, is as solid as a house.
Wherever the devil bares his claws, you feel them, too!"
And when someone reminded him of the second *finale* and of
the musical innovations in it, he said: "Yes, that's undoubtedly
so; but it affects me strangely. True, I can see what Weber is
trying to do, but he's put some confounded nonsense into it as
well! When I read it—for instance the wild chase—it makes me
laugh, yet I don't doubt that it's right." Then, deeply excited,
he added, pointing at his ear: "That kind of thing must be
heard, only heard, but as—I——"
The three men were moved when they entered the dreary,
almost sordid room inhabited by the great Ludwig. The room
was in the greatest disorder: music, money, clothes, lay on the
floor, linen in a heap on the unclean bed, the open grand piano
was covered in thick dust and broken coffee-cups lay on the
table.
Beethoven came forward to welcome them.

[1] *Der Wasserträger*, an opera by Cherubini.
[2] *La Vestale*, an opera by Spontini.

Benedict says: Lear or Ossian's bards must have looked like him. His hair dense, grey, standing up, quite white in places, forehead and skull extraordinarily wide and rounded, high as a temple, the nose square, like a lion's, the mouth nobly formed and soft, the chin broad and with those marvellous dimples which all his portraits show, formed by two jaw-bones which seemed capable of cracking the hardest nuts. A dark ruddiness coloured his broad, pock-marked face; beneath the bushy and sullenly contracted eyebrows, small, shining eyes were fixed benevolently upon the visitors; his square, Cyclopean figure, only a little taller than Weber's, was dressed in a shabby jacket torn at the sleeves.

Beethoven recognized Weber even before his name was mentioned, embraced him and exclaimed: "There you are at last, my dear fellow! You're the devil of a fellow! I'm delighted to see you!" and he at once handed him the famous slate; a conversation ensued, while Beethoven began by throwing all the music off the sofa and then proceeded to dress for the street, not in the least embarrassed by the presence of his guests.

Beethoven bitterly lamented the position he was in, cursed the theatre management, the promoters of concerts, the public, the Italians, the current bad taste and, above all, his nephew's ingratitude. Weber, who was very excited, advised him to break away from these repellent, discouraging conditions by going on a concert tour in Germany, where he would soon see how highly he was thought of in the world. "Too late!" cried Beethoven, made the gesture of playing the piano, and shook his head. "Well, go to England, then, where you're admired!" Weber wrote down. "Too late!" yelled Beethoven, seized Weber by the arm ostentatiously and dragged him away to the *Sauerhof*, where they lunched. . . .

When they parted, Beethoven embraced and kissed Weber several times, for a long time held Weber's slender hand in his fist and cried out: "Good luck for the new opera! If I can, I'll be at the first performance!"

CARL MARIA VON WEBER TO HIS WIFE

October 5th, 1823

. . . I was very tired and had to get up again at 6 o'clock yesterday morning, as our party was due to leave for Baden at 7.30. Haslinger, Piringer, Benedict and myself met at that time, as arranged; but we left in the most miserable rainy weather. Our main object was to see Beethoven. He received me with an affection which I found most moving; he embraced me cordially no less than seven or eight times and finally exclaimed, with the utmost enthusiasm: "Yes, you're the devil of a fellow, an excellent fellow!" We spent the late morning and noon together, very cheerful and gay. This rough, unsociable man literally courted me, served me at table with such attentiveness that I might have been his lady, etc. Briefly, this day will always remain a most memorable one for me, as for all the others who were present. It was curiously exalting to be overwhelmed with such affectionate attentions by this great man.

TO ANTON SCHINDLER

1823

Best of friends,

In accordance with the following hattisherif you will attend at the *Mariahilf* coffee-house at 4 o'clock this afternoon in order to be tried for various punishable offences. If this hs. should not reach you to-day, then it is your duty to attend at my house at 2 o'clock to-morrow afternoon, at which time, after partaking of bread and water, you will be placed under arrest for the duration of twenty-four hours.

L. V.! Beethoven

TO SCHINDLER

To Herr Schindler:
   I beg you not to come again until I send for you. Concert will
not take place.

                                                           B-vn.

TO SCHINDLER

Best of friends,
   You will find us in the Golden Pear, after that in the coffee-
house.

TO IGNAZ SCHUPPANZIGH

To Herr Schuppanzigh!
   Let him not visit me again. I am not giving a concert.
                                                        Beethoven

TO COUNT MORITZ LICHNOWSKY

   I despise treacheries. Do not visit me again. Concert not
taking place.
                                                        Beethoven

A PERSONAL NOTE

Foreign countries will make you gentler, more human, more reconciled to the world. Continually apply all your faculties, exert them; nor will so much be wasted, as in Vienna.

TO FRANZ GRILLPARZER

Vienna, 1823/24

Worthy, most worthy friend,

The management would like to know your terms for your Melusine;[1] they have already committed themselves thus far, and this is surely better than to be left with the initiative in such matters. For some time my household has been in the greatest disorder, else I should certainly have looked you up and also asked you to visit me. For the present, make known your terms in writing either to me or straight to the management; in the former event I shall pass them on myself. Overburdened, I could not approach you either lately or at present; I hope that one day it will become possible. My number is 323.

In the afternoons you will also find me in the coffee-house opposite the *Goldene Birne*. Should you wish to come there, I beg you to come alone; this obtrusive appendix known as Schindler has long been utterly repulsive to me, as you must have observed at Hetzendorf—*otium est vitium*. I embrace you cordially and honour you sincerely.

Wholly yours,
Beethoven

---

[1] The projected opera, for which Grillparzer had written the libretto.

AN ACCOUNT BY GEORG AUGUST GRIESINGER
(*according to Seyfried*)

The praise which, in spite of the critics, had been accorded
to the libretto (of "Der Freischütz") inspired Kind with the
wish to write librettos for other operas. But the poet of the
"Freischütz" was clever enough to see that good music was the
first requisite for the favourable reception of an opera and,
during a meeting at a spa, said to me that he would be very
pleased if Beethoven were willing to set a text written by him;
yet he did not feel inclined to write to him, as he had heard
much about Beethoven's refractory nature. I offered to
approach Beethoven in this matter at the first opportunity. As
soon as possible, therefore, I fulfilled my promise. Beethoven
answered me: "Thank you, thank you very much. I appreciate
the value of the 'Freischütz' libretto: it is as musical as it is
picturesque; I believe, too, that if Kind were to enter once more
into the realm of legend, he would be capable of writing another
excellent, truly popular libretto, but I'm not sufficiently
interested in such a drama to set it to music. My 'Fidelio'
was not understood by the public, but I know that it will yet
be valued; nevertheless, although I know what my 'Fidelio'
is worth, I know just as clearly that the symphony is my true
element. When sounds stir within me, I always hear the full
orchestra; I know what to expect of instrumentalists, who are
capable of almost everything, but with vocal compositions I
must always be asking myself: can this be sung? No, no! Herr
Friedrich Kind should not take it amiss, but I shan't write
any more operas."

We continued to converse about Weber, and Beethoven
praised him most fervently, so that I am firmly convinced that
the disparaging judgments of Weber attributed to Beethoven
have been put into his mouth.

TO B. SCHOTT'S SONS, MUSIC PUBLISHERS IN MAYENCE

Vienna, March 10th, 1824

. . . As regards those works of mine which you wish to have, I offer you the following: only the decision should not be delayed too long: a new great solemn Mass with solo voices and chorus (and) full orchestra. Difficult as it is for me to speak about myself, I must say that I regard it as my greatest work. The payment would be 1000 fl. in c.c.; a new great symphony which concludes with a finale (in the manner of my Piano Fantasia with Chorus, yet much more grand in conception) with solos and chorus of singing voices, the words from Schiller's well-known immortal Hymn to Joy. The payment 600 fl. c.c.; a new quartet for two violins, viola and 'cello, the payment 50 duc. in gold.

This negotiation only to oblige you. In connection with this announcement, do not consider me mercenary; yet even I, as a genuine artist, must not despise competition. For, indeed, it places me in a position in which I can be faithful to my Muses and provide for several other persons in a noble manner. As for the works announced, your reply should follow very soon.

I am, Sir, your most devoted

Beethoven

TO B. SCHOTT'S SONS

Vienna, end of July or beginning of August, 1824

Honourable Sir,

I write only to tell you that the works[1] will now surely be delivered next week. You will easily understand (my position) if you imagine that, owing to the unreliable copying, I had to examine every voice individually. For this trade, like so many things here, has deteriorated badly: the more taxes, the more difficulties, everywhere—poverty *spiriti* [*sic*] and of the purse.

---

[1] The Missa Solemnis and the Ninth Symphony.

I have not yet received your *Cäcilia*.[1] The overture[2] which my brother is sending to you was performed here some days ago. I received much praise, etc., for it. What is all this compared to the great Master Musician above—above—above—and, rightly, supreme, when down here it is nothing but an object of mockery. The little dwarfs supreme!!! ??? You will receive the quartet[3] at once with the other works. You are so candid and unpretending, qualities which I have never observed in publishers; I like this and shake hands with you because of it, very soon in person perhaps, who knows?! I should be pleased if you could now also remit the payment for the quartet to Fries;[4] for just at this moment I need a great deal of money, as everything due to me is coming from abroad and there may well be a delay here and there—caused by myself. My brothers will add all the necessary information about the works offered to you and accepted by you. My sincere regards. Junker,[5] I gather from your review, is still alive; he was one of the first to take notice of me, innocently and without any other motives; give him my regards.

In the greatest haste, with the greatest urgency and yet not with the greatest brevity,

Your

Beethoven

FROM AN ACCOUNT BY JOHANN ANDREAS STUMPFF

... When the door was opened, a shudder ran through me, as if I were about to approach some supernatural being. I sent my visiting card up to him and we were invited to enter. Now

---

[1] *Cäcilia* was a musical review published by Schott. A contribution by Beethoven appeared in it in 1825, but without his permission.

[2] *The Consecration of the House*, Op. 124. This overture, the Ninth Symphony and parts of the Missa Solemnis were performed at two concerts on May 7th and May 23rd, 1824.

[3] The String Quartet in E flat major, Op. 127.

[4] A firm of bankers in Vienna.

[5] Karl Ludwig Junker (1740–97) was the author of an account of the orchestra at Bonn, in which account Beethoven is mentioned. He was not, however, alive, as Beethoven supposed.

Beethoven came out to meet us with my card in his hand; he offered me his hand with a cheerful expression on his face, repeating my name: "Stumpff, Herr Stumpff from London? Of whom I have heard many fine things already from Herr Streicher; also I possess a letter of yours written to him in which I, too, am mentioned." Now he went to his writing-desk. "Ha, here it is, containing the text of a song for composition." It was the same letter which I had given to Herr Streicher two years previously.

... "Yes, to-day I'm happy and cheerful. Well, how are you faring in old Vienna? Where one eats and drinks, sleeps and——! Ah, everyone here lives in his own fashion, plays and sings what he's produced himself."

So, at last, I stood before Beethoven, who received me with an open heart in his daily attire, not in a clean, flowered dressing-gown. . . . Beethoven was fond of talking and not chary of words; he had an exaggerated opinion of London and of its highly cultured inhabitants. "England stands high in culture. In London every person knows something, and knows it well, but the Viennese, he can talk about eating and drinking and sings and strums music of little significance, though fashionable, or music which he himself has fabricated. . . . Of my nephew Karl I wish to make a man whom I have ransomed from his worthless mother, and wish to send him to a high school in Saxony, and every guilder which I can earn by exerting my faculties is destined for his education. Karl must learn English, too, and stay with you in London, so that he may come to something; but our clever superiors will not hear of it, they wish him to remain in Vienna, to become an everyday person for ever."

Beethoven now asked me with great concern how much it might cost to maintain a young man, like his Karl, in London for a year. So as to hear my opinion clearly, he provided me with his accessories and aids, a pencil and the conversation books, in which I was to write down my reply. His eyes followed the movements of my pencil and he uttered every word aloud before I had completed it; when he had gathered what he wished to know, he shook his head disconsolately and complained bitterly of the music publishers, who would give him next to nothing for his great compositions which had cost him so much time and effort.

"Remain at Baden," Beethoven continued, "and visit me as often as you like; there are many things I wish to discuss with you"—and I promised to do so. When I found that this audience, so ardently desired and yet feared, had passed so happily, I said in parting to my companion: "As you have such power over his spirit tormented by fantasies, my dear friend, do you think you could induce him to dine with me, that is, in my guest-house, where there is such a beautiful, shaded garden behind the new buildings?" "I'll try," was his answer, "and let you know as soon as possible."

Beethoven accepted the invitation on the condition that we should dine in the garden.

And now I had nothing better to do than to consult with the host about the dishes that we should eat. I asked him whether perhaps he knew the preferences of this strange man and begged him to give special consideration to these in choosing the menu. "Oh, yes, my dear Sir, I do know: fish, that's it, he's very fond of fish. Beethoven is certainly strange, but he's good! Everybody knows that, Sir."

Now the table, steaming, stood ready in a well-shaded garden, waiting to serve the guests with simple, but wholesome food. Only Herr Haslinger and some of his friends awaited the great artist, who now approached with his nephew Karl; he eyed the fish with evident pleasure and his nose caught their smell. After a short greeting, he seized the table with both hands and signified to us to do likewise on the opposite side, so that the large chair intended for him would be in the sun. Beethoven now sat down in this same chair and, laughing, removed the cover from the dish: "Excellent, excellent, I see fish here! Yes, I like eating fish; only, in this country they're no good. The fish that come out of the sea, like those they serve in London, these would be a fine dish!" Now he talked incessantly, cursed the Viennese cooks and wine merchants, who adulterate everything ("poison" was the word he used). "Yes, that's how it is!" Now he began to praise the English, who know how to appreciate everything that is strong, good and beautiful. The French, to whom he is not well disposed, received many blows, for he regarded them as bad judges of what is good, true and beautiful in music, as well as in politics, as they had proved sufficiently and were still proving!

Then the attack switched to the Viennese, to their taste, which had changed so much, deteriorated so much. "No one has any understanding now for what is good and strong, for true music, in fact! Yes, that's how it is, you Viennese! Rossini and his cronies, these are your heroes. They want none of my music now. Sometimes Schuppanzigh digs up a quartet of mine: they haven't time for the symphonies, and they don't care for "Fidelio". Rossini, Rossini means more than anything to you! Or perhaps your soulless strumming and singing, your own miserable bunglings, which you use to ruin yourselves for true art—that's your taste! Oh, you Viennese!" And so it went on in a good-natured way which revealed not the least trace of either malice or envy, which jeremiads we supported or contradicted in an equally good-natured manner, nodding or shaking our heads and laughing heartily. Now, when the (declining) sun warned us that it was time to go, Beethoven seized his hat and stick and, holding on to his nephew, he clasped my hand and asked me to dine with him three days later, as I gladly agreed to do.

I therefore appeared at his house at the appointed noon. I must permit myself to comment upon a certain circumstance which might excuse, if not justify, a rather surprising incident which occurred during the meal. Beethoven had repeatedly told his housekeeper that she must always set down everything that had been ordered for the midday meal upon the table and never under any circumstances bring in anything once he was seated at the table. Whether such a command was usual, reasonable or unreasonable does not concern me here: briefly, such was the command.

Now I sat alone with Beethoven at his well-appointed table.

Two tall, patriarchal bottles of reddish wine stood on either side of him and a smaller bottle glowed on his left, to glorify the dessert. "What you will find here is simple fare, not poisoned by the cook; the wine, too, is natural and unadulterated. Now help yourself, eat and drink what God has given us!"

I followed his example and showed little hesitation. The wine, which was pure and good, animated my host, who continued to fill up and empty the glasses with evident satisfaction and always served his guest first; and as he continued to talk incessantly, witty and droll conceits were brought to light, about many of which he himself laughed noisily, while I applauded them by clapping my hands. During one of these effusions a surly housekeeper crept into the room and placed a dish of noodles upon the table, thinking that her presence would escape notice, when suddenly Beethoven shouted at her. "You obstinate woman, who has allowed you to do the forbidden thing?" He pushed the dish of steaming noodles at her, and she caught it in her apron. The old woman, knowing her master, left the room as quickly as possible, and grumbling to herself, disappeared.

Now Beethoven seized the small bottle. It contained delicious Tokay wine and he filled the two glasses to the brim. "Well, my dear German Englishman, to your precious health!" After we had emptied the glasses, he gave me his hand. "Good luck for your journey, and may we meet soon in London!" I now asked him by signs to fill the glasses once more and hastily wrote down in his book: "Now for the health of the greatest living tone poet, Beethoven!" I rose from my chair, he followed my example, emptied his glass and, grasping my hand, said, "And to-day I am wholly myself, wholly what I should be, quite unbuttoned!" Now he poured out his thoughts about music, how music was debased at present and transformed into the play of vile and insolent emotions. True music, he said, received little welcome in this age of Rossini. Then I seized the pencil and wrote down very distinctly: "Whom do you regard as the greatest composer that ever lived?" "Händel," was his immediate reply, "before him I go on my knees"—and he touched the floor with one of them. "Mozart?" I now wrote. "Mozart", he continued, "is good and excellent." "Yes," I wrote, "and could even improve on Händel by composing a new accompaniment to the 'Messiah'." "Händel would have survived without it," was his reply. Now I wrote: "Sebastian Bach?" "Why is he dead?" I wrote at once: "He shall live again." "Yes, when people begin to study him again, but they haven't the time for it!"

I took the liberty of writing on: "As you place the merit of a Händel higher than everything else, when you yourself are an incomparable practitioner of a divine art, I take it that you possess the scores of his principal works?" "I? How should I have obtained them, a poor devil like me! Yes, the scores of his 'Messiah' and 'Alexander's Feast' have passed through my hands. . . ."

Our conversation now turned to keyboard instruments and compositions for these. Beethoven complained of the imperfection of the grand pianoforte, upon which one could not perform forcefully and effectively under present conditions. "I myself possess a London instrument, which, however, does not live up to my expectations. Come along, it's in the next room, in a most miserable state." When I opened it, what a sight confronted me! The upper registers were mute and the broken strings in a tangle, like a thorn bush whipped by the storm [sic]! Beethoven begged me to advise him as to what should be done to it. "Do you think that the piano-maker Stein could repair it, if you consulted him in this matter?" I promised to do my best. At that moment his brother, who owned an estate, entered the room; he had heard of me and seemed pleased to find me here: because he had several matters to discuss with me, he begged me in a flattering manner to visit him. As it was now evening, I said good-bye to Beethoven, who accompanied me as far as the front door. He seemed quite ill-tempered; with a gloomy expression, he said to me: "That's my brother—have nothing to do with him! He is not an honest man. I shall tell you about many evil actions of which he has been guilty. Farewell!" This was the brother to whom

Beethoven had to forfeit his compositions when he was in the greatest financial need, and who once proudly signed himself "land-owner" in a letter, whereupon the tone poet in his reply signed himself "brain-owner".

In the very early morning of the following day Beethoven, his brow gloomy and contracted, came to see me and complained very bitterly, in disjointed phrases, of the conduct of his brother who was obsessed with filthy avarice, saying that the plague of avarice was continually spreading, so that it was more and more difficult for an honest fellow to keep body and soul together. "Yes, indeed, that's how it is! Oh, you misers! When will you be sated?" He mentioned the names of two men who pollute even the divine art of music because of this plague, and called them "filthy skinflints".

"I must recuperate amid unspoilt nature and cleanse my mind. What are your plans for to-day? Would you like to come with me to-day to visit my unalterable friends, the green shrubs and the aspiring trees, the green hedges and bowers, with their murmuring streams? The vines, too, which on their hills offer their grapes to the sun that engendered them, so that they may grow ripe? Will you, my friend? Here there is no envy or competition or dishonesty. Do come—do come! What a glorious morning! It promises a fine day."

Now at a quick pace we made for the popular *Helenenthal*, the haunt of all classes, where the Emperor himself would divert himself with his noble retinue and where one was often obliged to squeeze past people walking in the opposite direction on a narrow path. On the way he spoke of his great works which, in order to cheer him up, I had expressly chosen to be our topic. I remarked to him what a great effect his symphonies invariably produced in our concert hall, and especially his Pastoral Symphony, the favourite of our London ladies, whose eyes sparkling with pleasure redoubled my own. "Yet it is a marvel to all how a Beethoven can represent the phenomena of nature in tones", adding that the art-lovers delighted by such creations longed for a Tenth Symphony. "Yes, in England, where greatness is still appreciated, compositions of great weight are still suitably performed—so I am told. I must go to London and shall be your guest."

We now passed a newly built palace which, as already mentioned, the Duke of C. had put up here. "Just look at our excellent good taste in choosing the site for a modern palace! The right site for them is at a place where one can see the ruins of some former palace, don't you agree? If only my arm were strong enough to move such buildings to where they belong!"

Now we were approaching a very romantic place. Tall, ancient, splendid trees raised their crests towards the blue sky, dark shrubs drank in the sun's rays and cast them back upon the green carpet of a lawn, on which the denizens of the shrubs hopped about, seeking the nourishment destined for them [*sic*]. One could hear a flowing brook, though invisible, which came cascading down from a height. Here Beethoven sat down on a grassy mound.

"Here, surrounded by the products of Nature, often I sit for hours, while my senses feast upon the spectacle of the conceiving and multiplying children of Nature. Here the majestic sun is not concealed by any dirty roof made by human hands, here the blue sky is my sublime roof. When in the evening I contemplate the sky in wonder and the host of luminous bodies continually revolving within their orbits, suns or earths by name, then my spirit rises beyond these constellations so many millions of miles away to the primal source from which all creation flows and from which new creations shall flow eternally. When, now and again, I endeavour to formulate my seething emotions in music—oh, then I find that I am terribly deceived: I throw my scrawled paper upon the ground and feel firmly convinced that never shall anyone born on this earth be able to express in sounds, words, colours or stone those heavenly images that hover before his excited imagination in his happiest hours."

In the course of this warm effusion he quickly rose from his seat and gazed up at the sun: "Yes, it must come from above, that which strikes the heart; otherwise it's nothing but notes, body without spirit, isn't that so? What is body without spirit?

Earth or muck, isn't it? The spirit must rise from the earth, in which for a time the divine spark is confined, and much like the field to which the ploughman entrusts precious seed, it must flower and bear many fruits, and, thus multiplied, rise again towards the source from which it has flown. For only by persistent toil of the faculties granted to them do created things revere the creator and preserver of infinite Nature. . . ."

Finally Beethoven accompanied me as far as the carriage which was to separate me from him on this side of the grave. After some silent minutes on the high road, near the carriage, which was preparing to leave, he drew a small scroll of paper out of his breast pocket: "Take this paper which is intended to represent my face, as a memento! True, it isn't good and done by a friend who is not a professional artist, a lithograph!" Now he looked at me fixedly, seizing my hand, which I withdrew, formed into a funnel and pressed to his left ear (an aid to communication which he had previously permitted me when in the open air). Now, articulating clearly, I called out the following words: "If in London I should encounter an artist to whom I am capable of expressing that which has left such a deep impression upon my soul, I shall add those details which are still lacking to the best possible portrait of yourself, for the sake of your admirers."

Now he embraced me in a kind of ecstasy, while a funeral procession moved towards us; he avoided it and vanished.

AN ACCOUNT BY KARL CZERNY
(as given to Otto Jahn)

Once the pianist Madame Cibbini remarked to Beethoven that he was the only one who had never written anything feeble or insignificant. "The deuce I haven't!" he replied. "There's a great deal which I'd gladly take back, if I could!"

Once he exclaimed: "They're always talking about my C sharp minor Sonata! Really, I have written better things than that. The F sharp major Sonata, for instance, is a very different matter!"

He could introduce a play on words anywhere. When listening to an overture by Weber, he said: "Hm! There's no doubt about it, it's a fine piece of weaving."[1]

In 1824, I once accompanied Beethoven to a coffee-house, where we found several newspapers on the table. In one of them I found an announcement of Walter Scott's *Life of Napoleon* and drew Beethoven's attention to it. "Napoleon!" he said. "Formerly I disliked him. Now I think quite differently. . . ."

Once Beethoven came across the score of Mozart's six quartets in my house. He opened the first (in A) and said: "That's what I call a work! In it, Mozart was saying: 'Look what I could do if you were ready for it!' " . . .

Once, talking of Schiller, he said to me: "Schiller's works are extremely difficult to set. The composer must be capable of rising far above the poet. Who can do so with Schiller? Now, Goethe is far easier."

When Weber had completed his "Euryanthe" in Vienna, Count Moritz Lichnowsky took the score to Beethoven (already deaf at that time), who said, after looking through it: "Weber has put far too much effort into this. . . ."

About the compositions of Prince Louis Ferdinand he said: "There are some fine tit-bits in them, here and there. . . ."

A CONVERSATION WITH HIS NEPHEW KARL ABOUT KARL'S FRIEND NIEMETZ
(*From the Conversation Books, Baden, Autumn, 1824*)

Beethoven. I am not all satisfied with your choice of a friend. Certainly, poverty deserves our sympathy, but not without exceptions in certain cases. I don't want to be unfair to him, but he strikes me as a Merry Andrew totally devoid both of property and propriety, and these, surely, are necessary attributes of well-bred boys and men.

[1] A pun on the name of Weber ("weaver").

Furthermore I suspect him of having a better understanding with the housekeeper than with myself.

Furthermore I am fond of silence; and this room is too small for a number of persons, as I am continually occupied and he is quite incapable of showing me any consideration.

Your character is still very weak.

Karl. As far as my choice is concerned, I should have thought that four years of intimate acquaintance would suffice to make one familiar with every aspect of a person's character, especially with that of a boy, who could hardly succeed in wearing a mask during all this time.

Beethoven. I think he is coarse and vulgar. Persons of that kind are not fit to be your friends.

Karl. If you think that he is coarse, you are mistaken. At least, I am not aware that he has given you any occasion to think so. Besides, I have no intention of exchanging him for another friend, for this would be a sign of that very weakness of character of which you accuse me, wrongly, I am sure; for among all the inmates at Blöchlinger's[1] I found that no one but he ever helped me to endure my time there, which was often miserable enough, and I should think that I owe him some gratitude at least.

Beethoven. You are not yet capable of discernment.

Karl. It seems useless to quarrel about a matter, especially about a character, concerning which I shall never change my convictions as long as I do not regard myself as a bad character.

I think that the best way to avoid such differences is to keep quiet about them.

I have never thrust him upon you. I did not expect to receive reproaches for something which I have made sufficiently clear

[1] Joseph Blöchlinger was the director of the educational institute in which Karl van Beethoven spent some time as a boarder.

to you. If you did not like him, you could have sent him away at once. He is too proud to beg for alms, nor does he need to do so, and will therefore cease to be a burden to you.

But you needn't quarrel about it. If you keep quiet about it, the matter will never be mentioned again.

I have no cause for further reflection.

TO B. SCHOTT'S SONS

Baden, near Vienna, September 17th, 1824

Honourable Sir,

I write only to inform you that I have not received your letter of August 19th; the reason for this has not yet been discovered. With regard to your last communication, containing the remittance to the house of Fries & Co., rest assured that as soon as I leave this place for Vienna, as I should do not later than the end of this month, I shall immediately attend to the works in question with all possible speed. The quartet, too, should reach you without fail before the middle of October. Overwhelmed with work and in poor health as I am, one must have a little patience with me. I am here for my health, or rather for my ailments, but there is already some improvement. Apollo and the Muses will surely preserve me from Death's clutches for a while; for I still owe them so much and before departing for the Elysian Fields I must leave behind what the spirit dictates to me and commands me to complete. It really seems to me as if I had scarcely written a single note of music. I hope that your exertions on behalf of Art may be crowned with every possible success. For, indeed, it is the Arts and the Sciences that indicate a higher life to us and give us the hope of attaining it. More soon!

In haste, Sir,
Your most devoted
Beethoven

TO HANS GEORG NÄGELI

In addressing your letter, write "in Vienna" as usual.

My very worthy friend,

The Cardinal-Archduke is in Vienna and I am here because of my health; not until yesterday did I receive a letter from him in which he states that he will gladly subscribe for your poems because of your meritorious efforts to encourage the rise of music, and that he is taking six copies. I shall send details of wording later. An anonymous person is also subscribing for them, and I am that person; for as you are doing me the honour of being my panegyrist, surely my name must not appear under any circumstances. How gladly I would have subscribed for several copies, yet my circumstances are too restricted. Father to an adopted son, the child of my deceased brother, I must think and act on his behalf both for the present and the future. I remember that you wrote to me before about subscriptions, but I was very ailing at the time; this sickliness lasted longer than three years, but now I am feeling better. Do not hesitate to send your collected lectures, also, to Archduke Rudolph, dedicate them to him if possible, you will certainly receive a present; true, it will not be a large one, but better than nothing; say some flattering words to him in the preface, for he does understand music, lives and has his being in music. I am really sorry on account of his talent, as I can no longer take as much interest in him as formerly.

From time to time I have made other attempts to find subscribers for you: should I receive any more, I shall let you know at once. I wish that you would also send your lectures to me here, as well as the Mass for five voices by Bach; I shall immediately remit the cost of both from here. Yet by no means think that self-interest has inspired any of my endeavours; I am free from every kind of petty vanity; only divine Art, only in this are the levers that give me strength to sacrifice the best part of my life to the heavenly Muses. Since my childhood it has been my greatest joy and pleasure to be able to work for others; you may, therefore, guess how pleased I am to be of help to you in something and to indicate to you how highly I value your deserts. I embrace you as one of the wise men of Apollo,

Cordially yours,
Beethoven

In the matter of the Archduke, write to me soon, so that I may at once make the necessary arrangements; you need not apply for permission to dedicate the book to him, for we shall, and must, surprise him.

TO B. SCHOTT'S SONS

Vienna, November, 1824

Honourable Sir,

I regret to inform you that it will take me a little longer still to prepare these works.[1] It is true that the copies did not require very much more revision; but as I did not spend the summer here, I must make up for it now by spending two hours daily in giving lessons to His Royal Highness the Archduke Rudolph. This makes such demands on me that I am unfit for almost everything else and, at the same time, I cannot live on my income, which my pen could otherwise supplement. In spite of all this, no consideration is given either to my health or to my precious time. I hope that this condition will not last long, in which case I shall immediately attend to what little remains of the revision and send you the two works without further delay. . . .

Vienna, December 5th,1824

. . . I shall let you have contributions to your journal. On no account mention anything about my lessons to the Cardinal

---

[1] The works in question (Missa Solemnis, Ninth Symphony and Quartet, Op. 127) were not delivered until January, 1825.

Archduke Rudolph in your journal. In the mean time I have tried once more to shake off this yoke in a decent manner. However, there is now a willingness to resort to a kind of authority[1] of which previously one never thought at all but which, it seems, these new times are about to establish. Let us thank God for the expected steam cannons and for the already present use of steamships. What distant swimmers will there be then to give us air and freedom?

FROM LUDWIG RELLSTAB'S "AUS MEINEM LEBEN"

On entering, my first glance fell upon him. He was sitting indolently on a disordered bed near the back wall of his room and seemed to have been lying down just before my arrival. He held Zelter's letter in one hand and extended the other to me in a very friendly manner, with an expression of such goodness and, at the same time, of such suffering in his eyes, that suddenly every barrier of shyness collapsed and I approached the deeply honoured artist with all the warmth of my love for him. He got up, shook hands with me, pressed mine cordially, in the German fashion, and said: "You've brought me a fine letter from Zelter! He is a true patron and protector of genuine art!" Accustomed to take charge of the conversation himself, as it was difficult for him to hear the other person, he continued: "I am not very well, and have been rather ill. You will have difficulty in conversing with me, for I am very hard of hearing."

Beethoven invited me to be seated. He himself sat down on a chair in front of the bed and moved it to a table which, two paces away, was entirely covered with treasures, with notes written in his own hand, with the works that occupied him at that time. I took a chair next to his. I shall cast a quick glance over the room: it is as large as the ante-room, has two windows; beneath them there is a grand piano; otherwise it reveals nothing at all suggestive of comfort, convenience, not to mention splendour or luxury. A writing-desk, a few chairs and

---

[1] A veiled allusion to the Metternich régime.

tables, white walls with old, dusty paper—that is Beethoven's room.

So I was seated at last beside the ailing, melancholic invalid. His hair, almost entirely grey, bushy and untidy, rose from his scalp; it was not smooth, not frizzled, not stiff, but a mixture of all these. At first sight the features did not seem very striking: the face was much smaller than I had imagined from the portraits, all of which are forced into arbitrary representations of wild genius. Nothing expressed that ruggedness, that unfettered tempestuousness which have been lent to his features so as to make them agree with his works. His complexion was brownish in colouring, but not that healthy, sturdy brown which the huntsman acquires, but mingled with a yellowish, sickly hue. The nose narrow, sharp, the mouth benevolent, the eyes small, pale grey, but expressive. Melancholy, suffering and kindness were stamped upon his features; yet, I repeat, not a single sign of hardness, nor of that great boldness which characterizes his spirit, was to be seen in his features, if only in passing. In spite of all this, he lost nothing of that mysterious attraction which draws us so powerfully and irresistibly to the exterior of great men. For the suffering, the grave, silent pain expressed in it was not the result of his present sickness, as I found this expression again and again even weeks later, when Beethoven felt very much better, but the sum of his entire, unique experiences.

When we were seated, Beethoven handed me his slate and a pencil, saying: "You need only write down the main substance of what you wish to say; I can do the rest, for I have been used to this for many years." As he now looked at me questioningly, I took the slate and wished to write down the words: "I asked Zelter to inform you that I wish to write the text of an opera for you." Beethoven followed my hand as I wrote and, quick to guess the rest, retorted when I had written less than half of this: "Zelter tells me so in his letter." Saying so, he passed it to me. Now I read it for the first time and the noble, dignified language, deepest reverence and bare conciseness of expression moved me all the more in the presence of him to whom they were addressed. Beethoven seemed to divine my feelings; for upon him, too, the letter had necessarily made a deep impression, as I could see from the reception he gave to me. He therefore repeated what he had said when he first greeted me: "That is a fine letter. Zelter is a worthy patron of genuine art. Give him my cordial regards when you return! You wish to write an opera for me," he continued, "that would be a great pleasure to me. It is so very difficult to find a good libretto. Grillparzer promised me one, he has already done one, but we can't quite agree: my own ideas are quite different from his. You will find me very troublesome."

I tried to convey to him by gestures that I should regard no labour too difficult, if only I might satisfy him. He nodded kindly to show that he had understood. I took up the slate again and wished to write down: "What kind of dramatic poem would you prefer?" but already at the word "kind" Beethoven resumed the conversation: "The kind would matter little, if only the subject attracted me: but I must be able to set about it with love and intense interest. Operas like 'Don Juan' and 'Figaro' I could not compose: I feel an aversion for them. I could never have chosen such subjects," he continued, "they're too frivolous for me."

. . . Beethoven spoke very frankly, with great intensity. I expressed my regret that during the whole of my sojourn in Vienna I had heard only one symphony by him, no quartet (except the one I had heard privately) nor any other of his compositions at a concert, that his "Fidelio" had not been performed. This gave him occasion to vent his feelings about the taste of the Viennese public. "Ever since the Italians (Barbaja) became firmly established here, all that is best has been pushed aside. The ballet is the principal interest of the aristocracy, as far as the theatre is concerned. One must not speak at all about artistic judgment: their interest is confined to horses and ballerinas. The good period is past. But I do not trouble about it; in future I wish to write only for my own pleasure. If I were well, I should be indifferent to everything else!" In those, and similar words, he expressed his thoughts.

TO DR. BRAUNHOFER

Honoured friend,

Doctor: How are you, patient?

Patient: We are not in a good state, still very weak, belching, etc. I think that in the end we shall need a stronger medicine, but one that does not constipate; I should be able to drink white wine with water! for this mephitic beer can only revolt me. My catarrhal condition has the following symptoms here: I cough up rather a lot of blood, probably only from the wind-pipe; but it does flow out of my nose more often, as was also the case several times this winter. There is no doubt at all, on the other hand, that my stomach has grown terribly weak, indeed, the whole of my system has done so. As far as I know my constitution, I should say that my faculties will scarcely recover unaided.

Doctor: I shall help them.

Patient: It would please me greatly to be able to sit at my writing-desk without too much difficulty. Give this matter your consideration.

Finis.

PS. As soon as I go into town, I shall see you—just tell Karl when I should meet you. But if you could tell Karl himself what I should do now (I took the last medicine only once and have lost it), this would be most agreeable.

With respect and gratitude, your friend

Beethoven

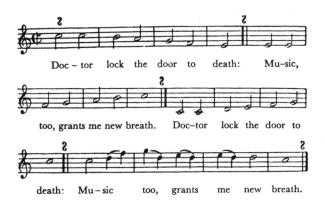

Doc – tor lock the door to death: Mu–sic,

too, grants me new breath. Doc–tor lock the door to

death: Mu – sic too, grants me new breath.

Written in Baden on May 11th, 1825. Helenenthal, by the
second Anton Bridge, towards Siechenfeld.

Beethoven

TO KARL VAN BEETHOVEN

Baden, May 31st, 1825

I intend to go to town on Saturday and to return here by
Sunday evening or Monday morning. I therefore ask you to
inquire at Dr. Bach's at what hour he can usually be seen at
present, also to obtain the key from our honourable brother the
baker, so as to ascertain whether the room owned by that
gentleman, our unbrotherly brother, contains so much furniture that I could spend the night there, whether the linen is
clean, etc. As Thursday is a holiday and you will hardly be
coming here—nor, indeed, do I demand that you should—
you could easily run these few errands for me. Upon my
arrival on Saturday you can tell me about them.

I am not sending you any money; for, if you are in difficulties,
you can borrow 1 fl. in the house. Sobriety is necessary for
young persons and you do not seem to have paid sufficient
attention to it, since you had money of which I did not, and
still do not know where you obtained it. A fine way to act! It

is not advisable to go to the theatre at present, as this would be too distracting, so I believe. The 5 fl. obtained from Dr. Reisser[1] will be paid off monthly without fail—and let that suffice! Spoilt as you are, it would do you no harm to strive after simplicity and truthfulness at last; for my heart has suffered too much by your sly conduct towards me and it is difficult for me to forget. And even if I should bear all this uncomplainingly, liked a yoked ox, your conduct, when directed against others in the same manner, would never win you the love of such persons. God is my witness, I dream only of one thing, to be entirely rid of you and this wretched brother of mine and this abominable family which has been foisted upon me. May God grant my wishes, for never again shall I be capable of suffering on your account.

Unfortunately your father
or rather not
Your father

BEETHOVEN AND A COPYIST
(according to Thayer)

An amusing illustration of how Beethoven could work himself into a rage even when alone is preserved at the Beethoven Museum in Bonn, in the shape of some extraordinary glosses on a letter from a copyist named Wolanek, who was in his employ in the spring of the year (1825). Wolanek was a Bohemian. Beethoven had railed against him whenever sending corrections to a publisher or apologizing for delays, and it is not difficult to imagine what the poor fellow had to endure from the composer's voluble tongue and fecund imagination in the invention and application of epithets. In delivering some manuscripts by messenger some time before Easter, Wolanek ventured a defence of his dignity in a letter which, though couched in polite phrases, was nevertheless decidedly ironical and cutting. He said that he was inclined to overlook Beethoven's conduct

---

[1] Vice-Principal of the Polytechnic where Karl began to study in the summer of 1825.

towards him with a smile; since there were so many dissonances in the ideal world of tones, why not also in the world of reality? For him there was comfort in the reflection that if Beethoven had been copyist to "those celebrated artists, Mozart and Haydn", he would have received similar treatment. He requested that he be not associated with those wretches of copyists who were willing to be treated as slaves simply for the sake of a livelihood, and concluded by saying that nothing that he had done would cause him to blush in the slightest degree in the presence of Beethoven. It did not suffice Beethoven to dismiss the man from his employ; such an outcome seemed anticipated in the letter. He must make him feel that his incompetency was wholly to blame and realize how contemptible he looked in the eyes of the composer. The reference to Mozart and Haydn was particularly galling. Beethoven read the letter and drew lines across its face from corner to corner. Then in letters two inches long he scrawled over the writing the words: "*Dummer, Eingebildeter, Eselhafter Kerl*" ("Stupid, Conceited, Asinine Fellow"). That was not enough. There was a wide margin at the bottom of the sheet, just large enough to hold Beethoven's next ebullition: "Compliments for such a good-for-nothing, who pilfers one's money? —better to pull his asinine ears!" Then he turned the sheet over. A whole page invited him—and he filled it, margin and all. "Dirty Scribbler! Stupid Fellow! Correct the blunders which you have made in your ignorance, insolence, conceit and stupidity—this would be more to the purpose than to try to teach me, which is as if a *Sow* were to try to give lessons to Minerva!" "Do YOU do honour to Mozart and Haydn by never mentioning their names." "It was decided yesterday and even before then *not to have you write any more* for me."

TO H. RAMPEL

The following note to a copyist is reproduced much as Beethoven wrote it, to give the reader some idea of how these letters were actually set out; it will also serve to counterbalance the Wolanek episode.

1825?

Dearest ramperl[1] do come to-morrow morning but the devil take your gracious sir *only God alone can be called gracious.*

I have already engaged the maidservant, only infuse her with honesty & devotion to me likewise with orderliness and punctuality in her little duties a

very devoted *Beethoven*

For H. Rampel copyist by the Danube river.

TO KARL HOLZ

Baden, August 24th, 1825

Dearest Mahogany Wood,[2]

Pens are unknown to us, we crave your indulgence. Your letter made me laugh. Yes, Tobias remains a T——[3], but we'll tobias him yet. Yes, yes, indeed, we must get Castelli[4] to help us. We'll have the thing printed and engraved for the benefit of every poor Tobias. I have just written to Karl, asking him to wait before sending off the letters to Peters and Schlesinger; that is to say, I am waiting to hear from Herr Artaria of Mannheim. I'm indifferent as to which of these hellhounds licks and gnaws at my brain, as one of them must, only we mustn't delay too long before replying. The hellhound in Leipzig[5] can wait and while away the time by conversing with Mephistopheles (the editor of the Leipzig Musical Review) in Auerbach's Cellar, while Beelzebub, the highest of all the devils, will seize the latter by the ears.

[1] The diminutive, used here as a form of endearment.
[2] "Holz" is German for "Wood".   [3] T for *Teufel* (devil)?
[4] Ignaz Franz Castelli (1781–1862), the author of comedies and farces.
[5] Peters.

Dearest Holz, the last quartet[1] contains six movements, too, and with these I intend to conclude this month. If only someone would prescribe something for my bad stomach! My esteemed brother has been a Paternosterian as well. Hi, ha! But, my dear fellow, we must see to it that these new words shall survive even to the third or fourth generation of our posterity. Come on Friday or Sunday. Come on Friday, when that Satan in my kitchen is slightly more tolerable.

Well, look after yourself. A thousand thanks for your devotion and kindness to me. I hope you will not be punished for them.

Yours, with love and friendship,

Beethoven

Do write again soon; or, better still, come yourself.

N'oubliez pas de rendre visite à mon cher Benjamin!

Oh, yes, the Paternoster Mews! And our Director was properly in the soup. It's a good thing to know, even if one doesn't gain anything by knowing.

AN ACCOUNT BY KARL GOTTLIEB FREUDENBERG

. . . Soon after, a stout person of medium height, benevolent in appearance and with a friendly expression in his eyes, came out and beckoned to me to enter his room. Here I was given a seat on the sofa and we spent an hour in pleasant conversation, over a cup of black coffee. The art of music and its disciples, of course, provided the subject for our conversation. I believed that Beethoven would deride Rossini, idolized at the time: not at all, he acknowledged that Rossini was a talented and melodious composer, that his music was suitable for the frivolous, sensual character of the age and that his productivity was such that he needed as many weeks as the Germans needed years to compose an opera. Spontini had many good

[1] String Quartet in B flat major, Op. 130.

points, he was an adept in theatrical effects and the uproar of battle. Spohr was too full of dissonances, and his chromatic melody lost him much of the public's approval. As for Sebastian Bach, Beethoven honoured him greatly: "Not Bach (brook), but Meer (sea) should be his name, because of his infinite, inexhaustible wealth of melodic combinations and harmonies." Bach, he said, was the ideal of all organists. "I, too," Beethoven told me, "played the organ frequently in my youth, but my nerves could not stand up to the power of this gigantic instrument. I should place an organist who is a master of his instrument at the very head of all virtuosi." Beethoven was very much incensed against the organists in Vienna: these posts were filled by favouritism or according to old, traditional observances. Such a post is accorded to those who have given the longest service, and in this way the organ-grinders were the ones who profited most. He criticized the organs with inadequate pedals and, lastly, the exalted and rich of this earth, who will not do anything for art or other good causes, because they know nothing about them. As for my questions about some of his works, for example, why his "Fidelio" was not appreciated everywhere, he answered them in these words: "We Germans have too few singers with a dramatic training which would enable them to sing the part of Leonora; they're too cold and unfeeling, while the Italians sing and act with all their bodies and souls." Beethoven uttered many truths about church music. Pure church music should be performed only by voices, with the exception of a *Gloria* or similar text. For that reason he preferred Palestrina; yet it was nonsense to imitate him without sharing his spirit and religious attitude; also, it might well be impossible for contemporary singers to sing the long-sustained notes purely and clearly. He would not express any opinion about the famous *Miserere* by Allegri, because he had not heard it; many listeners had been enchanted by it, many, too, had been left quite cold. The exemplary artists, to him, were those who combined nature and art in their works.

FROM THE DIARY OF SIR GEORGE SMART

Friday, September 9th (1825)... At twelve I took Ries to the hotel Wildemann,[1] the lodgings of Mr. Schlesinger, the music-seller of Paris, as I understood from Mr. Holz that Beethoven would be there, and there I found him. He received me in the most flattering manner. There was a numerous assembly of professors to hear Beethoven's second new manuscript quartette,[2] bought by Mr. Schlesinger. This quartette is three-quarters of an hour long. They played it twice. The four performers were Schuppanzigh, Holz, Weiss and Lincke. It is most chromatic and there is a slow movement entitled "Praise for the recovery of an invalid". Beethoven intended to allude to himself I suppose for he was very ill during the early part of this year. He directed the performers, and took off his coat, the room being warm and crowded. A staccato passage not being expressed to the satisfaction of his eye, for alas, he could not hear, he seized Holz's violin and played the passage a quarter of a tone too flat. I looked over the score during the performance. All paid him the greatest attention. . . .

Sunday, September 11th. From hence I went alone to Schlesinger's, at the "Wildemann", where was a larger party than the previous one. Among them was l'Abbé Stadler, a fine old man and a good composer of the old school, to whom I was introduced. . . . When I entered Messrs. C. Czerny, Schuppanzigh and Lincke had just begun the Trio, Op. 70, of Beethoven, after which the same performers played Beethoven's Trio, Op. 79, both printed by Steiner. Then followed Beethoven's quartet, the same that I had heard on September the 9th and it was played by the same performers. Beethoven was seated near the pianoforte beating time during the performance of these pieces. This ended, most of the company departed, but Schlesinger invited me to stop and dine with the following company of ten: Beethoven, his nephew, Holz,

[1] The inn *zum Wilden Mann*.
[2] The String Quartet in A minor, Op. 132.

238

Weiss, C. Czerny, who sat at the bottom of the table, Lincke, Jean Sedlatzek—a flute player who is coming to England next year, and has letters to the Duke of Devonshire, Count St. Antonio, etc.—he has been to Italy—Schlesinger, Schuppanzigh, who sat at the top, and myself. Beethoven calls Schuppanzigh Sir John Falstaff, not a bad name considering the figure of this excellent violin player.

We had a most excellent dinner, healths were given in the English style. Beethoven was delightfully gay but hurt that, in the letter Moscheles gave me, his name should be mixed up with the other professors. However he soon got over it. He was much pleased and rather surprised at seeing in the oratorio bill I gave him that the "Mount of Olives" and his "Battle Symphony" were both performed the same evening. He believes —I do not—that the high notes Händel wrote for trumpets were played formerly by one particular man. I gave him the oratorio book and bill. He invited me by his nephew to Baden next Friday. After dinner he was coaxed to play extempore, observing in French to me: "Upon what subject shall I play?" Meanwhile he was touching the instrument thus:

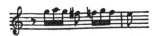

to which I answered, "Upon that". On which theme he played for about twenty minutes in a most extraordinary manner, sometimes very fortissimo, but full of genius. When he arose at the conclusion of his playing he appeared greatly agitated. No one could be more agreeable than he was—plenty of jokes. We all wrote to him by turns, but he can hear a little if you halloo quite close to his left ear. He was very severe in his observations about the Prince Regent never having noticed his present of the score of his "Battle Symphony". . . .

Friday, September 16th. . . . On our return (from the walk) we had dinner at two o'clock. It was a most curious one and so plentiful that dishes came in as we came out, for, unfortunately, we were rather in a hurry to get to the stage coach, it being the only one going to Vienna that evening. I overheard Beethoven say, "We will try how much the Englishman can drink". *He* had the worst of the trial. I gave him my diamond pin as a remembrance of the high gratification I received by the honour of his invitation and kind reception and he wrote me the following droll canon as fast as his pen could write in about two minutes of time as I stood at the door ready to depart.

(*Follows Canon on* "Ars longa vita brevis")

"Written on the 16th of September, 1825, in Baden, when my dear talented musical artist and friend Smart (from England) visited me here.

Ludwig van Beethoven"

TO KARL VAN BEETHOVEN

Baden, September 14th, 1825

Dear Son,

Don't forget to give Tobias the receipt, as well as the money. This Mr. Instructor should have come sooner—but as the matter stands at present you will have to obey him.

Also, I do not want you to visit me on September 14th. It would be better for you to finish these studies. God has never forsaken me. Surely someone will yet be found who may close my eyes for me when I am dead. Altogether, it seems to me that some preconcerted scheme is afoot in everything that has been happening, wherever my honourable brother (pseudo) has had a hand in it. I know, too, that later you will not feel inclined to stay with me. Naturally, for I do things rather too decently. Last Sunday, too, you borrowed another 1 fl. 15 kr. from the housekeeper, this ancient, vulgar baggage. I had already forbidden it. But that's the way with all things. I had made do with the morning coat for two years: true, I have the disgusting habit of putting on an old coat at home. But as for Mr. Karl, why, shame on it! and why? That old money-bag Mr. Ludwig van Beethoven only exists for that purpose. This Sunday, too, you need not come; for with your behaviour we shall never establish true agreement and harmony. Why all this concealment? Later you may become a better man; you need not dissemble, nor lie, which will be better in the end for your moral character. You see, that is how you are reflected in me, for what is the use of all my affectionate admonishments!! They make you angry on top of everything else. Incidentally, have no fear: I shall always provide for you incessantly, as I do now. Such scenes as these you provoke in me—when I found another 1 fl. 15 in the accounts.

Don't use those thin sheets of paper in future, for the housekeeper can read them against the light. I have just received this letter from Leipzig; but it is my opinion that the quartet should not yet be sent.[1] This can be discussed on Sunday. Formerly, three years ago, I demanded only 40 duc. for a quartet. So we must now investigate what was the real price which you mentioned.

Farewell! He who, it is true, did not give you life, but certainly maintained it and, what is more important than everything else, undertook the education of your mind, paternally, more than paternally, now implores you to keep to the only true way of goodness and righteousness. Farewell!

Your faithful, good father

Bring this letter with you on Sunday.

TO KARL VAN BEETHOVEN

Baden, October 5th, *1825*

Dear, beloved son,

I have just received your letter,[2] already full of apprehension and resolved to hasten to Vienna already to-day. Thank God, it is not necessary. Only obey me, and love, like spiritual joy,

---

[1] The String Quartet in B flat, Op. 130.

[2] After receiving the previous letter, Karl had run away and had not been seen for several days: later, he went to stay with his mother and wrote a letter of apology to Beethoven. The above is Beethoven's reply; yet shortly after writing it, he left Baden and returned to Vienna, as he could not endure his anxiety on Karl's account.

coupled with human joy, will always be with us, and you will couple your inner being with the outer one; yet it is better still that the former should have precedence over the latter. *Il fait trop froid.* On Saturday, then, I shall see you. Let me know still whether you are coming in the morning or the afternoon, when I shall hasten to meet you.

A thousand times I embrace you and kiss you, not my prodigal, but my new-born son. I shall write to Schlemmer:[1] don't be offended, I am still too full of apprehension.

My apprehension on your account, my dear, and my care for you, whom I have found again, are the only feelings which your loving father will show you now.

TO KARL VAN BEETHOVEN

Vienna, October, 1825

My dear son,

No more, I beg of you! Only come into my arms! You will not hear a single harsh word. Oh, God, do not seek your own undoing! You will always be received lovingly. Affectionately, we shall discuss all that calls for reflection, all that we must do in the future. My word of honour, there will be no reproaches, as in any case these would be fruitless now! You may expect only the most loving care and support from me. Only come! Come to the faithful heart of your father!

Beethoven

Come home at once upon receiving this letter.

Si Vous ne viendrez pas, Vous me tuerez sûrement.

Lisez la lettre et restez à la maison chez Vous. Venez de m'embrasser, Votre père Vous vraiment adonné. Soyez assuré, que tout cela restera entre nous.

Only, for God's sake, return home to-day! Who knows what dangers lie in wait for you, if you stay. Hurry, hurry!

[1] Karl's landlord.

TO B. SCHOTT'S SONS

Vienna, January 28th, 1826

Honourable Sirs,

In reply to your last letter I inform you that soon you will receive everything adapted for metronome. I beg you not to forget that the first quartet is dedicated to Prince Gallitzin. As far as I know, Matthias Artaria has already received two copies of the overture from you. I should be glad to receive several copies of this, as well as of the quartet. Should I have failed to thank you for the copies already sent to me, this is entirely due to forgetfulness. Also, let me assure you that I never sell a copy or use it in any way profitable to myself: it is simply that I give away copies to a few artists whom I respect, whereby you suffer no loss, as these artists cannot yet acquire these works. . . .

Lately you have been asking for works of mine?

Best of friends,

You have grossly insulted me! You are guilty of several errors! First, therefore, you must purify yourselves before my judge's seat here! As soon as the ice begins to thaw, Mayence will proceed to Vienna! Even the reviewing Chief Judge of Appeals will present himself here in order to justify himself! And so farewell!

We are not at all well disposed towards you! Given, without giving anything, on the heights of Black Spain,[1] on January 28th, 1826.

Beethoven

[1] Beethoven was living in the Schwarzspanierhaus (House of the Black Spaniards) so called because it had been built by Spanish Benedictines.

TO ABBÉ MAXIMILIAN STADLER

February 6th, 1826

Esteemed and venerable Sir,

It was a really good deed on your part to see that justice is done to Mozart's *manes* by writing so exemplary and penetrating an essay on the subject, and both lay and profane, all those who are musical or can in any way be counted among the musical have reason to be grateful to you.

Such gentlemen as Herr W.[1] require either no incentive at all or a very weighty one to raise such matters.

When one considers, too, that, as far as I know, such a gentleman has written a treatise on composition and yet attempts to attribute passages like the following:

to Mozart, and adds such passages as:

A - gnus De - i
pec - ca - ta mundi

and

qui tol - lis pec - ca - ta qui tol - lis pec - ca - ta

Herr W.'s amazing knowledge of harmony and melody reminds us of the late lamented Imperial Composers Sterkel, . . ., Kalkbrenner (the father), André (*nicht der gar Andere*[2]), etc.

Requiescat in pace. Once again, my esteemed friend, I thank you most especially on my own behalf for the pleasure that you

---

[1] Gottfried Weber, who had published an essay questioning the authenticity of Mozart's "Requiem". Abbé Stadler wrote a reply to this essay.
[2] An untranslatable pun.

have given me by sending me your essay. I have always counted myself among the greatest admirers of Mozart and shall remain such till my last breath. Reverend Sir, your blessing soon![1]

Yours, venerable Sir, with the deepest respect,

Beethoven

TO KARL VAN BEETHOVEN

Vienna, August 1st, 1826

Merely because you have at least obeyed me, all is forgiven and forgotten. More about this orally! Quite calm to-day! Do not think that I am dominated by any thought but that of your well-being, and judge me accordingly. Whatever you do, don't take any steps which will make you unhappy and kill me before my time. I could get no sleep until about three o'clock, for I was coughing all night. I embrace you cordially and am convinced that very soon you will cease to misjudge me. It is in this light, too, that I interpret your conduct yesterday. I expect you at one o'clock to-day without fail. Only, do not give me any further cause for sorrow or anxiety. Meanwhile, farewell!

Your true and faithful father

We shall be alone; for that reason I do not wish Holz to come, the more so as I wish that nothing shall transpire about yesterday. Do not fail to come—do not let my poor heart bleed any longer!

---

[1] In connection with this request, which in view of Beethoven's rather questionable orthodoxy seems a little strange, Thayer tells the following anecdote:

"Beethoven and Abbé Stadler once met at Steiner's (one of Beethoven's publishers). About to depart, Beethoven kneeled before the Abbé and said: 'Reverend Sir, give me your blessing.' Stadler, not at all embarrassed, made the sign of the cross over the kneeling man and, as if mumbling a prayer, said: 'Hilft's nix, schadt's nix' ('If it does no good, 'twill do no harm'). Beethoven thereupon kissed his hand amid the laughter of the bystanders."

TO DR. SMETANA

Vienna, Beginning of August, 1826

Most honoured Dr. Smetana,

A great calamity has occurred, accidentally inflicted by Karl upon himself. There is yet hope that he may be saved, especially by you, if only you come soon. Karl has a bullet in his head: how, you will learn in time. Only hurry, for God's sake, hurry!

Respectfully yours,

Beethoven

The urgency of the situation demanded that he should be taken to his mother's, where he is now. The address is enclosed.

TO KARL HOLZ

September 9th, 1826

My very dear friend,

One can see how much effect the better and purer air is having on you, not to mention the women, for it has taken your coating of ice rather less than three days to thaw, as I can see from yesterday's letter to me, for the one of September 7th is like a stockfish. I received it only last night, as I spent yesterday in Nussdorf because of the cooler, more pleasant climate there; I would go to Baden, too, and perhaps I shall be there tomorrow; with regard to the room, I would like to see it first, but I must finish the corrections for his Royal Majesty with all possible speed. Karl is quite intent on the military life, he wrote to me, I saw him too, it would still be better if he could first be accepted by a military institute such as Neustadt; should you be going there with your party, you need only ask Colonel Faber about this: whether the years are counted in the same way there. I don't think so, for there they pay and K. can leave straight away as an officer, for I don't think that it's a good thing to remain a cadet for too long a time, and if we want him to become an officer in this way, we must provide him with money to buy his commission, and add even more to it for his living expenses; nor must he be treated like a convict. Incidentally, I am not at all in favour of the military profession. If they are there, everything will have to go by special mail from now on. I am fatigued, and joy will evade me for a long time, the present expenses, and those that will be required later, worry me, all my hopes are vanishing. I had hoped to enjoy the company of one who might be like me, at least in my good qualities. Enjoy yourself in the open air, empty the cornucopia of all-enchanting Nature, and I hope to see and embrace you on Monday without fail.

As ever, gratefully yours,

Beethoven

FROM GERHARD VON BREUNING'S "AUS DEM SCHWARZSPANIERHAUSE"

After so many removals, the great man was now about to find his last lodgings in the "*Schwarzspanierhaus*", that is, at about Michaelmas, the time often chosen for removals. It was in the period between September 29th and October 12th, 1825, that Beethoven moved into this house on the *Alservorstadt Glacis*. . . .

Orderly as his household soon became, his own room remained as untidy as ever, his papers and possessions dusty and pell-mell, his clothes unbrushed, in spite of the dazzling whiteness and cleanliness of his linen and the frequent ablution of his body. This excessive washing may originally have caused, or at least furthered, the development of his deafness, perhaps through a rheumatic inflammation; more so than his susceptibility to abdominal disorders, which are often regarded as the true cause. It had always been his habit, when he had been seated at his table for a long time while composing and when his head felt hot, to hurry to the wash-basin, to pour jugs of cold water over his heated head and, after having cooled himself in this fashion and only hurriedly dried himself, to return to his work or even to go out for a walk in the mean time. How very hastily this function was performed, so that the flight of his imagination should not be interrupted, and how little care was taken to see that his abundant hair should be properly dried is proved by the circumstance that often, unknown to himself, considerable quantities of the water that had been poured over his head flowed upon the floor, even soaked through the floor, reappeared on the ceiling of the party living below and, at that time, had occasioned disagreeable comments from them, from the caretaker and finally from the owner; indeed, notice had been given for that reason. . . .

On the street, where there was often not time enough to write, conversation with him presented the greatest difficulty, and the following incident gave me striking proof of his complete deafness, if the latter had required such proof. Once he was expected to lunch at our house; it was already nearly two o'clock (our meal time). My parents, constantly suspecting that, engrossed in composition, he might be oblivious of time, sent me over to his lodgings to fetch him. I found him at his writing-desk, his face turned towards the open door that led to his music-room, working at one of the last (Gallitzin) quartets. Looking up briefly, he asked me to wait a little, until he had put his last idea on paper. I kept quiet for a while, then I moved my chair up to the Graf piano (with its superstructure of sounding-boards) and, not convinced of Beethoven's deafness to musical sounds, began to strum softly on the keys. I frequently looked at him to see whether he felt disturbed by my playing. However, when I observed that he was not even aware of my playing, I struck the keys with greater force on purpose, until I played quite loudly; there was no longer any doubt: he could not hear me at all, but continued to write undismayed, until, finished at last, he invited me to go. In the street he asked me a question: I shouted the reply into his ear; but it was rather my signs that he understood. Only, once at table my sister uttered a high-pitched, piercing cry and he was so happy to have heard this that he laughed loudly and joyfully, so that his dazzling white, perfectly preserved teeth could be seen.

Another of his characteristics was the liveliness with which he discussed matters of interest to him, on which occasions it sometimes happened that, walking up and down the room with my father, he would spit into the mirror without knowing it, instead of out of the window, as was his habit. . . .

On September 24th, 1826, my name-day, Beethoven was once again our guest at table, as well as my private tutor, Waniek. Before lunch Beethoven showed us the gold medal he had received from Louis XVIII. During the meal he told us that the Vienna Magistracy had nominated him a citizen of Vienna, on which occasion someone had remarked to him that he had become not a real citizen, but an honorary one, whereupon he had replied: "I never knew that one could also be nominated an infamous citizen of Vienna."

In the afternoon we all walked to Schönbrunn. My mother had to pay a visit at Meidling (adjacent to Schönbrunn). I accompanied her. My father, Beethoven and my tutor awaited us on the lower terrace of the Schönbrunn gardens, on one of the seats. When, after this, we went for a walk in the gardens, Beethoven pointing at the shrubs clipped in the French manner to look like walls, said: "All artifice, docked like those old farthingales. I only feel well when I'm surrounded by wild scenery." An infantry soldier passed by. Immediately he came out with the sarcastic remark: "A slave, who has sold his liberty for five kreutzers a day."

On our way home, several small boys were playing at skittles with a small ball on the right-hand avenue in front of the Schönbrunn bridge, and this ball accidentally struck Beethoven's foot. Thinking that this had been done on purpose to annoy him, he at once turned to them, crying out angrily: "Who gave you permission to play here? Do you have to choose this of all places for your noisome games?" and was about to rush at them and drive them away. My father, fearing the rudeness of these guttersnipes, soon calmed him.

TO TOBIAS HASLINGER

Best of all the To - bi - ases!

Best of all the To - bi - a - - - - - - ses!

We write to you here from the castle[1] of our *Signore Fratello.*
I must trouble you again in politely requesting you to post the
two enclosed letters at once.

Beginning with the piano school, I shall repay you for all the
expenses which I have occasioned you as soon as I return to
Vienna. The fine weather and the fact that I could not go to
the country all last summer are my reasons for prolonging my
stay here. The quartet[2] for Schlesinger is already finished;
only I do not yet know which is the safest way of sending it to
him, so perhaps you will be good enough to deliver it to
Tendler & Manstein[3] and also to receive the money for it.
Probably Schlesinger will not sign an order for gold: if you can
persuade him to do so, I shall be much obliged to you, as all
publishers pay me in gold. Meanwhile, dear Tobiasserl,[4] we
need money; for it is not quite the same thing to have money
and to have none.

If you should happen to meet Holz, put the peg in a different

[1] A facetious reference to his brother's estate at Gneixendorf, near Krems, where
Beethoven spent the autumn months with his nephew Karl.
[2] The quartet in F major, Op. 135, which was published by Schlesinger.
[3] A firm of bankers in Vienna.
[4] The diminutive, used as a form of endearment.

hole.[1] It is horribly afflicted with amorous inebriation; it has become almost inflamed with it, so that somebody wrote in jest that Holz is a son of the late Papageno.

Wholly amazing, unique, most admirable of all Tobiases, farewell! If it is not disagreeable to you, do write a line to me here. Is Dr. Spiker[2] still in Vienna?

With the most reverential reverence and fidelity, yours,

Beethoven

TO FRANZ WEGELER

Vienna, December 7th, 1826

My dear old friend,

I cannot express the pleasure that your and Lorchen's letter gave me. Certainly, a reply should have followed it at lightning speed: but I am generally somewhat remiss in my correspondence, because I think that the better people know me well enough in any case. Often I write the answer in my head; yet when I want to set it down I usually throw away my pen, because I am not capable of writing exactly what I feel. I remember all the kindness that you have always shown me, for example how you had my room distempered and gave me such a pleasant surprise: the same applies to the Breuning family. If we have drifted apart, this is due to the devious way of all things: each one of us must endeavour to pursue and fulfil the purpose of his own destiny. Nevertheless, the eternal, solid and unshakable principles of virtue have always remained a strong tie between us.

Unfortunately I cannot write to you to-day as fully as I should wish, as I am confined to bed, and must limit myself to answering some of the points in your letter. You tell me that somewhere I have been described as a natural son of the late King of Prussia: this had already been mentioned to me some

[1] Another weak pun on the name of Holz (wood); "the peg" refers to Holz, who had just got married.

[2] Samuel Heinrich Spiker (1786–1858) had come to Vienna from Berlin to acquire the manuscript of the Ninth Symphony for the library of Frederick William, King of Prussia.

time ago. However, I have made it one of my principles never to write anything about myself, nor even to reply to anything that has been written about me. I therefore gladly leave it to you to acquaint the world with the unsullied honour of my parents, and more especially of my mother. You write about your son. It goes without saying that, should he come here, I shall be a friend and a father to him, and wherever I am capable of helping him or being of service to him, I shall do so with pleasure.

Your Lorchen's silhouette is still in my possession, by which you can see how dear to me still is everything that dates from my youth.

As for my honours and awards, I shall only tell you briefly that I have been made an honorary member of the Royal Society of the Arts and Sciences in Sweden, also in Amsterdam, and that I have received the freedom of the city of Vienna.

Recently a certain Dr. Spiker took away my last grand symphony with chorus to Berlin: it is dedicated to the King, and I had to write the dedication in person. Some time previously I had applied at the embassy for permission to dedicate this work to the King, who granted it. At Dr. Spiker's request, I had to hand him the work myself, in manuscript and with my own corrections on it, to be delivered to the King, as it is intended for the royal library. In this connection I heard something about the Red Order of the Eagle, second class; I don't know what will come of this;[1] for I have never sought distinctions of this kind. Yet for various reasons this one would not be unwelcome to me in these times. Incidentally, I still adhere to the motto: *Nulla dies sine linea*, and if I let the Muse sleep, it is only so that she may be all the stronger when she awakes. I hope to give birth to a few more great works and then to conclude my earthly course among good people, like a child grown old in years. . . .

[1] Beethoven did not receive this award but, to his great disappointment, the King sent him a diamond ring instead; what is more, the diamond was not genuine; it is believed that the genuine one was stolen on the way and a false one substituted. Beethoven sold the ring for 300 florins.

When we entered, the poor man lay on his sick-bed, gravely ill with dropsy. He looked at me with wide and shining eyes, then, with a smile, extended his left hand to me and said: "So that's little Louis, and even engaged to be married now?" Thereupon he nodded to Nanny and said: "A pretty couple and, as I've heard and read, a pair of fine artists. Well, how is your dear mother?" He handed us paper and pencil; we conducted the ensuing conversation in writing, while he spoke at times, but rather unintelligibly. Then he asked us to sing something for him. Schindler sat down at one of the two grand pianos which stood close together in the centre of the room, and we stood facing Beethoven. I wrote down for him that I should sing his "Adelaide", which had really established my reputation as a singer. Beethoven nodded kindly. Yet when I was about to sing, my throat and gums had grown so dry with apprehension that it was impossible for me to sing. I asked Schindler to wait a few moments, while I collected myself. Beethoven asked what was going on, why I was not singing and laughed out loud when Schindler wrote down the reason for him. Then he said: "Do go ahead and sing, dear Louis! For, as you know, unhappily I can't hear anything, I only wish to see you sing." At last I plucked up courage and, with genuine emotion, sang the song of all songs, Beethoven's divine "Adelaide". When I had finished, Beethoven beckoned me over to his bed and, cordially pressing my hand, said: "I could see from your breathing that you sang correctly and I could read in your eyes that you feel what you are singing. You have given me great pleasure." I was overjoyed at the great man's judgment and had to dry a tear. When I wished to kiss his hand, he withdrew it quickly and said: "Do this to your good mother and give her my regards repeatedly and tell her what a great pleasure it was for me that she still remembers me and sent me little Louis."

Now Nanny sang the great aria by Leonora from "Fidelio", and with such feeling that Beethoven often beat time to her singing and seemed to devour her with his wide eyes. After the aria Beethoven kept his eyes covered with his hands for some time, then he said: "I am sure that you are a masterly singer and that you possess a voice which may well recall that of Milder, who, however, did not command such depth of feeling as I read distinctly on your face. What a great pity that I cannot——" Probably he wished to say "hear you", but he broke off and said :"I thank you, *Fräulein*, for this fine hour, and may you be very happy together!" Nanny also was deeply moved and pressed his hand to her heart. There was a little pause; then Beethoven said: "I do feel rather unwell."

We prepared to leave, but not without writing down our thanks with an apology for disturbing his rest and the wish that God might soon restore him to perfect health. To this Beethoven replied with a smile: "Then I shall write an opera for you both. Do convey all my good wishes to your father and to your dear little mother, and should I get well again I shall ask Schindler to fetch you. Adieu, my dear little Louis, and adieu, my dear Fidelio!" He pressed our hands again, gazed at us sorrowfully, but kindly, and finally turned his head to the wall.

TO B. SCHOTT'S SONS

Vienna, end of December, 1826

. . . The metronome marks will follow soon: do not fail to wait for them. In our century things of this kind are certainly needed. Also I learn from letters written by friends in Berlin that the first performance of the symphony received enthusiastic applause, which I ascribe mainly to the use of a metronome. It is almost impossible now to preserve the *tempi ordinari*; instead, the performers must now obey the ideas of unfettered genius. . . .

FROM ANTON SCHINDLER'S BIOGRAPHY OF BEETHOVEN

I submitted to him a collection of Schubert's songs and ballads, about 60 in number, and among them many that were still in manuscript at the time. I did so with the intention not only of providing him with an agreeable diversion, but also of giving him an opportunity to acquaint himself with the essential character of Schubert's works, so that he might receive a favourable impression of Schubert's talent, upon which doubt had been cast by those inwardly exalted persons who probably treated other contemporaries much in the same manner. The great Master, who previously had not known five songs by Schubert, was amazed by the number now shown to him and would not believe that up to that time (February, 1827) Schubert had already composed more than five hundred songs. But if the number amazed him, he began to marvel when he acquainted himself with their content. For several days he could not bear to part with them, and daily he spent hours in studying "*Iphigenias Monolog*", "*Grenzen der Menschheit*", "*Die Allmacht*", "*Die Junge Nonne*", "*Die Viola*", the Müller songs and many others. Repeatedly he exclaimed, full of joyous enthusiasm: "Truly, this Schubert is lit by a divine spark." "If I had seen this poem, I should have set it too!", and so forth in the same manner with most of these poems, whose subjects, contents and original treatment on Schubert's part he could not praise enough. Likewise, he could scarcely understand how Schubert had had sufficient leisure "to tackle such long poems, many of which contain ten others", as he expressed it.

FROM GERHARD VON BREUNING'S "AUS DEM SCHWARZSPANIERHAUSE"

. . . During his illness (mid-February, 1827) one morning Händel's complete works, in a fine quarto edition, bound, came to him as a present from the harp virtuoso Stumpff. He had long harboured the wish to possess these and the present had been made in order to fulfil this very wish. When I entered his room at noon as usual, he at once pointed out these works, piled up on the piano, while his eyes glowed with joy. "Look, these were given to me to-day. These works have given me great pleasure. For a long time I've been wishing to have them; for Händel is the greatest, the most capable of composers; there is still much to be learned from him. Just hand me those books again!" He continued to speak in this manner about the present, pleasantly excited. And now I began to hand them to him in his bed, one by one; he turned over the pages of one after the other, as I gave them to him, occasionally paused to ponder on some passage or other and immediately put down each volume on the right-hand side of his bed, next to the wall, until at last they all stood piled up there and remained thus for some hours; for I found them there when I returned in the afternoon. And again he began to pour out the most fervent encomiums of Händel, calling him the most classical and the most thorough of all tone poets.

Once I found him asleep, as was frequently the case. I would then sit down beside his bed, keeping quiet, so as not to rouse him from a sleep which, we hoped, might strengthen him, while I turned over and skimmed the conversation books which still lay on his little bedside table for the use of visitors, so as to find out who had been with him in the mean time and what had been discussed. There, among others, I found the following passage: "Your quartet played yesterday by Schuppanzigh was not well received." When, after a short time he awoke, I confronted him with this passage, asking him what he thought about it. "They'll like it one day!" was the laconic reply, to which he added, among other remarks to the effect that he wrote what he thought best and would not allow himself to be distracted by the judgments of his contemporaries. "I know that I'm an artist!"

. . . And further he said to me: "I wanted to write many other works. Now the Tenth Symphony, a requiem, too, I intended to compose, and the music to 'Faust'; even a piano school.

But this would have been quite different from the existing ones. Well, now I shall not be able to do any of these things, and altogether, as long as I'm ill I shall do no work, much as Diabelli and Haslinger press me to do so; for I must feel in the mood for it. Often I was unable to compose for a long time; then suddenly it comes back again."

A CONVERSATION WITH GERHARD VON BREUNING
(*from the Conversation Books, January, 1827*)

NOTE. *Generally, the authentic but one-sided material contained in the Conversation Books has not been included in this volume. An exception is made in this case, because there is no better account of Beethoven's last illness than the questions and remarks of Breuning, a boy of thirteen at the time; he had been granted the rare privilege of addressing Beethoven by the familiar "Du" and, in every respect, could be more candid in his dealings with Beethoven than any adult.*

G. v. Breuning:

How are you feeling?

I don't cough, except when I run up the stairs.

Has your belly grown smaller?

You should perspire more. All the time.

Who has just written this down?

I'm allowed to eat meat to-day.

How do you feel after the enema? You should have more of them.

Are you finished with Walter Scott?

Would you like to read Schiller perhaps?

Would you like "The History of the World" by Schröckh? Perhaps you'd like the travel book by Sommer. I'll show it to you to-morrow.

That's why she's so fond of gossiping. (The housekeeper.)

It would be better for you to have a manservant.

Do you still need this music?

If you don't need it any more, give it to me, I'd like to keep it.

257

Now I must go, I'll certainly come back to-morrow with the Sommer.

It is to be bought to-morrow.

It must be plums.

You and Father should both spend the summer at a spa.

Father will probably go to Baden—to Pischtien. (Pistyan in Hungary.)

Father says I write so badly; is that true?

That's the least important thing of all, if only you were well.

I do have great hopes for you before the summer.

Your system hasn't been at all weakened generally.

Does your belly still ache?

If there's no bandage on it, the wound will become inflamed.

You are getting another blanket.

My teacher, too, is going to the *Concert spirituel*.

I didn't know that.

To-night we're going to the Leopoldstadt Theatre; I don't know whether Father is going too, for he doesn't know himself.

I heard to-day that you're so plagued and disturbed by bugs that you wake up every moment; as sleep is good for you now, I'll bring you something to keep off the bugs.

You'll get the bolster to-morrow.

Was the operation carried out successfully?

The stove is very hot.

Is the operation painful?

Father, too, arrived in the middle of the first act, he laughed heartily.

To-day we are having people to lunch, the two Neustädters are coming, he and she and the three sons, and then the wife of Captain Gebauer.

But as a doctor he ought to ask you.

Wolfmayer[1] likes you very much; when he went away he said with tears in his eyes: Oh, the great man, the pity of it!

He asked whether you still have enough wine.

Did you like your lunch to-day?

[1] Johann Nepomuk Wolfmayer, a Viennese draper.

But here I must object that the *Schinkennudeln* (ham noodles) could not have been good, when you buy so little ham, they give you a bad piece, because then the people don't pay so much attention to it.

That's happened many times to Mother, too, that something quite different from what she had ordered was put on the table.

Schindler happened to say that he doesn't like *Schinkennudeln*.

Don't be angry about it; let's talk about something different.

No one can stand Holz; for everyone who knows him says he's treacherous. He pretends that he likes you ever so much.

He's very good at deceiving.

He can lie like a book.

You're the best of them all, all the others are scoundrels.

If you weren't so kind-hearted, you'd have the right to ask him to pay for his board.

He likes your wine best of all.

TO JOHANN ANDREAS STUMPFF

Vienna, February 8th, 1827

Most worthy friend,

My pen cannot describe the pleasure that you have given me by sending the works of Händel, by going so far as to make me a present of them (truly a royal present for me!). It has even been put into the newspaper here, and I enclose the cutting. Unhappily, for the last three months and until now I have been down with the dropsy. You can imagine the effect of this upon my circumstances! Usually I live only on the income derived from the products of my mind and depend upon them for everything that I need for myself and for my Karl. Unhappily, for the last three months and a half I have not been able to write a single note.

My salary amounts only to so much that it enables me to pay my half-yearly rent; after this I am left with a few hundred guilders in Viennese currency. Now consider also that the end of my illness cannot yet be determined and, lastly, that it will not be possible for me immediately afterwards to sail through the air on Pegasus with all my sails spread. Physician, surgeon, chemist, everything must be paid.

I remember quite well that several years ago the Philharmonic Society wished to give a concert for my benefit. It would be a great good fortune for me if they could now renew this intention: I might well be saved, after all, from all the embarrassments that await me. I am therefore writing to Herr Smart and if you, dear friend, can do anything to this end, I beg you to make common cause with Herr Smart. Moscheles, too, will be approached in this matter, and I do believe that with the united efforts of all my friends it should be possible to do something for me in this matter.

With regard to the works of Händel for His Imperial Highness Archduke Rudolph, I cannot yet tell you anything with certainty. I shall, however, write to him within the next few days and draw his attention to it.

While I thank you once again for your splendid present, I beg you now to command me: wherever I can be of service to you here, I shall be heartily glad to oblige you. Once more I appeal to your philanthropic heart in view of my position, as described in this letter, and, wishing you all that is fine and good, I send you my best regards.

With high esteem,

Your

Beethoven

TO B. SCHOTT'S SONS

Vienna, February 22nd, 1827

. . . Yet now I come to you with an important request. My physician ordered me to drink some very good, old hock. Here it is impossible to obtain anything of the kind, unadulterated, even at the greatest cost. If, therefore, I were to receive a small number of bottles, I should show you my gratitude by sending you something for your *Cäcilia*.[1] Something would be done for me at the customs, I believe, so that the transport would not cost me so much. As soon as I have sufficient strength, you will receive the Mass marked for metronome; for I am just in the period when the fourth operation is about to be performed. The sooner I receive this Rhine or Moselle wine, then, the more beneficial its effect can be in my present condition, and I beg you most cordially for this favour, for which I shall be gratefully obliged to you.

TO B. SCHOTT'S SONS

Vienna, March 1st, 1827

. . . I now repeat my request in my last letter, that is, my request for old, white Rhine or Moselle wine. Here it is infinitely difficult to obtain anything of the kind, pure and unadulterated, even at the greatest cost. Some days ago, on February 27th, I had my fourth operation, and still my complete improvement and recovery are not yet in sight. Pity your devoted and respectful friend,

Beethoven m.p.

NOTE. *These bottles of wine (Rüdesheimer Berg, 1806) arrived two days before Beethoven's death.*

FROM FERDINAND HILLER'S REMINISCENCES[2]

At first the conversation, as usual, touched upon the matter of lodgings, my journey and sojourn,[3] my relationship to Hummel and other things of the same kind. Beethoven enquired after Goethe's state of health with extraordinary concern and we were able to give a most favourable report. Indeed, only a few days previously the great poet had graced my album

[1] See footnote 1, p. 214.
[2] *Aus dem Tonleben unserer Zeit*, 1871.
[3] In Vienna.

261

with a few friendly verses which alluded to my journey. Beethoven complained bitterly about his own state of health. "Now I've been lying here for no less than four months!" he exclaimed; "one loses patience in the end!" In other respects, too, there was much that displeased him in Vienna and he made the most caustic comments upon "artistic taste in our time" and upon "the dilettantism which ruins everything in this place". Nor did he spare the Government, right up to the highest level. "Write a book of penitential songs and dedicate it to the Empress!" he said to Hummel, laughing grimly, but the latter did not make use of this advice.

. . . The Master continued to indulge in his wistful, yet passionate effusions without reticence. Partly, they concerned his nephew, of whom he was very fond, who, as was well known, had caused him a great deal of trouble and at that time had run foul of the authorities because of some trifle (so, at least, it seemed to Beethoven). "They hang the little thieves and let the big ones go", he called out peevishly. Enquiring about my studies and cheering up a little, he said: "Art must be propagated perpetually", and when I spoke of the exclusive interest claimed by the Italian Opera in Vienna at that time, he broke out into the memorable words: "They say: *vox populi, vox dei*— I have never believed in this."

On March 13th, Hummel took me to see Beethoven for the second time. We found that his condition had deteriorated considerably. He lay in his bed, seemed to be suffering great pain and at times uttered a deep groan; nevertheless, he spoke freely and vigorously. He seemed to be deeply concerned with his failure to enter the married state. Already during our first visit he joked about this with Hummel, whose wife he had known as a young and beautiful girl. This time he said to him, smiling: "You are a lucky fellow: you have a wife, she looks after you, she is in love with you—but I'm a poor bachelor!"—and he sighed deeply. Also, he begged Hummel to bring his wife, who had been unwilling to face in his present state a man whom she had known at the height of his powers. A short time before our visit, Beethoven had been given a picture of the house in which Haydn was born; he kept it near his bed and showed it to us. "It gave me an almost childish pleasure," he said, "the cradle of such a great man!"

Shortly after our second visit it became common knowledge that the Philharmonic Society in London had sent Beethoven the sum of a hundred pounds sterling, to alleviate his illness. It was added that this surprise had made such an impression upon the poor great man that even physically he felt a good deal better. When we stood beside his bed once more on the 20th, it was certainly clear from his remarks how greatly this attention had pleased him; but he was extremely weak and spoke only softly, in clipped sentences. "I rather think I shall soon be setting out on the upward journey", he whispered after our greeting. Similar exclamations occurred frequently; but, in between, he spoke of his plans and hopes, neither of which, unfortunately, were to be realized. Speaking of the noble conduct of the Philharmonic Society and praising the English, he said that it was his intention to leave for England as soon as his condition had improved. "I wish to compose a grand overture and a grand symphony for them." And then, too, he wished to visit Frau Hummel (who had come with her husband) and go to Heaven knows how many different places. It did not occur to us to write down anything for him. His eyes, which during our last visit had still been quite lively, were now drooping and only with difficulty could he sit up from time to time. We could no longer deceive ourselves: the worst was to be feared.

FROM ANTON SCHINDLER'S BIOGRAPHY

Towards the middle of March Hummel arrived in Vienna. Already on the following day he appeared at Beethoven's sickbed in the company of Andreas Streicher and of his pupil Ferdinand Hiller. The two artists had not met since 1814. Hummel, appalled at the sight of Beethoven in his sufferings, burst into tears; but Beethoven endeavoured to comfort him by showing him an engraving of the house in Rohrau in which

Haydn was born (it had been sent to him by Diabelli) with the words: "Look, dear Hummel, the house where Haydn was born; I was given it to-day, it gives me great pleasure; a wretched peasant hovel, in which such a great man was born!" Soon, however, he led the conversation to the concert in the Josephstadt Theatre which had been legally decreed, and his intention, now thwarted, to take part in it, concluding with the words: "Hummel, I count upon you, take my place in it, I shall be grateful to you." Hummel gave him his hand and Beethoven was visibly astonished at this readiness to oblige him. Indeed, considering the lack of sympathy which had previously marked the relationship between these two distinguished artists, this moment was an edifying one, worthy, in itself, of being recorded, even if no other circumstances had been connected with it.

Already a few days after this incident we conducted the great tone poet to his last resting-place, on which occasion Hummel was one of the pall-bearers. He fulfilled his promise faithfully on April 7th of that year.

TO IGNAZ MOSCHELES

Vienna, March 14th, 1827

My dear, good Moscheles,

I discovered lately from Herr Lewinger that in a letter of February 10th you asked him for news of my illness, about which such diverse rumours are current. Although I do not doubt at all that by now my letter of February 22nd has reached you safely, and that this letter will inform you of everything that you wish to know, I cannot refrain from thanking you heartily for your concern with my sad fate and from entreating you once more to give most serious consideration to my request,[1] which you know from my first letter—and I am almost certain in advance that, in unison with Sir Smart [*sic*]

[1] Beethoven's appeal for money. It should be mentioned that Beethoven still possessed securities to the value of 7000 guilders; but in order to be able to leave these to his nephew, he pretended that he was destitute.

Herr Neate and other friends of mine you will certainly succeed in obtaining a result favourable to me with the Philharmonic Society. Since this letter I have also written once more to Sir Smart, as I found his address by chance, and have once again reminded him of my request.

On February 27th I was operated upon for the fourth time, and already there are visible signs that soon I must expect my fifth. Where does all this lead to and what is to become of me, if things continue in this way for some time? Truly, a very hard lot has fallen to me! Yet I am resigned to what Fate has ordained and only implore God continually that in His divine justice He may see to it that, as long as I must suffer life in death on this earth, I may be preserved from want. This would give me sufficient strength to endure my lot, hard as it is, with resignation to the will of the Most High.

So, my dear Moscheles, once again I recommend my affairs to you and, with high esteem, remain as ever

Your friend,
Beethoven

Hummel is here and has already paid me several visits.

TO BARON JOHANN BAPTIST PASQUALATI

Vienna, the middle of March, 1827

Honoured friend,

How can I thank you enough for the glorious champagne! How greatly it has refreshed me and will continue to refresh me! To-day I need nothing and thank you for everything. I beg you to note whatever other results you wish to obtain with regard to the wines; I would gladly repay you myself as far as my means permit. I can write nothing more for to-day. May Heaven bless you generally and for your affectionate concern

With your respectful,
suffering Beethoven

TO IGNAZ MOSCHELES

Vienna, March 18th, 1827

My dear, good Moscheles,

I cannot describe the emotions with which I read your letter of March 1st. The generosity with which the Philharmonic Society almost forestalled my request has moved me to the very depths of my soul. I therefore beg you, dear Moscheles, to be the medium by which I may convey to the Philharmonic Society my heartfelt gratitude for their very special concern and assistance.

I found myself compelled to avail myself at once of the sum of 1000 fl. Convention Coin, for I was in the unpleasant position of being about to accept money which would have precipitated me into new embarrassments.

With regard to the concert which the Philharmonic Society has resolved to give for me, I beg the Society not to abandon this project on any account and to deduct these 1000 fl. Convention Coin, which they were kind enough to advance to me, from the proceeds of this concert. And should the Society be kind enough to remit the remainder to me, I guarantee to show the Society my most cordial gratitude by agreeing to write for them either a new symphony, a sketch of which is already lying in my desk, or a new overture or anything else which the Society may desire. May Heaven only restore my health to me soon, and I shall show the generous English how well I appreciate their concern with my sad fate.

Your noble conduct will remain unforgettable to me, and likewise I shall soon express my belated thanks especially to Sir Smart and Herr Stumpff.

Farewell! With the most friendly sentiments I remain

Your

Highly respectful friend,

Ludwig van Beethoven

My kindest regards to your honoured wife! In Herr Rau I owe a new friend to you and the Philharmonic Society.

(I beg you to deliver the symphony annotated for metronome to the Philharmonic Society. The marks are enclosed.)

March 24th, 1827

... His letter to you, with the exception of a few words at the beginning, was dictated by him word by word and will probably be the last of his life, although even to-day he whispered to me the incoherent words, "Smart—Stumpff—write". Should he be capable of so much as putting his name on paper, even this will yet be accomplished. He feels that his end is approaching, for yesterday he said to me and to Herr von Breuning: "*Plaudite amici! Comoedia finita est!*" Also we were fortunate enough yesterday to settle the matter of his will, although there is nothing here but a few pieces of old furniture and manuscripts. He was at work upon a quintet for strings and the Tenth Symphony, which is mentioned in his letter to you. Two movements of the quintet are quite finished. It was intended for Diabelli. For some days after receiving your letter he was most excited and spoke to me at length about his plans for a symphony which must now be all the more grand in conception as he would be writing it for the Philharmonic Society.

FROM GRILLPARZER'S "RECOLLECTIONS OF BEETHOVEN"

I saw him only once more, but cannot remember where. At that time he said to me: "Your opera is finished." I cannot say whether he meant: finished in my head, or whether those countless notebooks of his—in which he used to jot down isolated thoughts and passages for future use, in a manner intelligible only to himself—did perhaps contain the elements of this opera in the form of fragments. What is certain is that after his death not a single note of it was found, nor anything that could have been unquestionably related to our collaboration. Yet I remained true to my resolution never to remind him of it even in the most delicate manner and—as our written conversations were troublesome to me—never approached him again until, in a black suit and a burning torch in my hand, I walked behind his coffin.

Two days earlier, Schindler came to see me in the evening with the news that Beethoven was dying and that his friends wished me to prepare an oration which the actor Anschütz would deliver at his grave. I was all the more shattered as I had scarcely known that he was ill, yet I endeavoured to collect my thoughts and on the following morning began to write the oration. I had got to the second half when Schindler entered once more to fetch what he had ordered, for Beethoven had just died. At that moment there was a terrible commotion within me, tears poured from my eyes and—as was usually the case when I was overwhelmed by genuine emotion—I could not complete the oration as weightily as I had begun it. Incidentally, it was delivered, the funeral guests departed with awed emotion and Beethoven was no longer among us!

To be honest, I must say that I loved Beethoven. If I can recall very little of what he said to me, the main reason is that in the case of an artist I am not interested in what he says, but in what he does. If the value of art could be assessed by the amount of talk to which it gives rise, Germany at present would be just as full of artists as it is in fact lacking in them. Indeed, the creative faculty profits only from the kind of thought, already implied by talent, which is, as it were, bound, which expresses itself instinctively and is the source of life and of individual truth. The wider the circle, the more difficult its completion. The greater the mass (of material), the more difficult it is to give life to it. When Goethe knew very little as yet, he wrote the first part of *Faust*; when the whole realm of what is worth knowing was at his disposal, he wrote the second part. Of specific matters touched upon by Beethoven, I can only recall that he had a very high opinion of Schiller, that he considered the lot of poets happier than that of musicians, because they had a wider field of activity; lastly, that Weber's "Euryanthe", which was new at the time and displeased me, seemed to have impressed him no more favourably than it

268

impressed me. Yet, generally speaking, it may well have been Weber's success that inspired him with the wish to write another opera himself. But he had so accustomed himself to the unfettered flight of his imagination that no libretto in the world would have been capable of containing his effusions within the necessary bounds. He searched and searched and found none, because there was none that he could have used. . . .

FROM GRILLPARZER'S ORATION AT BEETHOVEN'S FUNERAL, March 29th, 1827

As we stand here at the grave of this departed, we are, as it were, the representatives of a whole nation, of the entire German people, mourning the fall of the one highly celebrated half of what remained to us of the vanished splendour of native art, the flower of our country's spirit. True, the hero of poetry in the German language[1] is with us still—and long may he remain with us! But the last Master of resounding song, the sweet lips that gave expression to the art of tones, the heir and successor of Händel's and Bach's, of Haydn's and Mozart's immortal fame, has ended his life, and we stand weeping beside the tattered strings of the silent instrument.

Of the silent instrument! Let me call him so! For he was an artist, and all that he was he became only by virtue of his art. The thorns of life had wounded him deeply, and as the ship-wrecked cling to the shore, so he fled into thy arms, glorious sister alike of goodness and truth, consoler of the suffering, Art, whose origins are above. He held fast to thee, and even when the gate was closed through which thou hadst entered into him and hadst spoken to him, when he had grown blind to thy features because of his deaf ears, still he bore thy image in his heart, and when he died still it lay upon his breast.

He was an artist, and who can bear comparison with him?

As Behemoth rushes, tempestuous, over the oceans, so he

[1] Goethe.

269

flew over the frontiers of his art. From the cooing of doves to the rolling of thunder, from the most subtle interweaving of the self-determined media of his art to the awe-inspiring point where the consciously formed merges in the lawless violence of the striving forces of Nature, all these he exhausted, all these he took in his stride. Whoever comes after him will not be able to continue, he will have to begin again, for his predecessor ended only where art itself must end. . . .

He was an artist, but he was a man, too, a man in every, in the highest sense. Because he shut himself off from the world, they called him malevolent, and because he avoided sentiment, they called him unfeeling. Oh, the man who knows himself to be hard does not flee! The finest points are those which are most easily blunted, bent or broken. Excessive sensibility recoils from sentiment. He fled the world because in the whole realm of his loving nature he could find no weapon with which to oppose it. He withdrew from men after he had given them everything and received nothing in return. He remained solitary because he could find no second I. But even unto his grave he preserved a human heart for all who are human, a paternal heart for those who were his kin, himself as a heritage to the whole world.

Thus he lived, thus he died, thus he shall live for ever.

ADDITION TO THE NOTE ON PAGE 114

According to Joseph Kerman and Alan Tyson (two leading Beethoven scholars) in the New Grove, *1812 is now established as the correct date of the letters, Teplitz as their place of origin and Karlsbad ('K' in the second letter) as their addressee's temporary residence. As to their intended recipient, they consider the most likely conjecture to be that of Maynard Solomon, namely Antonie Brentano, a Viennese aristocrat who 'fulfils all the chronological and topographical requirements'.*

INDEX

ALBRECHTSBERGER, JOHANN GEORG (1736–1809). Court Organist, theorist and composer in Vienna. Taught Beethoven counterpoint in 1794. 159

ALLEGRI, GREGORIO (1582–1652). The Italian composer. 237.

AMENDA, KARL (1771–1836). One of Beethoven's closest friends; studied theology, but abandoned it for music, before settling down as a country vicar. 4, 37, 137, 146, 147

ARISTOTLE. 168

ARTARIA. Music publishers in Vienna and Mannheim, originally a firm of art dealers founded by Carlo Artaria in 1769. 43, 126, 127, 173, 175, 235, 243

BACH, Dr. JOHANN BAPTIST (1779–1874). Barrister. Represented Beethoven in his law-suit over the guardianship of his nephew. 232–3

BACH, CARL PHILIPP EMANUEL (1714–1788). The composer. 30, 76, 94

BACH, JOHANN SEBASTIAN (1685–1750). The composer. 34, 37, 76, 94, 136, 197, 219, 226, 237, 269

BECHER, Dr. ALFRED JULIUS. 84

BEETHOVEN, KASPAR KARL VAN (1774–1815). The elder of Beethoven's two brothers. Bank official. In 1794 he settled in Vienna together with his younger brother, Johann. 48, 101, 142, 176

BEETHOVEN, JOHANN NIKOLAUS VAN (1776–1836). Left Vienna to work as a chemist in Linz, became prosperous and bought an estate at Gneixendorf. Was married and had one daughter. 48, 57, 188–9, 219–20, 240, 250

BEETHOVEN, JOHANNA VAN (d. 1867), née REISS. The wife of Beethoven's brother Kaspar Karl. 143, 163, 164, 168

BEETHOVEN, KARL VAN (1806–1858). Beethoven's nephew, the son of Kaspar Karl and Johanna. 55, 142, 143, 144, 145, 150, 151, 153, 164, 167–70, 176, 204, 208, 215–16, 223–5, 226, 231, 232–3, 235, 236, 238, 239, 240, 241–2, 245, 246, 259

BENEDICT, SIR JULIUS (1804–1885). Conductor and composer; born in Stuttgart, but lived mostly in England. Composed The Lily of Killarney, other operas and an oratorio. 205, 208

BERGE, RUDOLF VOM. Writer. 146

BIGOT, DE MOROGUES, MARIE (1786-1820). A distinguished pianist. Her husband, born in Berlin, was librarian to Count Rasumowsky in Vienna. In 1809 they left Vienna and settled in Paris. 69-71

BRAUNHOFER, Dr. Physician, Professor at the University of Vienna. Treated Beethoven in 1825 and 1826. 231-2

BREITKOPF UND HÄRTEL. Music Publishers in Leipzig; originally a firm of printers, founded in 1719 by B. C. Breitkopf. 36, 46, 51, 53, 75, 81, 93, 94, 97, 99, 100, 109, 118, 186

BRENTANO, BETTINA (1785-1859). Writer. In 1811 married the poet Achim von Arnim, the friend and collaborator of her brother Clemens. Beethoven was also friendly with her brother Franz and with his wife, Antonie. 1, 6, 85-92, 95, 97, 102

BREUNING, HELENE VON (1749-1838). Took an interest in the young Beethoven; at her house in Bonn he met Wegeler and became friendly with several of her children. 26, 43, 251

BREUNING, ELEONORE VON (1772-1841). Together with her brother Lenz, who died in 1769 while still a student of medicine, she took piano lessons from Beethoven. In 1792 she married Beethoven's friend Wegeler. 23, 24, 25, 41, 43, 251, 252

BREUNING, STEPHAN VON (1774-1827). Eleonore's elder brother, one of Beethoven's closest friends. Worked in the Ministry of War in Vienna. Beethoven's Violin Concerto is dedicated to him. 4, 42, 56, 58, 60, 248, 249, 251, 258, 267

BREUNING, GERHARD VON (1813-1892). Stephan's son. Later became a physician. 247-9, 251, 255-9

BRUNSWICK, COUNT FRANZ (1777-1849). One of Beethoven's friends of the Vienna period. 98, 111, 124

BRUNSWICK, COUNTESS THERESA (1775-1861). One of Count Franz's sisters. She remained unmarried and devoted her later life to charitable work. 95

BURSY, Dr. KARL VON (1791-1850). Physician. 145-9

CHERUBINI, LUIGI (1760-1842). The Italian composer. Settled in Paris in 1787. Visited Vienna in 1805-1806 and met Beethoven there. 62, 63, 80, 109, 160, 196-7, 207

CLEMENTI, MUZIO (1752-1832). Distinguished pianist and composer. Born in Rome, educated in England, where he founded a music shop. In 1807 and 1810 he visited Vienna, where he met Beethoven. 55, 66

COTTA, J. G. Publisher. 32

CRAMER, JOHN (1771–1858). Born in Mannheim, resident in London. Pianist, composer and piano teacher. Founded a publishing house in London. 139, 160

CRAMOLINI, LUDWIG (1803–1884). Tenor, resident in Vienna. 157, 253–4

CZERNY, KARL (1791–1857). Pianist and composer. Received lessons from Beethoven from 1800 to 1803. Became a distinguished and influential teacher; Liszt was one of his pupils. 29, 54, 62, 153, 155, 197, 222, 238

DIABELLI, ANTONIO (1781–1858). Music teacher and music publisher in Vienna. 257, 267

ERDÖDY, COUNTESS MARIE (1780–1837), née Countess Nisky. Patroness and friend of Beethoven, who lived in her house in 1808 and 1809. Banned from Vienna, 1819. 6, 137, 140, 142–4

ERTMANN, DOROTHEA VON (1778–1848). Amateur pianist. The Piano Sonata Op. 101 is dedicated to her. 154–5

ESTERHAZY, PRINCE NIKOLAUS (1765–1833). Field-Marshal in Vienna. His estate was at Eisenstadt, where Haydn conducted his orchestra. He commissioned Beethoven's Mass in C. 112

EURIPIDES. 75

FOERSTER, EMANUEL ALOIS (1748–1823). Composer and music teacher in Vienna. 159

FOUQUÉ, FRIEDRICH, BARON DE LA MOTTE (1777–1843). Poet and story-teller, resident in Berlin. Author of Undine. 140, 141

FREUDENBERG, KARL GOTTLIEB (1797–1869). Organist in Breslau. 236–7

FUSS, JOHANN EVANGELISTA (1777–1819). Composer and critic in Vienna. 132

GALITZIN, PRINCE NIKOLAUS. Russian nobleman, patron of the arts. Commissioned three of the last quartets. 243

GLEICHENSTEIN, IGNAZ VON (d. 1828). Amateur 'cellist and a close friend of Beethoven's. After his marriage to Anna Malfatti, in 1811, he returned to his native town, Freiburg, but visited Beethoven in Vienna on two occasions. The 'Cello Sonata Op. 69 is dedicated to him. 4, 67, 68, 74

GLUCK, CHRISTOPH WILLIBALD (1714–1787). The composer. 136

GOETHE, JOHANN WOLFGANG VON (1749-1832). The writer. 2, 3, 4, 32, 81, 84, 85-92, 93, 94, 96, 97, 102, 109, 110, 115, 116, 117, 118, 119, 152, 185, 186, 189-91, 223, 256, 261, 268, 269

GRIESINGER, GEORG AUGUST (1754-1828). Secretary at the Saxon Legation in Vienna. Haydn's friend and biographer. 32, 212

GRILLPARZER, FRANZ. The Austrian dramatist and poet. 1, 21, 29, 30, 31, 46, 76, 79, 100, 109, 114, 136, 160, 205, 219, 223, 230, 234, 244, 269

HÄNDEL, GEORG FRIEDRICH (1685-1759). The composer. 32, 75, 109, 114, 136, 160, 205, 218-19, 239, 255, 256, 259, 260, 269

HASLINGER, TOBIAS (1787-1842). Employé, partner, then sole proprietor of the Steiner publishing house. 177, 179, 206, 209, 216, 235, 240, 250, 257

HAUSCHA, VINZENZ (1766-1840). Amateur 'cellist, an intimate friend of Beethoven's. 165

HAYDN, JOSEPH (1732-1809). The composer. 5, 46, 47, 76, 80, 114, 136, 234, 263, 264, 269

HILLER, FERDINAND (1811-1885). The pianist and composer. 261, 263

HÖFEL, BLASIUS. Painter. 126, 127

HOFFMANN, ERNST THEODOR AMADEUS (1776-1822). The writer, music critic and composer. 174

HOFFMEISTER, FRANZ ANTON (1754-1812). Music publisher in Leipzig. 34, 26, 45

HOLZ, KARL (1798-1858). Violinist in the Schuppanzigh Quartet. Became Beethoven's adviser in business matters towards the end of the composer's life. 5, 235-6, 238, 245, 246, 250-1, 259

HOMER. 81, 136, 164

HUMMEL, JOHANN NEPOMUK (1778-1837). Famous pianist, conductor and composer; a pupil of Mozart's. 31, 32, 123, 124, 142, 261, 262, 263-4

KANKA, Dr. JOHANN NEPOMUK (1772-1864). Advocate in Prague; represented Beethoven in his law-suit against the heirs of Prince Kinsky. 125, 135

KANT, IMMANUEL (1724-1804). The philosopher. 6

KIND, FRIEDRICH (1768-1843). Librettist in Dresden. 212

KINSKY, PRINCE FERDINAND (1782-1812). One of Beethoven's noble patrons; contributed to the annual grant promised to him in 1809. The Songs Op. 75, 83 and 94 are dedicated to his widow, Princess Karoline Marie. 74, 75, 102, 110, 119, 125, 126, 176

KLOPSTOCK, FRIEDRICH GOTTLIEB (1724–1803). The German poet, author of *Der Messias*. 185–6

KOCH, BARBARA. Belonged to a Bonn family with whom Beethoven was on friendly terms. 24, 43

KOTZEBUE, AUGUST VON (1761–1819). German dramatist, very successful in his lifetime; lived in Weimar. 107, 109

KREUTZER, RODOLPHE (1766–1831). Violinist and composer, resident in Paris. Met Beethoven in Vienna in 1798. The Violin Sonata in A is dedicated to him. 61

KRUMPHOLZ, WENZEL (1750–1817). Violinist. 30, 54

LICHNOWSKY, PRINCE KARL (1758–1814). One of Beethoven's noble patrons and friends; once a pupil of Mozart's. 30, 38, 40, 50, 152

LICHNOWSKY, COUNT MORITZ (1770–1837). Brother of the Prince, a close friend of Beethoven's. 4, 210, 223

LINKE, JOSEPH (1783–1837). 'Cellist in Vienna, member of the Schuppanzigh Quartet. 143, 144, 238

LISZT, FRANZ (1811–1886). The composer and pianist. 197

LOBKOWITZ, PRINCE FRANZ MAXIMILIAN (1772–1816). One of Beethoven's noble patrons; contributed to the annual grant promised to him in 1809. Many of Beethoven's works, including the Third Symphony, are dedicated to him. 32, 64, 74, 135, 176

LOUIS FERDINAND, PRINCE OF PRUSSIA (1772–1806). Amateur composer and an admirer of Beethoven's works. 232

MALFATTI, THERESE (1793–1851). A friend of Beethoven's. 66, 82

MAELZEL, JOHANN NEPOMUK (1772–1838). Inventor of many mechanical devices, including a metronome and various aids to hearing used by Beethoven. Beethoven's *Battle of Vittoria* was written for another of his inventions, the "panharmonicon". 123, 161

MATTHISON, FRIEDRICH VON (1761–1831). Swiss poet, author of the ode *Adelaide*. 33

MAYSEDER, JOSEPH (1789–1863). Distinguished violinist in Vienna. A member of the Schuppanzigh Quartet, later solo violinist at the Vienna Opera. 123

MENDELSSOHN-BARTHOLDY, FELIX (1809–1847). The composer. 1

METTERNICH, PRINCE (1773–1859). The statesman. 5, 6, 228

MEYERBEER, GIACOMO (1791–1864). The composer; at that time famous only as a pianist. 131, 139

MILDER-HAUPTMANN, PAULINE ANNA (1785–1838). Singer. The part of Fidelio was written for her. 140, 254

MOLLO, TRANQUILLO. Music publisher in Vienna, at one time a partner in the firm of Artaria. 35, 46, 149

MOSCHELES, IGNAZ (1794–1870). Famous pianist, born in Prague; gave piano lessons to Mendelssohn; lived in London from 1821 to 1846. 132, 160, 239, 260, 264–5, 266–7

MOSEL, IGNAZ FRANZ (1772–1844). Amateur musician and writer on musical subjects. 161

MOZART, WOLFGANG AMADEUS (1756–1791). The composer. 1, 21, 29, 30, 31, 46, 76, 79, 100, 109, 114, 136, 160, 205, 219, 223, 230, 234, 244, 269

MÜLLER, WILHELM CHRISTIAN (1752–1831). Director of music in Dresden. 175

NÄGELI, HANS GEORG (1773–1836). Swiss musician and teacher, founder of a firm of music publishers. 102, 226

NAPOLEON BONAPARTE (1769–1821). 45, 47, 76, 77, 78, 80, 223

NEATE, CHARLES (1784–1877). English pianist, one of the founders of the Philharmonic Society. Met Beethoven in Vienna in 1815. 265

NIETZSCHE, FRIEDRICH (1844–1900). The philosopher. 6

OLIVA, FRANZ. Bank employé in Vienna. 97, 98, 99

OSSIAN. 81, 208

PACHLER-KOSCHAK, MARIE LEOPOLDINE (1792–1855). Excellent pianist. She met Beethoven in 1817 and 1824. 158

PAISIELLO, GIOVANNI (1740–1816). Italian composer, a master of the *opera buffa*. 100

PALESTRINA, GIOVANNI PIERLUIGI (*circa* 1525–1594). The composer. 237

PASQUALATI, BARON JOHANN BAPTIST (1777–1842). Friend and patron of Beethoven's. 59, 145, 265

PETERS, CARL FRIEDRICH (1779–1827). Founder of the firm of music publishers. 180–3, 201, 202, 235

PLEYEL, CAMILLE (1788–1855). Maker of pianos and dealer in musical instruments. Born in Paris, but the son of an Austrian composer. 66

PLUTARCH. 42, 167

POTTER, CIPRIANI (1792–1871). English pianist, composer and writer on musical subjects. 158–60

PÜCKLER-MUSKAU, PRINCE HERRMANN VON (1785–1871). Writer and landscape gardener. 116

RACHMANINOV, SERGE. The composer and pianist. 7

RADZIWILL, PRINCE. Polish nobleman in the service of the King of Prussia. 192

RAMPEL, H. Copyist. 235

REICHA, ANTON (1770–1836). Flautist in Bonn; author of a well-known work on the art of fugue. 38

RELLSTAB, LUDWIG (1799–1860). Novelist and music critic. 228

RICHTER, JEAN PAUL (1763–1825). The novelist. 146, 148

RIES, FERDINAND (1784–1838). Famous pianist and composer; at one time Beethoven's pupil. 43, 46, 56, 58, 59, 139, 186, 188, 197, 202, 238

RIO, GIANNATASIO DEL. Director of the educational institute where Beethoven's nephew boarded for a time. 150

RIO, FANNY DEL (1790–1868). The daughter of Giannatasio del Rio, who wrote an account of her conversations with Beethoven. 151–2

ROCHLITZ, JOHANN FRIEDRICH (1769–1842). Editor of the *Allgemeine Musikalische Zeitung* in Leipzig. 183–6

ROSSINI, GIOACCHINO (1792–1868). The composer. 109, 179, 217–18, 236

ROUSSEAU, JEAN-JACQUES (1712–1778). The philosopher and novelist. 6, 79

RUDOLPH, ARCHDUKE (1788–1831). The youngest brother of Francis II, Emperor of Austria; became a Cardinal in 1819. For many years received lessons in composition from Beethoven, who dedicated many works to him—among them the last two Piano Concertos, the Hammerklavier Sonata and the last Piano Sonata, Op. 111. 74, 85, 92, 94, 101, 102, 103, 117, 127, 152, 170, 171–2, 176, 198, 203, 226, 227, 228, 260

SALIERI, ANTONIO (1750–1825). A prolific composer of operas and choral music. His intrigues against Mozart are the subject of a drama by the Russian poet Pushkin; according to a rumour current at the time, he confessed on his death-bed that he had murdered Mozart by poisoning him. 123

SALOMON, JOHANN PETER (1745–1815). Born in Bonn, but settled in London as a violinist and promoter of concerts. 138

SCHILLER, FRIEDRICH (1759–1805). The German poet and dramatist. 81, 95, 96, 171, 223, 257, 268

SCHINDLER, ANTON (1797–1864). Beethoven's biographer and "unpaid private secretary" during the last twelve years of the composer's life. Performed as a violinist and conductor, already during Beethoven's lifetime, when he conducted all the nine symphonies. 5, 174, 199, 200, 204, 209, 210, 211, 253, 254, 255, 259, 263, 267, 268

SCHLEGEL, WILHELM AUGUST (1767–1845). German man of letters; in collaboration with Ludwig Tieck, he produced an excellent translation of Shakespeare's plays. However, Beethoven preferred an earlier prose version of the plays. 84

SCHLESINGER, ADOLF MARTIN (1769–1848) and MORITZ (1798–1859). Publishers of music and books. The original firm, founded by Adolf S., was in Berlin; a French branch was opened by Moritz S., in 1822. 5, 172, 182, 195, 235, 238, 239, 250

SCHLÖSSER, LOUIS (1800–1886). Musician from Darmstadt, who visited Beethoven in 1822–1823. 193–5

SCHNYDER VON WARTENSEE, XAVER (1786–1868). Swiss musician and teacher. 102–5, 156

SCHOTT, ANDREAS (1781–1840) and JOHANN JOSEPH (1782–1855). Directors of the publishing house in Mainz. 5, 213–14, 225, 227, 243, 254, 260–1

SCHUBERT, FRANZ (1797–1828). The composer. 183, 255

SCHULZ, EDWARD. English musician. 205

SCHUMANN, ROBERT (1810–1856). The composer. 1

SCHUPPANZIGH, IGNAZ (1776–1830). His quartet, in which he played the first violin, was in the service of Prince Lichnowsky; later, from 1808 to 1816, it was in the service of Count Rasumowsky and first performed several of Beethoven's works. 32, 123, 124, 175, 185, 210, 217, 238, 239, 256

SCOTT, SIR WALTER (1771–1832). The novelist. 223, 257

SEBALD, AMALIE (1787–1839). Singer. She met Beethoven at Teplitz in 1812. 119–21

SEYFRIED, IGNAZ RITTER VON (1776–1841). Studied music under Mozart, Haydn and Albrechtsberger; became the conductor of a Vienna orchestra. 32, 84, 108, 129, 179, 205, 212

SHAKESPEARE, WILLIAM. 2, 79, 84, 208

SIMROCK, NIKOLAUS (1752–1834). Played the French horn. Founded a firm of music publishers and dealers established in Bonn. 26, 52, 61

SMART, SIR GEORGE (1776–1867). English composer, conductor, singer and organist. Musical director at Covent Garden. 238–40, 260, 264, 265, 266, 267

SOCRATES. 110

SPOHR, LOUIS (1785-1859). Composer, conductor and violinist, born in Brunswick. 110, 123, 133, 237

SPONTINI, GASPARO (1774-1851). Italian composer of operas, active in Paris, then—after 1820—in Berlin. 207, 236

STADLER, ABBÉ MAXIMILIAN (1748-1833). Benedictine; composer of church music. Mozart and Haydn were his friends. 205, 238, 244-5

STEINER, SIEGMUND ANTON (1773-1838). Founder of the firm of music publishers of that name. 5, 153, 173, 178, 179, 180, 182, 194, 205, 206, 238

STREICHER, ANDREAS (1761-1833) and NANETTE (1769-1833), his wife. It was with Andreas Streicher that Schiller fled from Stuttgart when they were at school together; after his marriage, Streicher settled in Vienna as a manufacturer of pianos. His wife helped Beethoven in household matters. 145, 159, 162-3, 215, 263

STUMPFF, JOHANN ANDREAS. Born in Thuringia; settled in London as a maker of musical instruments. Was introduced to Beethoven by Streicher during his visit to Vienna and became a fervent admirer of Beethoven's music. 1, 214-22, 255, 259, 266, 267

TOMASCHEK, JOHANN WENZEL (1774-1850). Composer, organist and music teacher in Prague. 31, 128

TRÉMONT, BARON DE (1779-1852). French civil servant. 76-80

TROXLER, IGNAZ PAUL (1780-1866). Swiss physician and philosopher, professor at Lucerne, then Bâle, then Berne. 66, 103

UHLAND, JOHANN LUDWIG (1787-1862). The German poet. 200

UMLAUF, MICHAEL (1781-1842). Violinist and conductor at the Vienna Opera. Assisted Beethoven in his last efforts to practise as a conductor; conducted the first performance of the Ninth Symphony. 130

VARENA, *KAMMERPROKURATOR*. Civil servant in Graz. 7

VOGLER, ABBÉ (1749-1814). Organist, pianist and composer. In 1803, he and Beethoven competed publicly as pianists. 62, 63

VOLTAIRE, FRANÇOIS-MARIE AROUET (1694-1778). The writer. 6

WAGNER, RICHARD (1813-1883). The composer. 1

WEBER, FRIEDRICH DIONYS (1766-1842). Music teacher and Director of the Prague Conservatoire. 141

WEBER, CARL MARIA VON (1786-1826). The composer. 109, 199, 205, 206, 207-9, 212, 223, 268, 269

WEGELER, FRITZ, BERNARD (1765-1848). One of Beethoven's oldest and closest friends. Became Professor of Medicine at the University of Bonn at the age of nineteen; later practised as a physician. Lived in Vienna from 1794 to 1796. 4, 28, 40, 44, 58, 59, 85, 251

WIEDEBEIN, GOTTLIEB. Composer. 55

WIELAND, CHRISTOPH MARTIN (1733–1813). The German poet and novelist. 81

WIMPFFEN, COUNTESS. 187

WOLANEK, FERDINAND. Copyist. 3, 233–4, 235

ZELTER, KARL FRIEDRICH (1758–1832). Director of the Berlin Academy of Vocal Music. Goethe's adviser in musical matters. Beethoven made his acquaintance during his visit to Berlin in 1796. 116, 191, 192, 228, 229, 230

ZMESKALL VON DOMANOVETZ (1759–1833). Civil servant in Vienna; amateur violinist. One of Beethoven's more intimate friends. 4, 29, 92, 122, 150